"I pledge allegiance to the flag of the United States of America and to the Republic for which it stands, one Nation under God, indivisible, with liberty and justice for all."

I

ARNOLD SCHWARZENEGGER
GOVERNOR OF CALIFORNIA
Elected at a Statewide Special Election October 7, 2003

CRUZ BUSTAMANTE
LIEUTENANT GOVERNOR

DON PERATA
PRESIDENT PRO TEMPORE OF THE SENATE

FABIAN NUÑEZ
SPEAKER OF THE ASSEMBLY

LELAND Y. YEE
SPEAKER PRO TEMPORE OF THE ASSEMBLY

Memoranda

VIII

CALIFORNIA LEGISLATURE

AT SACRAMENTO

Biographies and Photographs of

SENATE AND ASSEMBLY MEMBERS AND OFFICERS

List of

SENATE AND ASSEMBLY MEMBERS, OFFICERS, ATTACHES, COMMITTEES

and

RULES OF THE TWO HOUSES

and

Standards of Conduct of the Senate

Together With a List of the Members of Congress, State Officers, Etc.

2005–06 REGULAR SESSION

(2005 Edition)

Convened December 6, 2004
Published August 2005

GREGORY SCHMIDT
Secretary of the Senate

E. DOTSON WILSON
Chief Clerk of the Assembly

CONTENTS

CONTENTS—Continued

CALIFORNIA REPRESENTATIVES IN CONGRESS

UNITED STATES SENATE

Boxer, Barbara (D) .... San Francisco
       Term expires January 3, 2011.

Feinstein, Dianne (D) .... San Francisco
       Term expires January 3, 2007.

HOUSE OF REPRESENTATIVES

Dist.

1. Thompson, Mike (D) .... Del Norte
       Humboldt, Lake, Mendocino, Napa, Sonoma, Yolo.

2. Herger, Wally (R) .... Butte
       Colusa, Glenn, Shasta, Siskiyou, Sutter, Tehama, Trinity, Yolo, Yuba.

3. Lungren, Dan (R) .... Alpine
       Amador, Calaveras, Sacramento, Solano.

4. Doolittle, John T. (R) .... Butte
       El Dorado, Lassen, Modoc, Nevada, Placer, Plumas, Sacramento, Sierra.

*5. Matsui, Doris (D) .... Sacramento

6. Woolsey, Lynn (D) .... Marin
       Sonoma.

7. Miller, George (D) .... Contra Costa
       Solano.

8. Pelosi, Nancy (D) .... San Francisco

9. Lee, Barbara (D) .... Alameda

10. Tauscher, Ellen (D) .... Alameda
       Contra Costa, Sacramento, Solano.

11. Pombo, Richard W. (R) .... Alameda
       Contra Costa, San Joaquin, Santa Clara.

12. Lantos, Tom (D) .... San Francisco
       San Mateo.

13. Stark, Fortney "Pete" (D) .... Alameda

* Doris Matsui elected March 8, 2005 Special Election.

HOUSE OF REPRESENTATIVES—Continued

Dist.

14. Eshoo, Anna G. (D) .... San Mateo
    Santa Clara, Santa Cruz.

15. Honda, Michael M. (D) .... Santa Clara

16. Lofgren, Zoe (D) .... Santa Clara

17. Farr, Sam (D) .... Monterey
    San Benito, Santa Cruz.

18. Cardoza, Dennis (D) .... Fresno
    Madera, Merced, San Joaquin, Stanislaus.

19. Radanovich, George (R) .... Fresno
    Madera, Mariposa, Stanislaus, Tuolumne.

20. Costa, Jim (D) .... Fresno
    Kern, Kings.

21. Nunes, Devin (R) .... Fresno
    Tulare.

22. Thomas, Bill (R) .... Kern
    Los Angeles, San Luis Obispo.

23. Capps, Lois (D) .... San Luis Obispo
    Santa Barbara, Ventura.

24. Gallegly, Elton (R) .... Santa Barbara
    Ventura.

25. McKeon, Howard P. (R) .... Inyo
    Los Angeles, Mono, San Bernardino.

26. Dreier, David (R) .... Los Angeles
    San Bernardino.

27. Sherman, Brad (D) .... Los Angeles

28. Berman, Howard (D) .... Los Angeles

29. Schiff, Adam (D) .... Los Angeles

30. Waxman, Henry (D) .... Los Angeles

31. Becerra, Xavier (D) .... Los Angeles

32. Solis, Hilda (D) .... Los Angeles

33. Watson, Diane (D) .... Los Angeles

34. Roybal-Allard (D) .... Los Angeles

35. Waters, Maxine (D) .... Los Angeles

HOUSE OF REPRESENTATIVES—Continued

Dist.

36. Harman, Jane (D) .... Los Angeles

37. Millender-McDonald, Juanita (D) .... Los Angeles

38. Napolitano, Grace (D) .... Los Angeles

39. Sanchez, Linda (D) .... Los Angeles

40. Royce, Ed (R) .... Orange

41. Lewis, Jerry (R) .... Riverside
    San Bernardino.

42. Miller, Gary (R) .... Los Angeles
    Orange, San Bernardino.

43. Baca, Joe (D) .... San Bernardino

44. Calvert, Ken (R) .... Orange
    Riverside.

45. Bono, Mary (R) .... Riverside

46. Rohrabacher, Dana (R) .... Los Angeles
    Orange.

47. Sanchez, Loretta (D) .... Orange

48. Cox, Christopher (R) .... Orange

49. Issa, Darrell (R) .... Riverside
    San Diego.

50. Cunningham, Randy (R) .... San Diego

51. Filner, Bob (D) .... Imperial
    San Diego.

52. Hunter, Duncan (R) .... San Diego

53. Davis, Susan (D) .... San Diego

(D) Democratic 33, (R) Republican 20.

DIRECTORY OF STATE OFFICERS

CONSTITUTIONAL OFFICERS

Governor

ARNOLD SCHWARZENEGGER....................445-2841
Patricia T. Clarey, *Chief of Staff*
Marybel Batjer, *Cabinet Secretary*
Randal J. Hernandez, *Appointments Secretary*
Peter Siggins, *Legal Affairs Secretary*
Margita Thompson, *Press Secretary*
Margo Reid Brown, *Scheduling Secretary*
Richard Costigan, *Legislative Secretary*..............445-4341
www.governor.ca.gov

Governor's Cabinet

A. G. Kawamura, *Secretary*
Department of Food and Agriculture
    1220 N Street, A400
    Sacramento 95814
    654-0433
    www.cdfa.ca.gov

Roderick Q. Hickman, *Secretary*
Youth and Adult Correctional Agency
    P.O. Box 13908
    Sacramento 95853
    323-6001
    www.yaca.ca.gov

Fred Aguiar, *Secretary*
State and Consumer Services Agency
    915 Capitol Mall, Suite 200
    Sacramento 95814
    653-2636
    www.scsa.ca.gov

Tom Campbell, *Director*
Department of Finance
    State Capitol, Room 1145
    Sacramento 95814
    445-4141
    www.dof.ca.gov

Victoria Bradshaw, *Secretary*
Labor and Workforce Development Agency
  801 K Street, Suite 2101
  Sacramento 95814
  327-9064
  www.labor.ca.gov

Alan Lloyd, *Secretary*
California Environmental Protection Agency
  1001 I Street
  P.O. Box 2815
  Sacramento 95812-2815
  445-3846
  www.CalEPA.ca.gov

S. Kimberly Belshé, *Secretary*
Health and Human Services Agency
  1600 Ninth Street, #460
  Sacramento 95814
  654-3345
  www.chhs.ca.gov

Mike Chrisman, *Secretary*
Resources Agency
  1416 Ninth Street, Room 1311
  Sacramento 95814
  653-5656
  www.resources.ca.gov

Sunne Wright McPeak, *Secretary*
Business, Transportation and Housing Agency
  980 9th Street, Suite 2450
  Sacramento 95814
  323-5401
  www.bth.ca.gov

Alan Bersin, *Secretary*
Office of Secretary of Education
  1121 L Street, Suite 600
  Sacramento 95814
  323-0611
  www.ose.ca.gov

Lieutenant Governor

Cruz M. Bustamante, *Lieutenant Governor*

Offices: State Capitol, Room 1114
Sacramento 95814
445-8994

300 S. Spring St., Suite 12702
Los Angeles 90013
(213) 897-7086
www.ltg.ca.gov

Secretary of State

Bruce McPherson, *Secretary of State*

Office: 1500 11th Street
Sacramento 95814
653-7244
www.ss.ca.gov

State Controller

Steve Westly, *Controller*

Office: 300 Capitol Mall
Sacramento 95814
445-3028
www.sco.ca.gov

State Treasurer

Philip Angelides, *Treasurer*

Office: 915 Capitol Mall, Room 110
Sacramento 95814
653-2995
www.treasurer.ca.gov

Attorney General

Bill Lockyer, *Attorney General and Head
of Department of Justice*

Offices: 1300 "I" Street
Sacramento 95814
(916) 445-9555

300 South Spring Street
Los Angeles 90013
(213) 897-2000

455 Golden Gate Avenue, Suite 1100
San Francisco 94102-7004
(415) 703-5500

1515 Clay Street, Suite 2000
Oakland 94612-0550
(510) 622-2100

2550 Mariposa Mall, Room 5090
Fresno 93721
(559) 477-1691

110 West A Street, Suite 1100
San Diego 92101
(619) 645-2001
www.ag.ca.gov

Insurance Commissioner

John Garamendi, *Insurance Commissioner*

Offices: 45 Fremont Street
San Francisco 94105
(415) 538-4010

300 Capitol Mall, Suite 1700
Sacramento 95814
(916) 492-3500

300 S. Spring Street
Los Angeles 90013
(213) 346-6464
www.insurance.ca.gov

Superintendent of Public Instruction

Jack O'Connell, *Superintendent of Public
Instruction and Director of Education*

Office: 1430 N Street, Room 5602
Sacramento 95814
319-0791
www.cde.ca.gov

State Board of Equalization

Betty Yee, *First District,* San Francisco (Interim)

Bill Leonard, *Second District,* Sacramento

Claude Parrish, *Third District,* Torrance

John Chiang, *Fourth District,* Los Angeles (Chair)

Main Office: 450 N Street
                Sacramento 95814
                445-6464
                www.boe.ca.gov

LEGISLATIVE DEPARTMENT

Legislative Analyst's Office
  Elizabeth G. Hill, *Legislative Analyst*
  Hadley Johnson, Jr., *Deputy Legislative Analyst*
  Mac Taylor, *Deputy Legislative Analyst*

    Office: 925 L Street, Suite 1000
              Sacramento, 95814
              445-4656
              www.lao.ca.gov

Legislative Counsel
  Diane F. Boyer-Vine, *Legislative Counsel*
  Jeffrey A. DeLand, *Chief Deputy*
  Daniel A. Weitzman, *Chief Deputy*
  Receptionist, 341-8000

    Office: Room 3021, State Capitol
              Sacramento 95814
              www.legislativecounsel.ca.gov

Legislative Bill Room
  Lily Hitomi, *Legislative Liaison*

    Office: Bill Room, Room B-32
              State Capitol
              Sacramento 95814
              445-2323

The Senate

List of

MEMBERS, OFFICERS, COMMITTEES, AND THE RULES

2005–06

REGULAR SESSION

Published August 2005

Compiled Under the Direction of

GREGORY SCHMIDT
Secretary of the Senate

By

DAVID VALVERDE
Chief Assistant Secretary of the Senate

DAVID KNEALE
History Clerk

PAULA ROSSETTO
Minute Clerk

MARLISSA HERNANDEZ
File Clerk

JAMIE TAYLOR
Assistant File Clerk

KIPCHOGE RANDALL
Reading Clerk

BERNADETTE C. McNULTY
Assistant Secretary of the Senate

HOLLY DAWN HUMMELT
Amending Clerk

ZACH TWILLA
Assistant Amending Clerk

SUSAN DeLaFUENTE
Assistant to the Secretary of the Senate

BIOGRAPHIES AND PHOTOGRAPHS

of

OFFICERS AND MEMBERS

OF THE SENATE

2005–06

Regular Session

CRUZ BUSTAMANTE
LIEUTENANT GOVERNOR

Re-elected as 45th Lieutenant Governor in 2002. Sued energy companies for gouging taxpayers; made higher education more accessible; expedited the 10th UC Campus. Serves as UC Regent; CSU Trustee; and Chairs the State Lands Commission and Economic Development Commission. Created the first public-private partnerships to promote international trade and the "Commission for One California" to improve race relations; the "Contract to Fight Breast Cancer," an employer-awareness program; formed a partnership between truck drivers and "Amber Alert." Speaker of Assembly from 1996–1998. As Speaker, he protected California's coast, wrote law to sue tobacco companies and cut college tuition. Elected Assemblymember in 1993—authored legislation to provide $1 billion for textbooks. Married to Arcelia, three daughters, two grandchildren.

DON PERATA
PRESIDENT PRO TEMPORE OF THE SENATE

(D-Oakland) 9th District, elected to the State Senate in 1998 after two years in the State Assembly. A lifelong Democrat, he was born on April 30, 1945 in the City of Alameda. He graduated from St. Mary's College and became a teacher in the Alameda public schools from 1966 to 1981. Don served on the Alameda County Board of Supervisors from 1986 to 1994 and as a Senator was elected by his colleagues to the position of Senate Majority Leader in 2002. Senator Perata has twice been unanimously elected President pro Tempore by the members of the 2003–04 Session of the California State Senate, and then again by the members of the 2005–06 Session. Senator Perata's experiences as a teacher and local elected representative have shaped his legislative priorities. He continues to fight for quality education, affordable housing, access to health care and In Home Supportive Services for seniors and people with disabilities, and has created new legislation to increase local control of education and to combat sprawl, reduce traffic, protect open space, and improve air quality in California. Senator Perata has two children, Rebecca and Nick, and two grandchildren.

GLORIA ROMERO
SENATE MAJORITY LEADER

(D-East Los Angeles) 24th District. As Senate Majority Leader, Senator Gloria Romero is the highest ranking woman in the California Legislature, and is the first woman to hold this leadership position. She is a legislator, an educator, a dedicated social activist, an aggressive prison reformer, and a forceful advocate for California's most disadvantaged citizens. She is Chair of the Senate Select Committee on the California Correctional System where she has taken on the formidable task of investigating and authoring reforms for the state's massive array of youth and adult correctional facilities which constitutes over 6 billion dollars of the state's general fund. Elected first to the State Assembly in 1998 and then to the Senate in a special election in March 2001, she has gained a reputation as one of the hardest working legislators in Sacramento. Senator Romero has risen quickly to positions of leadership. In the Assembly, upon her election, she was appointed Majority Whip, and during her first term in office was named a rising star in politics by the *California Journal*. Senator Romero is a graduate of Barstow Community College and California State University Long Beach. She earned her Ph.D. in psychology from the University of California, Riverside. She currently serves on the Senate committees on Budget and Fiscal Review; Education; Public Safety; Health; Elections, Reapportionment, and Constitutional Amendments; Natural Resources and Water; and the Joint Legislative Audit Committee.

DICK ACKERMAN
SENATE REPUBLICAN LEADER

(33rd District) Elected to the Senate in 2000. Represented Orange County in the Assembly from 1995 to 2000. Business Attorney currently Of Counsel with Rutan and Tucker. Elected Senate Republican Leader, May 2004. Born in Long Beach, December 5, 1942. Graduated U.C. Berkeley, 1964 (B.A. Mathematics); Hastings College of Law, 1967 (J.D.). Former city council member and Mayor of Fullerton (1980–92). Senator Ackerman's public service and effective advocacy have been recognized throughout the community. He has received several awards, including the Legislator of the Year Award from the University of California; the Legislator of the Year Award from the California Charter Schools Association; the Distinguished Service Award from the Black Chamber of Commerce of Orange County; the Legislator of the Year Award from the Orange County League of Cities; the Fullerton Chamber of Commerce Educator of the Year Award; and the Spotlight Award from the Regional Centers of Orange County for outstanding service to people with developmental disabilities. As leader, Senator Ackerman will push for reform in the state budget, education and tort law. He will continue pursuing reforms to free small businesses from over-regulation and fight to protect California's taxpayers. Senator Ackerman and his wife Linda were married in 1968, have three children, Lauren, Marc, and Brett and two grandchildren, Caitlin and Elizabeth.

THE SENATE RULES COMMITTEE

From left to right: Senator Debra Bowen; Senator Ray Ashburn; Senator Don Perata (Chair); Senator James Battin (Vice Chair); Senator Gil Cedillo.

AANESTAD, Samuel (R), Fourth District. Elected to the Senate in 2002, after serving four years in the Assembly. Served 11 years on the Nevada County School Board of Trustees. Oral Surgeon. Attended University of California Los Angeles: B.A. and Doctor of Dental Surgery degrees, MA Public Administration, Golden Gate University. Married to Susan; children: Kaesa, Eric, and Kirsten. Committees: Appropriations (Vice-Chair); Business, Professions and Economic Development; Health; Human Services; Natural Resources and Water. Select: Capitol Area Flood Protection; Defense and Aerospace Industry; Jt. Comm. on Boards, Commissions, and Consumer Protection. Subcommittees: Aging and Long Term Care; Delta Resources.

ALARCÓN, Richard (D) 20th District. Represents the San Fernando Valley. Elected November of 1998. Serves as Senate Majority Whip. Previously served on the Los Angeles City Council (1993–98). Full time legislator. Life-long resident of the San Fernando Valley. Attended Cal State University, Northridge. Father of four; children: Armando, Claudia, Antonio, and Andrea. Major accomplishments: secured $5.4 billion in unemployment insurance benefits, $548 million for affordable housing, 2000 budget; secured $218 million for teacher recruitment and retention, redevelopment of General Motors Plant site; initiated establishment of Valley Transit Zone; Committees: Labor and Industrial Relations (Chair); Energy, Utilities and Communications; Human Services; Public Employment and Retirement.

ALQUIST, Elaine Kontaminas (D) 13th District, *The Heart of Silicon Valley.* Representing San Jose, Sunnyvale, Santa Clara, Mountain View, and Gilroy. Elected 2004. Served in the Assembly from 1996–2002. First Greek-American woman legislator. Born August 21, 1944. Raised in Saint Louis, MO. B.A. in Mathematics, Mac
Murray College; M.A. in Education, Washington University in St. Louis. Children: two sons, Peter (M. Anju Chowdhry) and Bryan White. Grandaughter: Jasmine White. Married to former Senator Al Alquist. Former Algebra teacher, school board member, businesswoman, Stanford University financial analyst. First woman to Chair Senate Public Safety Com. Chair: Sub-Com. on Aging and Long Term Care; Select Committee on Emerging Technologies and Economic Competitiveness. Member: Committees on Appropriations; Education; Health; Human Services; and Revenue and Taxation. Sub-Com. on Stem Cell Research Oversight. Select Coms. on Defense and Aerospace Industry; and Mobile and Manufactured Homes.

ASHBURN, Roy A. (R) 18th District. Elected to Senate 2001, after serving 6 years in the Assembly and 12 years as a Kern County Supervisor. Vice Chair of the Senate Republican Caucus. Represents Kern, Tulare, Inyo and San Bernardino Counties. Native Californian, born March 21, 1954 in Long Beach. Attended College of the Sequoias and
graduated from CSU Bakersfield with a degree in Public Administration. Children: Shelley, Shannon, Stacy, and Suzannah. Legislative interests: PERS Reform, Military Support, Economic Development and Job Creation, Welfare Reform, Adoption, Public Safety, and Valley Fever. Committees: Rules; Public Employees and Retirement (Vice Chair); Appropriations; Transportation and Housing; Government Modernization, Efficiency & Accountability; Senate Select Committee on Defense and Aerospace Industry (Chair).

BATTIN, James F. (R) 37th District. Elected to Senate 2000, after serving 6 years in the Assembly. Business Owner and Former Television Executive. Born July 28, 1962 in Billings, Montana. Attended University of Oregon, B.S., Psychology. Married to Mary; children: Christopher, Bailey, and Kelsey. Member of Palm Desert Presbyterian Church. Legislative Priorities include: Victims' rights (especially children), government responsibility and accountability, and investment into California's infrastructure and economy. Committees: Appropriations; Elections, Reapportionment and Constitutional Amendments (Vice-Chair); Energy, Utilities and Communications; Governmental Organization; Rules (Vice-Chair).

BOWEN, Debra (D) 28th District. Elected in 1998 and 2002 after serving in the Assembly 1992–98. Born in Rockford, Illinois; B.A., Michigan State, 1976; J.D., Virginia, 1979. Authored law giving people Internet access to California legislative information. Helped combat identity theft by precluding companies from using people's Social Security numbers as public identifiers. Gave people the ability to fight back against unsolicited e-mail ads and outlawed sending junk fax ads to people without their permission. Wrote laws requiring strict emissions standards for small, on-site power plants, and promoting energy conservation and renewable power. Wrote laws restricting the use of psychotropic medication on foster children and requiring counties to maintain up-to-date health & education records for foster children. Committees: Elections, Reapportionment and Constitutional Amendments (Chair); Appropriations; Energy, Utilities and Communications; Government Modernization, Efficiency and Accountability; Natural Resources and Water; Revenue and Taxation; and Rules.

CAMPBELL, John (R) 35th District. Elected 2004. Businessman/CPA. Native Californian born July 19, 1955, in Los Angeles. Graduate of U.C.L.A. with B.A. in Economics in 1976; Master's degree in Business Taxation U.S.C., 1977. Married, wife, Catherine; two children. Member, Young Presidents Organization; California Motor Car Dealers Association; Breakfast Club of Newport Beach; Irvine Presbyterian Church. Past Chairman, Orange County Overall Economic Development Program Committee. Serves on California Republican Party Central Committee. Judiciary (Chair); Budget and Fiscal Review; Elections, Reapportionment and Constitutional Amendments; Energy, Utilities and Communications; Governmental Organization; Labor and Industrial Relations; Public Employment and Retirement; Veterans' Affairs.

CEDILLO, Gilbert (D-Los Angeles) 22nd District. Elected 2002. Assembly 1998–2002. Native Californian born in Barstow in 1954. Raised in Boyle Heights. Son, Gilbert Cedillo, Jr.; Bachelors Degree, UCLA; Juris Doctorate, People's College of Law. General Manager of S.E.I.U., 660, 1991–1996; Former Field Representative to Mayor Tom Bradley; Democratic National Convention Delegate for Jackson 1988, Clinton 1996, Gore 2000. Awarded: The CBIA Legislator of the Year 2004; The CCPOA Legislator of the Year 2004. Committees: Senate Rules Committee; Joint Legislative Audit Committee; Public Safety; Revenue and Taxation; Transportation and Housing; and Judiciary Committees; Select Committee on Immigration and the Economy (Chair); College and University Admissions and Outreach; California's Horseracing Industry.

CHESBRO, Wesley (D-Arcata) 2nd District. Chesbro is a native Californian and 35-year resident of Humboldt County. He was elected in 1998 to represent the diverse Second Senate District. He serves as Chair of the Senate Budget & Fiscal Review Committee. He also Chairs the Senate Select Committee on California's Wine Industry and the Senate Select Committee on Developmental Disabilities and Mental Health. He serves as a member of the following Senate committees: Environmental Quality; Governmental Organization; Health; Human Services; and Veterans Affairs. Chesbro, a former Humboldt County Supervisor and Arcata City Council member, has continued to be an advocate for local governments, access to health care, improved school facilities and protection of the California coastline.

COX, Dave (R) 1st District. Elected 2004. Served in the California Assembly 1998–2004. Assembly Republican Leader March 26, 2001–December 31, 2003. Businessman. Born February 20, 1938 in Oklahoma; California resident since 1956. B.A. Business Administration, University of San Diego, 1961; M.S., Golden Gate University, 1983. Married, wife, Maggie; three daughters; five grandchildren. Former member, Sacramento County Board of Supervisors, 1992–1998. Past Director, Sacramento Municipal Utility District. Former member, Board of Directors, American Red Cross; Sacramento Metropolitan Chamber of Commerce; Easter Seals; Rotary Club of Sacramento; KVIE-Channel 6. Vice-Chair, Senate Banking, Finance and Insurance; Senate Local Government Committees. Member, Senate Energy, Utilities and Communications; Environmental Quality; Governmental Organization; and Health Committees.

DENHAM, Jeffrey J. (R-Merced) 12th District. Elected to Senate 2002, is a Merced Farmer and owns a Salinas based Agricultural Plastics firm. Born July 29, 1967 in Hawthorne, CA. Attended California Polytechnic University, San Luis Obispo, B.A. Political Science. During his first term, he has focused on sale of state surplus proper-

ties and identifying waste in government. A 16-year U.S. Air Force veteran, he served in the first Gulf War. Married to Sonia; children: Austin and Samantha. Honored as legislator-of-the-year by peace officers, education and engineering groups. Committees: Agriculture (Chair); Governmental Organization (Vice Chair); Banking, Finance and Insurance; Education; Veteran's Affairs.

DUCHENY, Denise Moreno (D) 40th District. She was elected to the California State Senate on November 5, 2002, to represent the 40th District. The district incorporates portions of San Diego and Riverside Counties and all of Imperial County. Senator Ducheny Chairs the Senate Budget Subcommittee on Health and Human Services and is Vice

Chair of the Committee on Agriculture. She also serves on Transportation and Housing; Government Modernization, Efficiency and Accountability; and the Joint Legislative Budget Committee. Senator Ducheny chairs the Senate Select Committees on California-Mexico Cooperation; the Colorado River; and Oversight of UC Energy Laboratories, and serves on several other select committees. She served in the State Assembly from 1994–2000 and on the San Diego Community College Board from 1990–94.

DUNN, Joseph L. (D-Garden Grove) 34th District. Elected in 1998. Consumer attorney. Graduated with honors from College of St. Thomas (B.A., 1980) and the University of Minnesota School of Law (J.D., 1983). Lives in Santa Ana with wife, Diane, and two children. Senator Dunn has been honored with legislator-of-the-year awards from many organizations, including military veterans, peace officers, firefighters, probation officers, physicians, seniors, Latinos, children's hospitals, judges, attorneys, homebuilders, affordable housing advocates, conservationists, mobile-home owners, University of California alumni and others. Committees: Judiciary (Chair); Budget and Fiscal Review; Elections, Reapportionment and Constitutional Amendments; Energy, Utilities and Communications; Governmental Organization; Labor and Industrial Relations; Public Employment and Retirement; Veterans Affairs.

DUTTON, Bob (R) 31st District. Senator Bob Dutton was elected to represent the 31st Senate District in November 2004. Born and raised in Nebraska, Senator Dutton moved to California in 1969. In addition to being a member of the California Legislature, Senator Dutton is a local business owner. He is the CEO of a real estate investment firm—Dutton & Associates, Inc. in Rancho Cucamonga. Senator Dutton was elected to the Rancho Cucamonga City Council and then reelected in November 2000. The Senator's rise in politics continued when he was elected to the California State Assembly in November 2002. The senator married his wife, Andrea Guillen, in 1981 and the couple has one daughter, Kara. Committees: Government Modernization, Efficiency and Accountability (Vice Chair); Revenue and Taxation (Vice Chair); Appropriations; Budget and Fiscal Review; Education; Natural Resources and Water.

ESCUTIA, Martha M. (D) 30th District. Elected in 1998. Former Assembly Member, 50th District 1992–1998. Attorney. Native Californian born in Los Angeles. Received B.S., USC, 1979; J.D., Georgetown University Law School, 1982; Certificate, Private and Public International Law, The World Court, The Hague, Netherlands, 1986. Married, husband, Leo Briones; sons, Andres and Diego. A staunch consumer and children's advocate, Escutia has authored landmark legislation to prevent age discrimination, created California's first low cost auto insurance program and establishing the first children's environmental health standards in the nation. Founding Member, Southeast Community Development Corporation; Latino Lawyers Committee. Member, National Women's Political Caucus, Latino Legislative Caucus, 2002 Women's Legislative Caucus (Chair). Committees: Energy, Utilities and Communications (Chair); Appropriations; Environmental Quality; Judiciary.

FIGUEROA, Liz (D) 10th District. Elected in 1998. Member of the Assembly from 1994–1998. Businesswoman. Native Californian, born in San Francisco. Attended College of San Mateo. Mother of AnaLisa Luippold and Aaron Bloom and the grandmother of Andrew and Cameron. A leader in consumer and privacy protection, Figueroa authored legislation creating the nation's first "Do Not Call List," as well as protecting victims of identify theft, reforming HMOs, and improving access to healthcare. Appointed to the City of San Mateo Human Relations Commission at age 18. First woman elected to Union Sanitary District Board (1987). Member of the Little Hoover Commission, Women in Government, Mexican American Legal Defense and Educational Fund (MALDEF), CEWAER, Centro Legal de la Raza Advisory Board, 2004 Women's Legislative Caucus (Chair). Committees (Chair); Business, Professions, and Economic Development; Government Modernization, Efficiency, and Accountability (Chair); Joint Committee on Boards, Commissions, and Consumer Protection, Subcommittees on International Trade. Committees (member); Banking and Finance; Environmental Quality; Health; Judiciary.

FLOREZ, Dean R. (D) 16th District. Elected in 2002. Previously served two terms in the Assembly, beginning in 1998. Investment Banker. Born in Shafter on April 5, 1963. Attended Bakersfield College. Graduated UCLA with honors (B.A. in Political Science, '87) and Harvard School of Business (M.B.A., '93). Married to Elsa; two children, Sean and Faith. Past member of the California High-Speed Rail Authority. Committees: Governmental Organization (Chair); Agriculture; Business, Professions and Economic Development; Government Modernization, Efficiency and Accountability; Human Services.

HOLLINGSWORTH, Dennis (R) 36th District; Riverside, San Diego. Served one Assembly term, 2000–02; elected to the State Senate November 2002. Farmers' Representative, businessman. Native Californian born January 12th, 1967 in Hemet. Attended Cal Poly State University, San Luis Obispo; Cornell University. Married, wife, Natalie; sons Kenneth Hunter and Nathan Clark. Served as Legislative Director for the Riverside County Farm Bureau. Named Legislator of the Year by the California Rifle and Pistol Association, the California Building Industry Association, the League of Off-Road Voters, California Sexual Assault Investigators Association. Vice Chair, Budget & Fiscal Review Committee. Member, Committees on Agriculture; Banking, Finance and Insurance; Natural Resources and Water; Public Employment and Retirement. Co-chair Outdoor Sporting Caucus.

KEHOE, Christine (D) 39th District. Elected 2004. Full-time Legislator. B.A., State University of New York. Chair, Committee on Local Government. Member, Committee Budget & Fiscal Review, Natural Resources & Water, Transportation & Housing, Energy, Utilities and Communications. Vice Chair Women's Caucus. Member State Assembly 2000–2004. First Chair of the LGBT Legislative Caucus 2002. Speaker pro Tempore 2003. Governor's Blue Ribbon Fire Commission 2004. Councilmember, San Diego City Council 1993–2000. California Coastal Commissioner 1997–2000. Clean Water Champion 2002 by Project Clean Water; River Park Champion by San Diego River Park Foundation 2003; BIOCOM Legislator of the Year 2004; Legislator of the Year California Federation of Teachers 2004; Calstart Blue Sky Award 2004, California Small Business Association Legislator of the Year 2004.

KUEHL, Sheila James (D) 23rd District. Elected in 2000. Elected to the Assembly in 1994. Born February 9, 1941 in Tulsa, Oklahoma. B.A., UCLA 1962; J.D., Harvard University, 1978, Co-founder and managing attorney, California Women's Law Center. Former law professor, Loyola Law School and UCLA Law School. First woman in California history named Assembly Speaker pro Tempore. Authored 134 bills signed into law including paid family leave, child support redesign, and numerous bills concerning child custody, domestic violence, discrimination prevention, and natural resource protection. Committees: Natural Resources and Water (Chair); Budget Subcommittee on Resources, Energy, and Water (Chair); Budget and Fiscal Review; Environmental Quality; Health; Judiciary; Labor; and Government Modernization, Efficiency and Accountability.

LOWENTHAL, Alan (D) 27th District. Alan Lowenthal was elected to represent the 27th District of the California State Senate in November of 2004 following six years in the California State Assembly. As Chair of the Senate Environmental Quality Committee as well as Chair of the Transportation and Housing Committee's Sub Committee on California Ports and Goods Movement, Senator Lowenthal is committed to protecting the environment through innovative policy solutions and strong stewardship of public lands. A resident of Long Beach, Senator Lowenthal is married to Dr. Debbie Malumed, a family practice physician. He has two adult sons, and one grandson. He graduated with a B.A. from Hobart College and earned a Ph.D. from Ohio State University. Committees: Environmental Quality (Chair); Banking, Finance and Insurance; Budget and Fiscal Review; Education; Labor and Industrial Relations; Natural Resources and Water; Transportation and Housing.

MACHADO, Michael J. (D) 5th District. Elected to the Senate in November 2000. Full time farmer and legislator. Owns and operates family farm in Linden, California. Served in California State Assembly from 1994 to 2000. Native Californian. Born in Stockton, California on March 12, 1948. Attended Stanford University and graduated with a degree in economics. Earned his master's degree in agricultural economics from the University of California at Davis. Married to Diana Machado. Children: Erahm and Melissa, and Christopher (deceased). Committees: Revenue and Taxation (Chair); Banking, Finance and Insurance; Budget and Fiscal Review; Local Government; Natural Resources and Water; Transportation and Housing.

MALDONADO, Abel (R) 15th District. Senator Abel Maldonado is the oldest son of immigrant field workers. As a child, Abel worked in the fields alongside his father to help support the family. Maldonado was first elected into office by the Santa Maria City Council in 1994. Maldonado was elected to the State Assembly in 1998.

As the 15th District State Senator, Abel is committed to represent his constituents to the best of his ability and provide them with the best possible customer service. Abel's track record has proven that he is a man of his word and will keep his commitments. Senator Abel Maldonado remains committed to the fundamental values of family, fiscal responsibility, personal accountability, integrity, and a strong work ethic. Committees: Education (Vice Chair); Human Services (Vice Chair); Agriculture; Banking, Finance and Insurance; Health; Transportation and Housing.

MARGETT, Bob (R) 29th District. Re-elected to Senate November 2004. Member State Assembly April 1995–Nov. 2000. Arcadia Council Member 1976–1980 & 1992–1995; Mayor 1979–80. Engineering contractor and partner in industrial properties. Native Californian, born in Los Angeles. Attended Hoover H.S. and U.C. Berkeley.

Major: Econ. and Bus. Admin. Married to Beverly Sidel. Seven children: Dennis, Jeff, Jim, Richard, Kenneth, Mindy, and Phil; eleven grandchildren. 39 year resident of Arcadia. Rotarian of the Year 1992; Los Angeles County Distinguished Legislative Service Award 1997. Legislator of the Year: Safari Club International, California Women in Agriculture, American Subcontractors Association of California, Inc., University of California, and Crime Victims United. Member: American Roadbuilders; Building Industry Association; Association of General Contractors; Rotary Club of Arcadia. Committees: Natural Resources and Water (Vice Chair); Budget and Fiscal Review; Governmental Organization; Public Safety; Transportation and Housing.

McCLINTOCK, Thomas (R) 19th District. Elected in 2000. Served in the Assembly 1982–1992 and 1996–2000. Taxpayer advocate. Received B.A. in Political Science from the University of California, Los Angeles. Married, wife Lori. Children: Shannah and Justin. Served as Director of Economic and Regulatory Affairs for the Claremont Institute's Golden State Center for Policy Studies, 1995–96; Director of the Center for the California Taxpayer, 1992–94; Chief of Staff, State Senator Ed Davis, 1980–82; Former Chair, Ventura County Republican Central Committee, 1979–81; Resolutions Chair for the California Republican Party, 1985–92. Served as political columnist, Thousand Oaks News Chronicle, 1976–80. Received Medal of Merit for Heroism, Ventura County Peace Officers Association, 1985. Committees: Transportation and Housing (Vice Chair); Budget and Fiscal Review; Government Modernization, Efficiency and Accountability; Governmental Organization; Local Government.

MIGDEN, Carole (D) 3rd District. Elected 2004, limit 2012; born 8/14/48 New York, NY. Full-time Legislator. Received B.A. Adelphi University; Master's Degree in Clinical Psychology, CSU at Sonoma. Married, spouse: Cristina Arguedas. Former Member, Board of Equalization, 2002–04. Former Assembly Member, 1996–2002. Former Member, San Francisco Board of Supervisors, 1990–1996. Member, Democratic National Committee. Former Chair, California Democratic Party Platform Committee; former Chair, San Francisco Democratic Party; Delegate and Platform Committee member of last four Democratic National Conventions. Formerly directed two community mental health agencies and served as a state health commissioner. Served as Director of the Golden Gate Bridge Highway and Transportation District and as Vice Chair of Finance on the San Francisco County Transportation Authority. Chair, Committee on Appropriations. Member, Committees on Natural Resources and Water, Public Safety, Joint Committee on Legislative Budget, Select Committees on California's Wine Industry, Bay Area Infrastructure, Select Committee on California's Horse Racing Industry.

MORROW, Bill (R) 38th District. Elected in 1998. Small Business Attorney. State Assembly 1992–98. Married Barbara on February 24, 2001. Native Californian born in Monterey Park. B.A. Political Science, UCLA; J.D., Pepperdine School of Law. Eight years as U.S. Marine Corps Officer, Military Judge Advocate. "Legislator of the Year" for Orange County League of Cities, Pro-Life PAC of Orange County, Orange County Citizens Against Lawsuit Abuse, Golden State Mobile Home Owners League, CA Republican Assembly, and "Legislator of the Decade" by Off-road Legislative Coalition of CA. Kiwanis, AMVETS, American Legion, Vista Masonic Lodge, Chamber of Commerce, Volunteer for Y.M.C.A., Salvation Army, Special Olympics, Boys and Girls Club. Committees: Veterans (Chair); Energy, Utilities & Communications (Vice Chair); Judiciary (Vice Chair); Business, Professions and Economic Development, Education and Joint Legislative Audit Committee.

MURRAY, Kevin G. (D) 26th District. Elected to the State Senate in 1998, previously to the Assembly in 1994. Full time legislator. Native of California, lifelong resident of the 26th Senate District. Born March 12, 1960. B.S. in Business Administration/Accounting, Cal State Northridge, 1981; M.B.A., Loyola Marymount, 1983; J.D. Loyola  Law School 1987. Married to Janice Jamison. Son of former Assemblyman Willard Murray. Former talent agent with the William Morris Agency. Member of American Bar Association, Phi Beta Sigma Fraternity, American MENSA, and the CA Bar Association. Committees: Appropriations; Banking, Finance and Insurance; Energy, Utilities and Communications; Government Modernization, Efficiency and Accountability; Governmental Organization; Elections, Reapportionment and Constitutional Amendments; Transportation and Housing.

ORTIZ, Deborah (D) 6th District. Elected in 1998. Author of nationally-recognized stem cell research law, laws guaranteeing college scholarships, access to health services, and fighting cancer and childhood obesity. Chairs Senate Health Committee, Subcommittee on Stem Cell Research Oversight, Subcommittee on Mental Health and Neurodevelopmental Disorders. Serves on Senate Appropriations; Banking, Finance and Insurance; Agriculture committees, and Joint Legislative Audit and Joint Rules committees. Sacramento native, attended University of California, Davis, graduated McGeorge School of Law. Sacramento City Council, 1993–96; California Assembly, 1996–98. Vice-president, National Association of Latino Elected & Appointed Officials Educational Fund Board; Chair, National Hispanic Caucus of State Legislators Health Policy Task Force; Board member, Commission on Status of Women.

POOCHIGIAN, Charles (R) 14th Senate District. Elected 1998. Assistant Republican Leader and Vice Chair of Public Safety and Joint Legislative Audit Committees; serves on Agriculture, Appropriations, Elections, Joint Rules, and Revenue and Taxation Committees. Senator Poochigian is a strong advocate for business and agriculture, education reform, and tough criminal justice policies. He authored landmark legislation in 2004 reforming California's broken workers' compensation system, and has been committed to sound fiscal policies, improving educational achievement, and enhancing law enforcement effectiveness. Born in Fresno, Senator Poochigian is a third generation resident of the Valley, where his family has farmed since 1914. B.A. CSU Fresno, 1972; J.D. University of Santa Clara, 1975. He and his wife, Debbie, were married in 1977 and have three grown children.

RUNNER, George (R) 17th District. George Runner was first elected to the State Senate in 2004. As a thoughtful conservative, Runner's priorities in the Legislature are to focus on improving economic prosperity, business growth, education excellence, and family preservation for all Californians. He currently is the Senate Republican Caucus

Chair, and serves as the Vice Chair of Health and Environmental Quality, and as a member of Budget, Transportation and Housing, Revenue and Taxation, Select Committee on Defense and Aerospace Industry. Prior to his election to the State Senate, Senator Runner served in the State Assembly for three terms, where he authored the well-known Amber Alert in California. He is married to Assemblywoman Sharon Runner who represents the 36th Assembly District. George and Sharon are the first husband and wife in California history to serve concurrently in the Legislature. They have a son, Micah, daughter-in-law, Sandy, and daughter Rebekah.

SCOTT, Jack (D) 21st District. Elected to the Senate in 2000. Educator. Born August 24, 1933 in Sweetwater, Texas. Established residency in California in 1962. B.A., Abilene Christian University; Master of Divinity, Yale University; Ph.D., Claremont University. Married, wife Lacreta; children: Sharon Mitchell, Sheila Head, Amy

Schones, Greg Scott, and Adam Scott (deceased). Former President of Pasadena City College, 1987–1995. Distinguished Professor of Higher Education, Pepperdine University; Board of Directors, Coalition for a Non-Violent City. Assemblymember (1996–2000). Committees: Education; Banking, Finance & Insurance; Budget and Fiscal Review; Senate Revenue & Taxation.

SIMITIAN, S. Joseph (D) 11th District. Elected 2004. Full-time Legislator. B.A., Colorado College; M.A., Stanford University; M.C.P. and J.D., U.C. Berkeley. Co-Chair, Silicon Valley Leadership Group Housing Leadership Council. Member, Bd. of Advisors, Adolescent Counseling Services; Trustee Emeritus, Junior Statesmen Foundation. Former Member, Steering Committee, Bay Area Council; Bd. of Directors, Joint Venture: Silicon Valley Network. Election observer/supervisor in El Salvador and Bosnia. Refugee relief and resettlement efforts in Albania and Kosovo in 1999 with the International Rescue Committee. "Scientific American 50" Leaders in Science and Technology; AeA (American Electronics Association) High-Tech Legislator of the Year; Community Hero Award by Peninsula Interfaith Action; Outstanding Legislator of the Year by the California School Boards Association; Environmental Leadership Award by Bluewater Network; Coastal Champion by Vote the Coast. Former State Assemblymember; Santa Clara County Board of Supervisors; Mayor, City of Palo Alto; President, Palo Alto School Board. Chair, Human Services Committee; Select Committee on Coastal Protection and Watershed Conservation; Joint Committee on the Master Plan for Education. Member, Committees on Budget and Fiscal Review; Business, Professions and Economic Development; Education; Energy, Utilities and Communications; Environmental Quality; Transportation and Housing.

SOTO, Nell (D) 32nd District. Elected March 7, 2000, Special Election. Full-time legislator. Native Californian born June 18, 1926 in Pomona. 1st Inland Empire woman elected to the Assembly in 1998. Pomona City Council (1987–98); Board of Directors, SCAQMD (1994–98). Attended Mount San Antonio College in Walnut. Public Affairs Representative Southern California Rapid Transit District (15 years). Widow of former Assembly Member Philip Soto, six children, grandmother of 12; great-grandmother to 4. Awards: "2004 Lady Bird Johnson Award," City of Riverside and Greater Riverside Chamber of Commerce; "2004 Elected Official Public Service Award" San Bernardino/Highland Chapter of MAPA. Committees: Public Employment and Retirement (Chair); Veterans Affairs (Vice-Chair); Education; Governmental Organization; Local Government; Transportation and Housing.

SPEIER, Jackie (D) 8th District. Elected 1998. Chairs Banking, Finance and Insurance Committee; serves on Appropriations and Education. Chairs Select Committee on Government Cost Control. Has more than 300 bills signed into law, including landmark financial privacy protections, the country's first Prescription Drug Discount Program

for seniors and the disabled, California's first low-cost auto insurance plan, bills related to workers compensation reform, prison reform and accountability, consumer protection, domestic violence, insurance, child support, HMO reform, and the environment. *The San Jose Mercury News* reported in 1996 that "no one comes close to Speier's remarkable record of getting substantive legislation signed into law." Served on the San Mateo County Bd. of Supervisors, 1981–86. BA, Univ. of Calif. at Davis; JD, Hastings College of Law, 1976. Member CA State Bar, Dist. of Columbia Bar. Married to Barry Dennis 2001. Two children, Jackson Sierra, 16 and Stephanie Sierra, 10. First member of the legislature to give birth while in office.

TORLAKSON, Tom (D) 7th District. Elected to the Senate in 2000. Educator/ Legislator. Born July 19, 1949 in San Francisco, CA. Received Bachelor of Arts in History; Life Secondary Teaching Credential; Master of Arts in Education from UC-Berkeley. Married in 1970 to the former Diana Bravos. An-

tioch City Council, Mayor Pro Tem, 1978–81. Contra Costa County Board of Supervisors, 1981–1996 (Chair, 1984, 1989, and 1994). California State Assembly, 1997–2000. Association of Bay Area Governments, President, 1994–95. Chairman, Delta Protection Commission, 1993–95. Member, Metropolitan Transportation Commission. Served as fireman in Merchant Marines, 1967–68. Recipient, Merchant Marines Vietnam Service Medal. Committees: Transportation and Housing, (Chair); Local Government; Education; and Budget and Fiscal Review.

VINCENT, Edward (D) 25th District. Elected 2000. Served in State Assembly 1996–2000. Full-time Legislator. Born June 23, 1934, Steubenville, Ohio. Attended University of Iowa, 1952–56; CSU Los Angeles, 1964–66; B.A. in Social Work and Corrections. Married March 28, 1957; wife, Marilyn; children: Valerie and Dawn, three grandchildren. Served in U.S. Army 1957–59. Served on Inglewood Unified School District's Board of Trustees. Member, NAACP; Urban League; Probation Officer's Union; Former Inglewood City Council Member and Mayor (1982–1996). Former Member, Calif. World Trade Commission; California Coastal Commission. Received All American Football honors from the University of Iowa in 1955. All Big Ten 1954–55; Holds longest touchdown run from scrimmage in Big Ten Conference history (96 yards against Purdue 1954); All Army-All Service 1958; Drafted by Los Angeles Rams 1956. Committees: Agriculture; Governmental Organization; Health.

OFFICERS OF THE SENATE
(Nonmembers)

Gregory Schmidt, Secretary of the Senate. Born in Oakland, California, May 3, 1947. B.A. Santa Clara University, 1969. M.A. University of California, Berkeley, 1973. Served as Consultant to Assembly Committees on Human Resources; Labor, Employment and Consumer Affairs, 1974–82, Senate Committee on Elections and Reapportionment, 1983–84. Staff Director of Senate Judiciary Committee, 1985–94. Chief of Staff to the President pro Tempore, 1994. Executive Officer of Senate Rules Committee, 1995 to present. Staff Chair, NCSL Criminal Justice Committee 1992–93. Chair, California International Relations Foundation. Member, American Society of Legislative Clerks and Secretaries. Elected Secretary August 31, 1996. Married to Charlotte Haynes Schmidt, children Jeffrey, Korina, John, Thomas, grandsons Kai, Jaden, Damon, Nathan, and Parker.

Tony Beard, Jr., Chief Senate Sergeant at Arms. Born in Glendale, California. Attended Sacramento schools. A.A. degree in Mathematics and Physical Science from American River College; B.A. degree in Political Science from California State University, Sacramento. Has served as Chief Sergeant at Arms since December 1979. Married to Laura Bahlhorn, daughter Kristin Marie. Grand Children Chloe and Charlie. Attended U.S. Secret Service Dignitary Protection School, Washington, D.C. California Highway Patrol Protection of Public Officials School, Los Angeles, California. Board member of Association of Threat Assessment Professionals. Associate Member of Bomb Technicians and Investigators, Associate Member Sacramento Explosive Ordinance Disposal Team, Member Northern California Peace Officers Association. Past President National Legislative Security and Services Association. Staff Chair, NCSL Criminal Justice Committee—Advisory Board Member University of Southern California.

The Rev. Canon James D. Richardson
Chaplain; Born: Berkeley, Calif., 1953;
B.A. UCLA 1975; Alicia Patterson
Foundation Fellow, Visiting Scholar,
UC Berkeley Institute of Governmental
Studies, 1993; M.Div. Church Divinity
School of the Pacific, Berkeley, 2000;
Episcopal priest, Associate Dean, Trin-
ity Cathedral, Sacramento. Staff Writer,
Riverside Press-Enterprise, 1976–1983, Capitol Bureau
Chief 1985–1988; San Diego Union, 1983–1985; Sacra-
mento Bee Capitol Bureau 1988–1997. Author, *Willie
Brown: A Biography*, UC Press 1996; co-author, three
editions of California Political Almanac. Life member,
UCLA Alumni Assoc.; Board member Francis House, Sac-
ramento. Appointed Chaplain Dec. 2004.

SENATORIAL DISTRICTS

1. Alpine, Amador, Calaveras, El Dorado, Lassen, Modoc, Mono, Nevada, Placer, Plumas, Sacramento, Sierra—Cox (R)

2. Humboldt, Lake, Mendocino, Napa, Solano, Sonoma—Chesbro (D)

3. Marin, San Franciso, Sonoma—Migden (D)

4. Butte, Colusa, Del Norte, Glenn, Nevada, Placer, Shasta, Siskiyou, Sutter, Tehama, Trinity, Yuba—Aanestad (R)

5. Sacramento, San Joaquin, Yolo—Machado (D)

6. Sacramento—Ortiz (D)

7. Contra Costa—Torlakson (D)

8. San Francisco, San Mateo—Speier (D)

9. Alameda, Contra Costa—Perata (D)

10. Alameda, Santa Clara—Figueroa (D)

11. San Mateo, Santa Clara, Santa Cruz—Simitian (D)

12. Madera, Merced, Monterey, San Benito, Stanislaus—Denham (R)

13. Santa Clara—Alquist (D)

14. Fresno, Madera, Mariposa, San Joaquin, Stanislaus, Tuolumne—Poochigian (R)

15. Monterey, San Luis Obispo, Santa Barbara, Santa Clara, Santa Cruz—Maldonado (R)

16. Fresno, Kern, Kings, Tulare—Florez (D)

17. Los Angeles, San Bernardino, Ventura—Runner (R)

18. Inyo, Kern, San Bernardino, Tulare—Ashburn (R)

19. Los Angeles, Santa Barbara, Ventura—McClintock (R)

20. Los Angeles—Alarcón (D)

21. Los Angeles—Scott (D)

22. Los Angeles—Cedillo (D)

23. Los Angeles, Ventura—Kuehl (D)

24. Los Angeles—Romero (D)

25. Los Angeles—Vincent (D)

SENATORIAL DISTRICTS—Continued

26. Los Angeles—Murray (D)
27. Los Angeles—Lowenthal (D)
28. Los Angeles—Bowen (D)
29. Los Angeles, Orange, San Bernardino—Margett (R)
30. Los Angeles—Escutia (D)
31. Riverside, San Bernardino—Dutton (R)
32. San Bernardino, Los Angeles—Soto (D)
33. Orange—Ackerman (R)
34. Orange—Dunn (D)
35. Orange—Campbell (R)
36. Riverside, San Diego—Hollingsworth (R)
37. Riverside—Battin (R)
38. Orange, San Diego—Morrow (R)
39. San Diego—Kehoe (D)
40. Imperial, Riverside, San Diego—Ducheny (D)

(D) Democratic 25, (R) Republican 15

Total 40.

MEMBERS OF THE SENATE—FORTY SENATORS

LIEUTENANT GOVERNOR CRUZ M. BUSTAMANTE, President of the Senate

DON PERATA, President pro Tempore   GREGORY SCHMIDT, Secretary of the Senate

TONY BEARD JR., Sergeant at Arms

(R., Republican; D., Democratic; I., Independent)

Capitol Address of Senators: State Capitol, Sacramento 95814

Name	Occupation	Party	Dist.	District Address	Legislative Service
A					
Aanestad, Sam	Oral Surgeon	R	4	200 Providence Mine Road, Ste. 108, Nevada City 95959	Dec. 1998–05
Ackerman, Dick	Business Lawyer	R	33	17821 East 17th Street, Suite 180, Tustin 92780	Sept. 1995–05
Alarcón, Richard	Full-time Legislator	D	20	6150 Van Nuys Blvd., Suite 400, Van Nuys 91401	Dec. 1998–05

MEMBERS OF THE SENATE—FORTY SENATORS—CONTINUED

Name	Occupation	Party	Dist.	District Address	Legislative Service
Alquist, Elaine	Educator	D	13	100 Paseo de San Antonio, Suite 209, San Jose 95113	1996–2002 Dec. 2004–05
Ashburn, Roy	Full-time Legislator	R	18	5001 California Avenue, Ste. 105, Bakersfield 93309	Dec. 1996–05
B					
Battin, Jim	Businessman	R	37	73–710 Fred Waring Drive, Ste. 112, Palm Desert 92260; 13800 Heacock, Suite C112, Moreno Valley 92553	Dec. 1994–05
Bowen, Debra	Public Law Attorney	D	28	2512 Artesia Blvd. Suite 200, Redondo Beach 90278	Dec. 1992–05
C					
Campbell, John	Businessman/Legislator	R	35	950 S. Coast Dr., Ste. 240 Costa Mesa 92626	Dec. 2000–05
Cedillo, Gilbert	Full-time Legislator	D	22	617 S. Olive Street, Ste. 710, Los Angeles 90014	Jan. 1998–05

Chesbro, Wesley	Full-time Legislator	D	2	1040 Main Street, Suite 205, Napa 94559; 50 D St. Suite 120A, Santa Rosa 95404; 710 E Street, Suite 150, Eureka 95502; 444 Georgia Street, Vallejo 94590; P.O. Box 785, Ukiah 95482	Dec. 1998–05
Cox, Dave	Businessman/Legislator	R	1	2140 Professional Drive, Ste. 140, Roseville 95661	Dec. 1998–05
D					
Denham, Jeff	Agri-Businessman	R	12	1620 N. Carpenter Road, Suite A-4, Modesto 95351; 2824 Park Ave., #C, Merced 95348; 369 Main Street, #208, Salinas 93901	Dec. 2002–05

MEMBERS OF THE SENATE—FORTY SENATORS—CONTINUED

Name	Occupation	Party	Dist.	District Address	Legislative Service
Moreno Ducheny, Denise	Attorney	D	40	637 3rd Ave., Ste. C, Chula Vista 91910; 53-990 Enterprise Way. Ste. 14, Coachella 92236; 1224 State Street, Suite D, El Centro 92243	1994–2000 Dec. 2002–05
Dunn, Joseph L.	Consumer Attorney	D	34	12397 Lewis Street, Suite 103, Garden Grove 92840	Dec. 1998–05
Dutton, Bob	Small Business Owner	R	31	8577 Haven Ave., Ste. 210, Rancho Cucamonga 91730	Dec. 2002–05
E Escutia, Martha M.	Attorney	D	30	12440 E. Imperial Hwy., Suite 125, Norwalk 90650	Dec. 1992–05
F Figueroa, Liz	Businesswoman	D	10	43801 Mission Blvd., Suite 103, Fremont 94539	Dec. 1994–05

Florez, Dean	Businessman	D	16	2550 Mariposa Mall, Ste. 2016, Fresno 93721	Dec. 1998–05
H					
Hollingsworth, Dennis	Farmer's Rep/Businessman	R	36	27555 Ynez Rd., Suite 204, Temecula 92591	Dec. 2000–05
K					
Kehoe, Christine	Full-time Legislator	D	39	1010 University Ave., Ste. C207, San Diego 92103	Dec. 2000–05
Kuehl, Sheila James	Full-time Legislator	D	23	10951 W. Pico Blvd., # 202, Los Angeles 90064	Dec. 1994–05
L					
Lowenthal, Alan S.	Professor	D	27	16401 Paramount Blvd., 1st Flr., Paramount 90723; 115 Pine Ave., Suite 430, Long Beach 90802	Dec. 1998–05
M					
Machado, Mike	Farmer/Businessman	D	5	1020 N Street, Suite 506, Sacramento 95814; 31 East Channel Street, Room 440, Stockton 95202	Dec. 1994–05

MEMBERS OF THE SENATE—FORTY SENATORS—CONTINUED

Name	Occupation	Party	Dist.	District Address	*Legislative Service*
Maldonado, Abel	Businessman	R	15	100 Paseo de San Antonio, Suite 206, San Jose 95113; 1356 Marsh Street, San Luis Obispo 93401	Dec. 1998–05
Margett, Bob	Businessman	R	29	23355 E. Golden Springs Dr., Diamond Bar 91765	June 1995–05
McClintock, Tom	Budget Reduction Analyst	R	19	223 E. Thousand Oaks Blvd., Ste. 326, Thousand Oaks 91360	Dec. 1982–92, Dec. 1996–05
Migden, Carole	Full-time Legislator	D	3	455 Golden Gate Ave. Ste. 14800, San Francisco 94102; 3501 Civic Center, Rm. 425, San Rafael 94903	Mar. 1996–02, Dec. 2005
Morrow, Bill	Attorney	R	38	27126 A Paseo Espada, Suite 1621, San Juan Capistrano 92675; 2755 Jefferson Street, Suite 101, Carlsbad 92008	Dec. 1992–05

Murray, Kevin	Full-time Legislator	D	26	600 Corporate Point, Ste. 1020, Culver City 90230; 700 State Drive, Suite 108, Los Angeles 90037	Dec. 1994–05
O					
Ortiz, Deborah V.	Full-time Legislator	D	6	1020 N Street, Suite 578, Sacramento 95814; 5951 Birdcage Center Lane, Ste. 145, Citrus Heights 95610	Dec. 1996–05
P					
Perata, Don	Teacher	D	9	1515 Clay Street, Suite 2202, Oakland 94612; 300 S. Spring St., Ste. 8501, Los Angeles 90013	Dec. 1996–05
Poochigian, Charles	Attorney	R	14	4974 E. Clinton, Suite 100, Fresno 93727; 1308 W. Main, Ripon 95366	Dec. 1994–05

MEMBERS OF THE SENATE—FORTY SENATORS—CONTINUED

Name	Occupation	Party	Dist.	District Address	Legislative Service
R					
Romero, Gloria	Professor	D	24	149 South Mednik Ave., Ste. 202, Los Angeles 90022; 14403 E. Pacific Ave. #327, Baldwin Park 91706; 1444 W. Garvey Ave. Rm. 305, W. Covina 91790	Dec. 1998–05
Runner, George C.	Full-time Legislator	R	17	848 W. Lancaster Blvd., Ste. 101, Lancaster 93534; 23920 Valencia Blvd. Ste. 250, Santa Clarita 91355; 14343 Civic Drive, 1st Flr., Victorville 92392	Dec. 1996–02 Dec. 05
S					
Scott, Jack	Legislator/Professor	D	21	215 N. Marengo Avenue, Suite 185, Pasadena 91101	Dec. 1996–05

Simitian, Joe	Full-time Legislator	D	11	160 Town and Country Village, Palo Alto 94301; 701 Ocean St., Room 318A, Santa Cruz 95060	Nov. 2000–05
Soto, Nell	Full-Time Legislator	D	32	822 N. Euclid Avenue, Ontario 91762; 357 West 2nd Street, Ste. 1, San Bernardino 92401; 505 S. Garey Ave., 2nd Floor, Pomona 91766	Dec. 1998–05
Speier, Jackie	Attorney/Legislator	D	8	400 S. El Camino Real, Suite 630, San Mateo 94402; 455 Golden Gate Avenue, Ste. 14200, San Francisco 94102	Dec. 1986–96 Dec. 1998–05
T					
Torlakson, Tom	Educator	D	7	2801 Concord Blvd., Concord 94519; 420 W. 3rd Street, Antioch 94509	Dec. 1996–05

MEMBERS OF THE SENATE—FORTY SENATORS—CONTINUED

Name	Occupation	Party	Dist.	District Address	Legislative Service
V					
Vincent, Edward	Legislator	D	25	1 Manchester Blvd., Suite 600, Inglewood 90301	Dec. 1996–05

Senatoris Est Civitatis Liberatem Tueri—It is the Duty of the Senators to Protect the Liberty of the People

LIEUTENANT GOVERNOR CRUZ M. BUSTAMANTE, PRESIDENT
SENATOR DON PERATA, PRESIDENT PRO TEMPORE

Clerks / Officers (rostrum)

| DAVID M. KNEALE HISTORY CLERK | JAMES TAYLOR ASSISTANT FILE CLERK | MARISELA HERNANDEZ DAILY FILE CLERK | PAULA ROBERTO JOURNAL CLERK | KIP KENDALL READING CLERK | DAVID VALVERDE CHIEF ASSISTANT SECRETARY OF SENATE | GREGORY SCHMIDT SECRETARY OF THE SENATE | SUSAN DELAPLAINE ASSISTANT SECRETARY OF SENATE | CONTROL CONSOLE |

Senator Desks

Column 1
- DENHAM of Merced
- MORROW of Oceanside
- RUNNER of Antelope Valley

Column 2
- HOLLINGSWORTH of Murrieta
- COX of Fair Oaks
- ASHBURN of Bakersfield

Column 3
- MARGETT of Arcadia
- AANESTAD of Grass Valley
- CAMPBELL of Orange

Column 4
- DUTTON of Inland Empire
- MALDONADO of Santa Maria
- BATTIN of Palm Desert

Column 5
- FLOREZ of Shafter
- McCLINTOCK of Thousand Oaks
- POOCHIGIAN of Fresno
- MIGDEN of San Francisco

Column 6
- DUCHENY of San Diego
- VINCENT of Los Angeles
- ACKERMAN of Tustin
- PERATA of Oakland

Column 7
- CHESBRO of Arcata
- KEHOE of San Diego
- ALARCON of Los Angeles
- FIGUEROA of Fremont

Column 8
- BOWEN of Redondo Beach
- SOTO of San Bernardino
- SIMITIAN of Palo Alto
- MURRAY of Los Angeles
- MACHADO of Linden

Column 9
- DUNN of Santa Ana
- LOWENTHAL of Long Beach

Column 10
- CEDILLO of Los Angeles
- ROMERO of Los Angeles
- KUEHL of Santa Monica

Column 11
- SPEIER of San Francisco
- ESCUTIA of Norwalk
- ORTIZ of Sacramento
- SCOTT of Pasadena
- ALQUIST of Santa Clara
- TORLAKSON of Antioch

USUAL ORDER OF EVENTS

ROLL CALL
PRAYER BY THE CHAPLAIN
COMMUNICATIONS AND MESSAGES
COMMITTEE REPORTS
MOTIONS AND RESOLUTIONS
CONSIDERATION OF BILLS
ANNOUNCEMENTS
ADJOURNMENT

TONY BEARD, JR., SERGEANT AT ARMS
REV. CANON JAMES RICHARDSON, CHAPLAIN

SENATE PUBLICATIONS
(OBTAINABLE AT LEGISLATIVE BILL ROOM)

THE FILE—DAILY
PROGRAM OF THE DAY'S BUSINESS

THE JOURNAL—DAILY
RECORD OF THE DAY'S BUSINESS

THE HISTORY—DAILY
SHOWS LATEST ACTION ON BILLS

STANDING COMMITTEES OF THE SENATE

AGRICULTURE—(9)—Denham (Chair), Ducheny (Vice-Chair), Chesbro, Florez, Hollingsworth, Maldonado, Ortiz, Poochigian and Vincent. Consultant: John Chandler. Assistant: Jane Leonard Brown. Phone (916) 651-1508. 1020 N Street, Suite 244.

APPROPRIATIONS—(13)—Migden (Chair), Aanestad (Vice-Chair), Alquist, Ashburn, Battin, Bowen, Dutton, Escutia, Florez, Murray, Ortiz, Poochigian and Speier. Staff Director: Bob Franzoia. Consultants: George Cate, Miriam Barcellona Ingenito, Nora Lynn, Lisa Matocq, Mark McKenzie and Maureen Ortiz. Assistant: Sally Ann Romo and Krimilda Hodson. Phone (916) 651-4101. Room 2206.

BANKING, FINANCE AND INSURANCE—(11)—Speier (Chair), Cox (Vice-Chair), Denham, Figueroa, Hollingsworth, Lowenthal, Machado, Maldonado, Murray, Ortiz, and Scott. Staff Director: Brian Perkins. Consultants: Eileeen Roush, Erin Ryan and Soren Tjernell. Committee Assistant: Inez Taylor. Phone (916) 651-4102. Room 2032.

BUDGET AND FISCAL REVIEW—(17)—Chesbro (Chair), Hollingsworth (Vice-Chair), Campbell, Ducheny, Dunn, Dutton, Kehoe, Kuehl, Lowenthal, Machado, Margett, McClintock, Romero, Runner, Scott, Simitian, and Torlakson. Staff Director: Daniel Alvarez. Consultants: Brian Annis, Keely Martin Bosler, Kim Connor, Anastasia Dodson, Alex MacBain, Dave O'Toole, Amy Supinger and Diane Van Maren. Assistants: Glenda Higgins and Rose Morris. Phone (916) 651-4103. Room 5019.

Republican Fiscal Office: Phone (916) 651-1501. 1020 N Street, Room 234.

BUSINESS, PROFESSIONS AND ECONOMIC DEVELOPMENT—(7)—Figueroa (Chair), Campbell (Vice-Chair), Aanestad, Florez, Morrow, Murray, and Simitian. Chief Consultant: Bill Gage. Principal Consultant: Jay DeFuria. Consultants: G.V. Ayers, Doug Brown and Robin Hartley. Assistant: Kathy Sullivan. Phone (916) 651-4104. Room 2053.

STANDING COMMITTEES OF THE SENATE—Continued

EDUCATION—(12)—Scott (Chair), Maldonado (Vice-Chair), Alquist, Denham, Dutton, Lowenthal, Morrow, Romero, Simitian, Soto, Speier, and Torlakson. Chief Consultant: James Wilson. Principal Consultants: Nancy Rose Anton, Kathleen Chavira, Lisa J. Giroux, Diane Kirkham and Lynn Lorber. Assistants: Sandy Malosh and Barbara Montero. Phone (916) 651-4105. Room 2083.

ELECTIONS, REAPPORTIONMENT AND CONSTITUTIONAL AMENDMENTS—(6)—Bowen (Chair), Battin (Vice-Chair), Dunn, Murray, Poochigian, and Romero. Chief Consultant: Darren Chesin. Consultant: Fran Tibon-Estoista. Assistant: Diana Ramirez. Phone (916) 651-4106. Room 2203.

ENERGY, UTILITIES AND COMMUNICATIONS—(11)—Escutia (Chair), Morrow (Vice-Chair), Alarcón, Battin, Bowen, Campbell, Cox, Dunn, Kehoe, Murray, and Simitian. Chief Consultant: Randy Chinn. Principal Consultant: Lawrence Lingbloom. Assistant: Melanie Gutierrez. Phone (916) 651-4107. Room 5046.

ENVIRONMENTAL QUALITY—(9)—Lowenthal (Chair), Runner (Vice-Chair), Campbell, Chesbro, Cox, Escutia, Figueroa, Kuehl, and Simitian. Consultants: Bruce Jennings and Randy Pestor. Assistant: Ann Boone. Phone (916) 651-4108. Room 2205.

GOVERNMENT MODERNIZATION, EFFICIENCY AND ACCOUNTABILITY—(10)—Figueroa (Chair), Dutton (Vice-Chair), Ashburn, Bowen, Campbell, Ducheny, Florez, Kuehl, McClintock, and Murray. Chief Consultant: Ed Howard. Assistant: Angela Baber. Phone (916) 651-1518. 1020 N Street, Suite 521.

GOVERNMENTAL ORGANIZATION—(11)—Florez (Chair), Denham (Vice-Chair), Battin, Chesbro, Cox, Dunn, Margett, McClintock, Murray, Soto, and Vincent. Consultants: Steve Hardy and Arthur Terzakis. Assistant: Brenda K. Heiser. Phone (916) 651-1530. 1020 N Street, Suite 584.

STANDING COMMITTEES OF THE
SENATE—Continued

HEALTH—(11)—Ortiz (Chair), Runner (Vice-Chair), Aanestad, Alquist, Chesbro, Cox, Figueroa, Kuehl, Maldonado, Romero, and Vincent. Staff Director: Peter Hansel. Consultants: Roger Dunstan, Rachel Machi, Andrea Margolis, and Nicole Vazquez. Assistant: Amofia "Moe" Katsimbras. Phone (916) 651-4111. Room 2191.

HUMAN SERVICES—(7)—Simitian (Chair), Maldonado (Vice-Chair), Aanestad, Alarcón, Alquist, Chesbro, and Flores. Consultants: Jack Hailey and Sue North. Assistant: Joy Traylor. Phone (916) 651-4112. Room 2195.

JUDICIARY—(7)—Dunn (Chair), Morrow (Vice-Chair), Ackerman, Cedillo, Escutia, Figueroa, and Kuehl. Chief Counsel: Gene Wong. Deputy Chief Counsel: Gloria Megino Ochoa. Counsels: Alexandra Montgomery, Amanda Taylor, and Melinda Myers. Assistants: Carol Thomas and Emily Crossland. Phone (916) 651-4113. Room 2187.

LABOR AND INDUSTRIAL RELATIONS—(8)—Alarcón (Chair), Campbell (Vice-Chair), Ackerman, Bowen, Dutton, Hollingsworth, Lowenthal, and Runner. Staff Director: Frances T. Low. Principal Consultant: Rodger Dillon. Consultant: Nick Hardeman. Assistant: Rosa M. Castanos Padilla. Phone (916) 651-4114. Room 4035.

LOCAL GOVERNMENT—(9)—Kehoe (Chair), Cox (Vice-Chair), Ackerman, Kuehl, Machado, McClintock, Perata, Soto, and Torlakson. Consultants: Peter Detwiler and Jennifer Swenson. Assistant: Elvia Diaz. Phone (916) 651-4115. Room 410.

NATURAL RESOURCES AND WATER—(11)—Kuehl (Chair), Margett (Vice-Chair), Aanestad, Bowen, Hollingsworth, Kehoe, Lowenthal, Machado, Migden, and Romero. Chief Consultant: Bill Craven. Principal Consultants: Julia McIver and Dennis O'Connor. Consultant: Tam Ma. Assistants: Patricia Hanson and Cathy Cruz. Phone (916) 651-4116. Room 407.

PUBLIC EMPLOYMENT AND RETIREMENT—(5)—Soto (Chair), Ashburn (Vice-Chair), Alarcón, Dunn, and Hollingsworth. Consultant: David Felderstein. Assistant: Irene Reteguin. Phone (916) 651-4117. Room #B-31.

STANDING COMMITTEES OF THE
SENATE—Continued

Public Safety—(7)—Alquist (Chair), Poochigian (Vice-Chair), Cedillo, Margett, Midgen, Perata, and Romero. Chief Counsel: Simon Haines. Counsels: Alison Anderson, Mary Kennedy and Jerome McGuire. Associate Consultant: Tammy Lin. Assistants: Mona Cano and Barbara Reynolds. Phone (916) 651-4118. Room 2031.

Revenue and Taxation—(8)—Machado (Chair), Dutton (Vice-Chair), Alquist, Bowen, Cedillo, Poochigian, Runner and Scott. Consultants: Martin Helmke and Gayle Miller. Assistant: Marisa Lanchester. Phone (916) 651-4119. Room 408.

Rules—(5)—Perata (Chair), Battin (Vice-Chair), Ashburn, Bowen and Cedillo. Executive Officer: Greg Schmidt. Assistant: Pat Webb. Phone (916) 651-4120. Room 400.

Transportation and Housing—(14)—Torlakson (Chair), McClintock (Vice-Chair), Ashburn, Cedillo, Ducheny, Kehoe, Lowenthal, Machado, Maldonado, Margett, Murray, Runner, Simitian and Soto. Chief Consultant: Carrie Cornwell. Staff Director: Steven Schnaidt. Principal Consultant: Randall Henry. Consultant: Mark Stivers. Assistant: Tracey Hurd-Parker. Phone (916) 651-4121. Room 2209.

Veterans Affairs—(5)—Morrow (Chair), Soto (Vice-Chair), Chesbro, Denham and Dunn. Consultant: Donald Wilson. Assistant: Cindy Johnston. Phone (916) 651-1503. 1020 N Street, Room 251.

COMMITTEE ON LEGISLATIVE
ETHICS

Legislative Ethics—(6)—Vacancies. Chief Counsel: Ann Bailey. Assistant: Jean Myers. Phone (916) 651-1507. 1020 N Street, Suite 238.

SENATORS' STANDING
COMMITTEE MEMBERSHIPS

Aanestad—(5)—Appropriations (Vice-Chair); Business, Professions and Economic Development; Health; Human Services; Natural Resources and Water.

Ackerman—(3)—Judiciary; Labor and Industrial Relations; Local Government.

SENATORS' STANDING COMMITTEE
MEMBERSHIPS—Continued

ALARCÓN—(4)—Labor and Industrial Relations (Chair); Energy, Utilities and Communications; Human Services; Public Employment and Retirement.

ALQUIST—(6)—Public Safety (Chair); Appropriations; Education; Health; Human Services; Revenue and Taxation.

ASHBURN—(5)—Public Employment and Retirement (Vice-Chair); Appropriations; Government Modernization, Efficiency and Accountability; Rules; Transportation and Housing.

BATTIN—(5)—Elections, Reapportionment and Constitutional Amendments (Vice-Chair); Rules (Vice-Chair); Appropriations; Energy, Utilities and Communications; Government Organization.

BOWEN—(7)—Elections, Reapportionment and Constitutional Amendments (Chair); Appropriations; Energy, Utilities and Communications; Government Modernization, Efficiency and Accountability; Natural Resources and Water; Rules; Revenue and Taxation.

CAMPBELL—(6)—Business, Professions and Economic Development (Vice-Chair); Labor and Industrial Relations (Vice-Chair); Budget and Fiscal Review; Energy, Utilities and Communications; Environmental Quality; Government Modernization, Efficiency and Accountability.

CEDILLO—(5)—Judiciary; Public Safety; Revenue and Taxation; Rules; Transportation and Housing.

CHESBRO—(7)—Budget and Fiscal Review (Chair); Agriculture; Environmental Quality; Governmental Organization; Health; Human Services; Veterans' Affairs.

COX—(6)—Banking, Finance and Insurance (Vice-Chair); Local Government (Vice-Chair); Energy, Utilities and Communications; Environmental Quality; Governmental Organization; Health.

DENHAM—(5)—Agriculture (Chair); Governmental Organization (Vice-Chair); Banking, Finance and Insurance; Education; Veterans' Affairs.

DUCHENY—(4)—Agriculture (Vice-Chair); Budget and Fiscal Review; Government Modernization, Efficiency and Accountability; Transportation and Housing.

SENATORS' STANDING COMMITTEE
MEMBERSHIPS—Continued

Dunn—(8)—Judiciary (Chair); Budget and Fiscal Review; Elections, Reapportionment and Constitutional Amendments; Energy, Utilities and Communications; Governmental Organization; Labor and Industrial Relations; Public Employment and Retirement; Veterans' Affairs.

Dutton—(4)—Government Modernization, Efficiency and Accountability (Vice-Chair); Revenue and Taxation (Vice-Chair); Appropriations; Budget and Fiscal Review; Education; Natural Resources and Water.

Escutia—(4)—Energy, Utilities and Communications (Chair); Appropriations; Environmental Quality; Judiciary.

Figueroa—(7)—Business, Professions and Economic Development (Chair); Government Modernization, Efficiency and Accountability (Chair); Banking, Finance and Insurance; Environmental Quality; Health; Judiciary; Labor and Industrial Relations.

Florez—(5)—Governmental Organization (Chair); Agriculture; Business, Professions and Economic Development; Government Modernization, Efficiency and Accountability; Human Services.

Hollingsworth—(5)—Budget and Fiscal Review (Vice-Chair); Agriculture; Banking, Finance and Insurance; Natural Resources and Water; Public Employment and Retirement.

Kehoe—(5)—Local Government (Chair); Budget and Fiscal Review; Energy, Utilities and Communications; Natural Resources and Water; Transportation and Housing.

Kuehl—(8)—Natural Resources and Water (Chair); Budget and Fiscal Review; Environmental Quality; Government Modernization, Efficiency and Accountability; Health; Judiciary; Labor and Industrial Relations; Local Government.

Lowenthal—(7)—Environmental Quality (Chair); Banking, Finance and Insurance; Budget and Fiscal Review; Education; Labor and Industrial Relations; Natural Resources and Water; Transportation and Housing.

Machado—(6)—Revenue and Taxation (Chair); Banking, Finance and Insurance; Budget and Fiscal Review; Local Government; Natural Resources and Water; Transportation and Housing.

SENATORS' STANDING COMMITTEE
MEMBERSHIPS—Continued

MALDONADO—(6)—Education (Vice-Chair); Human Services (Vice-Chair); Agriculture; Banking, Finance and Insurance; Health; Transportation and Housing.

MARGETT—(5)—Natural Resources and Water (Vice-Chair); Budget and Fiscal Review; Governmental Organization; Public Safety; Transportation and Housing.

McCLINTOCK—(5)—Transportation and Housing (Vice-Chair); Budget and Fiscal Review; Government Modernization, Efficiency and Accountability; Governmental Organization; Local Government.

MIGDEN—(3)—Appropriations (Chair); Natural Resources and Water; Public Safety.

MORROW—(5)—Veterans Affairs (Chair); Energy, Utilities and Communications (Vice-Chair); Judiciary (Vice-Chair); Business, Professions and Economic Development; Education.

MURRAY—(7)—Appropriations; Banking, Finance and Insurance; Energy, Utilities and Communications; Government Modernization, Efficiency and Accountability; Governmental Organization; Elections, Reapportionment and Constitutional Amendments; Transportation and Housing.

ORTIZ—(4)—Health (Chair); Agriculture; Appropriations; Banking, Finance and Insurance.

PERATA—(3)—Rules (Chair); Local Government; Public Safety (Serves Ex Officio on all Standing and Joint Committees).

POOCHIGIAN—(5)—Public Safety (Vice-Chair); Agriculture; Appropriations; Elections, Reapportionment and Constitutional Amendments; Revenue and Taxation.

ROMERO—(6)—Budget and Fiscal Review; Education; Elections, Reapportionment and Constitutional Amendments; Health; Natural Resources and Water; Public Safety.

RUNNER—(6)—Environmental Quality (Vice-Chair); Health (Vice-Chair); Budget and Fiscal Review; Labor and Industrial Relations; Revenue and Taxation; Transportation and Housing.

SCOTT—(4)—Education (Chair); Banking, Finance and Insurance; Budget and Fiscal Review; Revenue and Taxation.

SIMITIAN—(7)—Human Services (Chair); Budget and Fiscal Review; Business, Professions and Economic Development; Education; Energy, Utilities and Communications; Environmental Quality; Transportation and Housing.

SENATORS' STANDING COMMITTEE
MEMBERSHIPS—Continued

Soto—(6)—Public Employment and Retirement (Chair); Veterans Affairs (Vice-Chair); Education; Governmental Organization; Local Government; Transportation and Housing.

Speier—(3)—Banking, Finance and Insurance (Chair); Appropriations; Education.

Torlakson—(4)—Transportation and Housing (Chair); Budget and Fiscal Review; Education; Local Government.

Vincent—(3)—Agriculture; Governmental Organization; Health.

SENATE SELECT COMMITTEES

AIR QUALITY—(6)—(Exp. 11-30-2006)—Florez (Chair), Denham, Escutia, Lowenthal, Machado, and Maldonado. Room 5061. Phone (916) 651-4016.

ASIA/PACIFIC RIM TRADE, COMMERCE AND CULTURE—(7)—(Exp. 11-30-2006)—Romero (Chair), Ackerman, Battin, Margett, Perata, Simitian, and Torlakson. Consultant: Teddi Chann. Assistant: Irma Morales. 1020 N Street, Room 510. Phone (916) 651-1514.

BAY AREA INFRASTRUCTURE—(5)—(Exp. 11-30-2006)—Torlakson (Chair), Machado, Migden, Perata, and Simitian. 1020 N Street, Room 533. Phone (916) 651-1535.

CALIFORNIA-EUROPEAN TRADE—(7)—(Exp. 11-30-2006)—Ackerman (Chair), Battin, Cox, Kehoe, Lowenthal, Margett, and Scott.

CALIFORNIA CORRECTIONAL SYSTEM—(5)—(Exp. 11-30-2006)—Romero (Chair), Denham, Kuehl, Machado, and vacancy. Consultants: Rosalinda Rosalez and Heather Scott. 1020 N Street, Suite 586. Phone (916) 651-1532.

CALIFORNIA'S HORSE RACING INDUSTRY—(15)—(Exp. 11-30-2006)—Vincent (Chair), Battin, Cedillo, Cox, Denham, Ducheny, Figueroa, Kehoe, Maldonado, Margett, Migden, Murray, Romero, Soto, and Torlakson. Room 5052. Phone (916) 651-4025.

CALIFORNIA-MEXICO COOPERATION—(7)—(Exp. 11-30-2006)—Ducheny (Chair), Aanestad, Ashburn, Battin, Escutia, Morrow, and Soto.

CALIFORNIA'S WINE INDUSTRY—(16)—(Exp. 11-30-2006)—Chesbro (Chair), Ackerman, Ashburn, Campbell, Cox, Denham, Dunn, Figueroa, Florez, Hollingsworth, Machado, Maldonado, Margett, Migden, Perata, and Poochigian. Principal Consultant: Susan Boyd. Room 5035. Phone (916) 651-4334.

CAPITAL AREA FLOOD PROTECTION—(6)—(Exp. 11-30-2006)—Ortiz (Chair), and vacancies. Room 5114. Phone (916) 651-4006.

CENTRAL VALLEY ECONOMIC DEVELOPMENT—(5)—(Exp. 11-30-2006)—Poochigian (Chair), Ashburn, Denham, Florez, and Machado. Room 5087. Phone (916) 651-4014.

CITIZEN PARTICIPATION—(5)—(Exp. 11-30-2006)—Dunn (Chair), Escutia, Maldonado, Morrow, and Romero. Room 2080. Phone (916) 651-4034.

SENATE SELECT COMMITTEES—Continued

COASTAL PROTECTION AND WATERSHED CONSERVATION—( )—
(Exp. 11-30-2006)—Simitian (Chair), Denham, Kehoe,
Lowenthal, and Maldonado. Room 4062. Phone (916)
651-4011.

COLLEGE AND UNIVERSITY ADMISSIONS AND OUTREACH—(7)—
(Exp. 11-30-2006)—Alarcón (Chair), Cedillo, Chesbro,
Denham, Maldonado, Scott, and Vincent. Room 4035. Phone
(916) 651-4020.

COLORADO RIVER—( )—(Exp. 11-30-2006)—Ducheny (Chair),
Ashburn, Battin, Florez, Hollingsworth, and Soto. Room 4081.
Phone (916) 651-4040.

DEFENSE AND AEROSPACE INDUSTRY—(11)—(Exp. 11-30-2006)—
Ashburn (Chair), Aanestad, Alquist, Ducheny, Kehoe,
Lowenthal, Machado, Maldonado, Morrow, Perata, and
Runner. Room 5094. Phone (916) 651-4018.

DEVELOPMENTAL DISABILITIES AND MENTAL HEALTH—(7)—
(Exp. 11-30-2006)—Chesbro (Chair), Ashburn, Kehoe, Kuehl,
Maldonado, Perata, and Speier. Principal Consultant: Peggy
Collins. Room 5035. Phone (916) 651-4002.

EMERGING TECHNOLOGIES AND ECONOMIC COMPETITIVENESS—(8)—
(Exp. 11-30-2006)—Alquist (Chair), Bowen, Kehoe,
Maldonado, Perata, Simitian, Torlakson, and one vacancy.
Consultant: Robert McLaughlin. Assistant: Lynda Hancock.
1020 N Street, Room 552. Phone (916) 651-1553.

ENTERTAINMENT INDUSTRY—( )—(Exp. 11-30-2006)—Murray
(Chair), and vacancies. Room 5050. Phone (916) 651-4026.

GLOBAL ENVIRONMENT—( )—(Exp. 11-30-2006)—Escutia
(Chair), Denham, Ducheny, Margett, and Torlakson. Room
5080. Phone (916) 651-4030.

GOVERNMENT COST CONTROL—(5)—(Exp. 11-30-2006)—Speier
(Chair), Ashburn, Poochigian, Scott, and Soto. Staff Director:
Richard Steffen. Consultant: Melissa Kludjian. Room 2032.
Phone (916) 651-4008.

HEALTH INSURANCE CRISIS IN CALIFORNIA—(6)—(Exp. 11-30-
2006)—Kuehl (Chair), Ashburn, Cedillo, Escutia, Ortiz, and
Runner. Room 5108. Phone (916) 651-4023.

IMMIGRATION AND THE ECONOMY—(6)—(Exp. 11-30-2006)—
Cedillo (Chair), and vacancies. Room 3048. Phone (916)
651-4022.

SENATE SELECT COMMITTEES—Continued

LEGAL, SOCIAL AND ETHICAL CONSEQUENCES OF EMERGING TECHNOLOGIES—( )—(Exp. 11-30-2006)—Bowen (Chair), Campbell (Vice-Chair), Dunn, Machado, Morrow, and Simitian. Room 4040. Phone (916) 651-4028.

MOBILE AND MANUFACTURED HOMES—(6)—(Exp. 11-30-2006)—Dunn (Chair), Alquist, Chesbro, Ducheny, Morrow, and vacancy. 1020 N Street, Room 520. Phone (916) 651-1517.

OVERSIGHT OF THE UC ENERGY LABS—( )—(Exp. 11-30-2006)—Ducheny (Chair), and vacancies. Room 4081. Phone (916) 651-4040.

PERCHLORATE CONTAMINATION—(7)—(Exp. 11-30-2006)—Soto (Chair), Ducheny, Dutton, Kuehl, Maldonado, Romero, and Simitian. Room 4074. Phone (916) 651-4032.

RETIREMENT INVESTMENT PROTECTION AND CORPORATE RESPONSIBILITY—(5)—(Exp. 11-30-2006)—Florez (Chair), Dunn, Escutia, Morrow, and Soto. Room 5061. Phone (916) 651-4016.

SCHOOL SAFETY—(3)—(Exp. 11-30-2006)—Kuehl (Chair), Alquist, and Margett. Room 4032. Phone (916) 651-4023.

URBAN ECONOMIC DEVELOPMENT—(7)—(Exp. 11-30-2006)—Soto (Chair), Alarcón, Escutia, Machado, Margett, Vincent, and vacancy. Room 4074. Phone (916) 651-4032.

URBAN SCHOOL GOVERNANCE—(5)—(Exp. 11-30-2006)—Romero (Chair), Maldonado (Vice-Chair), Scott, Torlakson, and vacancy.

WEST NILE VIRUS—(8)—(Exp. 11-30-2006)—Florez (Chair), Ashburn (Vice-Chair), Aanestad, Battin, Cox, Hollingsworth, Soto, and Vincent. Room 5061. Phone (916) 651-4016.

SUBCOMMITTEES OF SENATE STANDING COMMITTEES

BUDGET AND FISCAL REVIEW

SUBCOMMITTEE No. 1 ON EDUCATION—( )—Scott (Chair), Margett, and Simitian. Room 5019. Phone 651-4103.

SUBCOMMITTEE No. 2 ON RESOURCES, ENVIRONMENTAL PROTECTION AND ENERGY—( )—Kuehl (Chair), Dutton, and Lowenthal. Room 5019. Phone 651-4103.

SUBCOMMITTEE No. 3 ON HEALTH AND HUMAN SERVICES—( )—Ducheny (Chair), Runner, and Torlakson. Room 5019. Phone 651-4103.

SUBCOMMITTEE No. 4 ON STATE ADMIN., GENERAL GOVT., JUDICIAL, AND TRANSPORTATION—( )—Dunn (Chair), McClintock, and Kehoe. Room 5019. Phone 651-4103.

SUBCOMMITTEE No. 5 ON PUBLIC SAFETY, LABOR, AND VETERAN AFFAIRS—( )—Romero (Chair), Campbell, and Machado. Room 5019. Phone 651-4103.

BUSINESS, PROFESSIONS AND ECONOMIC DEVELOPMENT

SUBCOMMITTEE ON INTERNATIONAL TRADE POLICY AND STATE LEGISLATION—( )—Figueroa (Chair), Aanestad, and Simitian. Consultant: Laura Metune. 1020 N Street, Room 551. Phone 651-1694.

SUBCOMMITTEE ON TECHNOLOGICAL CRIME AND THE CONSUMER—( )—Figueroa (Chair), Morrow, and Murray.

EDUCATION

SUBCOMMITTEE ON HIGHER EDUCATION—(6)—Scott (Chair), Denham, Lowenthal, Maldonado, Romero, and Speier. Room 2082. Phone 651-4021.

HEALTH

SUBCOMMITTEE ON AGING AND LONG-TERM CARE—( )—Alquist (Chair), Aanestad, Cox, Kuehl, and Ortiz. Consultant: Robert MacLaughlin. Assistant: Lynda Hancock. 1020 N Street, Room 545. Phone 651-1541.

**SUBCOMMITTEES OF SENATE STANDING
COMMITTEES—Continued**

SUBCOMMITTEE ON MEDICINE AND HEALTH CARE—( )—Ortiz (Chair), vacancies. Room 2191. Phone 651-4111.

SUBCOMMITTEE ON MENTAL HEALTH AND NEURODEVELOPMENTAL DISORDERS—( )—Ortiz (Chair), vacancies. Room 2191. Phone 651-4111.

SUBCOMMITTEE ON STEM CELL RESEARCH OVERSIGHT—( )—Ortiz (Chair), Alquist, Kuehl, and Runner. Room 2191. Phone 651-4111.

JUDICIARY

SUBCOMMITTEE ON ADMINISTRATION OF JUSTICE—( )—Escutia (Chair), and two vacancies. Room 5080. Phone 651-4030.

SUBCOMMITTEE ON ANTI-COMPETITIVE CONDUCT AND THE MARKETPLACE—( )—Dunn (Chair), and two vacancies. Room 2187.

SUBCOMMITTEE ON BAD FAITH LIABILITY AND CONSUMER RIGHTS—( )—Dunn (Chair), and two vacancies. Room 2187.

NATURAL RESOURCES AND WATER

SUBCOMMITTEE ON DELTA RESOURCES—( )—Machado (Chair), Aanestad, Kehoe, Kuehl, and Margett. Room 5066. Phone 651-4005.

TRANSPORTATION AND HOUSING

SUBCOMMITTEE ON CALIFORNIA PORTS AND GOODS MOVEMENT—( )—Lowenthal (Chair), Ducheny, Runner, and Torlakson. Consultant: Norman Fassler-Katz. Room 2205. Phone 651-4414.

SUBCOMMITTEE ON LOS ANGELES COUNTY METROPOLITAN TRANSPORTATION AUTHORITY—( )—Murray (Chair), Cedillo, Lowenthal, Margett, Runner, and Torlakson.

JOINT COMMITTEES

Joint Committee on Arts—Resolution Chapter 101, Statutes of 1984. Continuous existence.
Senate Members (6): vacant (Chair), Ashburn, Battin, Kehoe, Kuehl, Maldonado, and Scott.
Assembly Members (6): Vacancies.
Room 2082. Phone 651-4021.

Joint Committee on Boards, Commissions and Consumer Protection—Business and Professions Code Section 473. (Exp. 01-01-2012).
Senate Members (3): Figueroa (Chair), Aanestad, and Vincent.
Assembly Members (3): Negrete McLeod, Koretz, and Spitzer.
1020 N Street, Room 521. Phone 651-1518.

Joint Committee to Develop a Master Plan to End Poverty in California—Resolution Chapter 117, Statutes of 2003. (Exp. 12-31-2005).
Senate Members (7): Vacancies.
Assembly Members (7): Vacancies.
1020 N Street, Room 560. Phone 651-1526.

Joint Committee on Fairs Allocation and Classification—Food and Agricultural Code Section 4531, 4532, 4533. Continuous existence.
Senate Members (7): Vacancies.
Assembly Members (7): Vacancies.

Joint Committee on Fisheries and Aquaculture—Resolution Chapter 88, Statutes of 1981. Continuous existence.
Senate Members (4): Vacancies.
Assembly Members (4): Vacancies.

Joint Committee on Legislative Audit—Government Code Sections 10501, 10502, J.R. 37.3. Continuous existence.
Senate Members (7): Poochigian (Vice-Chair), Cedillo, McClintock, Morrow, Ortiz, Romero, and Speier.
Assembly Members (7): Parra (Chair), Aghazarian, Cogdill, Goldberg, Klehs, Leslie, and Nava.
Assistant: Elise Flynn.
1020 N Street, Room 107. Phone 319-3300.

JOINT COMMITTEES—Continued

Joint Committee on Legislative Budget—Government Code
Sections 9140, 9141. Continuous existence.
Senate Members (8): Chesbro (Chair), Battin, Ducheny, Dunn,
Hollingsworth, McClintock, Migden, and Scott.
Assembly Members (8): Chu, De La Torre, Goldberg, Keene,
Laird, McCarthy, Nava, and Runner.
Room 5035. Phone 651-4002.

Joint Committee on Rules—Joint Rule 40. Continuous
existence.
Senate Members (11): Battin (Vice-Chair), Ashburn, Bowen,
Cedillo, Dunn, Escutia, Murray, Ortiz, Perata, Poochigian, and
Romero.
Assembly Members (11): Montañez (Chair), Baca, Benoit,
Cogdill, Coto, Dymally, Frommer, Karnette, McCarthy,
Núñez, and Villines.
Room 3016. Phone 319-2804.

WEEKLY COMMITTEE SCHEDULE

MONDAY

Committee	Time	Room
APPROPRIATIONS		
(Every Monday)	1:30 P.M.	4203
PUBLIC EMPLOYMENT AND RETIREMENT		
(2nd and 4th Mondays)	2:00 P.M.	2040
BUSINESS, PROFESSIONS AND ECONOMIC DEVELOPMENT		
(2nd and 4th Mondays)	2:00 P.M.	3191
ENVIRONMENTAL QUALITY		
(1st and 3rd Mondays)	1:30 P.M.	112

TUESDAY

Committee	Time	Room
PUBLIC SAFETY		
(Every Tuesday)	9:30 A.M.	4203
ENERGY, UTILITIES AND COMMUNICATIONS		
(1st and 3rd Tuesdays)	9:30 A.M.	3191
AGRICULTURE		
(1st and 3rd Tuesdays)	9:30 A.M.	113
GOVERNMENTAL ORGANIZATION		
(2nd and 4th Tuesdays)	9:30 A.M.	3191
NATURAL RESOURCES AND WATER		
(Every Tuesday)	9:00 A.M.	112
JUDICIARY		
(Every Tuesday)	1:30 P.M.	112
TRANSPORTATION AND HOUSING		
(1st and 3rd Tuesdays)	1:30 P.M.	4203
HUMAN SERVICES		
(2nd and 4th Tuesdays)	1:30 P.M.	3191
VETERANS AFFAIRS		
(2nd and 4th Tuesdays)	1:30 P.M.	2040

WEEKLY COMMITTEE SCHEDULE—Continued

WEDNESDAY

Committee	Time	Room
EDUCATION		
(Every Wednesday)	9:30 A.M.	4203
LOCAL GOVERNMENT		
(1st and 3rd Wednesdays)	9:30 A.M.	112
ELECTIONS, REAPPORTIONMENT AND CONSTITUTIONAL AMENDMENTS		
(1st and 3rd Wednesdays)	9:30 A.M.	3191
LABOR AND INDUSTRIAL RELATIONS		
(2nd and 4th Wednesdays)	9:30 A.M.	2040
RULES		
(Every Wednesday)	1:30 P.M.	113
HEALTH		
(Every Wednesday)	1:30 P.M.	4203
BANKING, FINANCE AND INSURANCE		
(1st and 3rd Wednesdays)	1:30 P.M.	112
REVENUE AND TAXATION		
(2nd and 4th Wednesdays)	1:30 P.M.	3191
GOVERNMENT MODERNIZATION, EFFICIENCY AND ACCOUNTABILITY		
(1st and 3rd Wednesdays)	4:00 P.M.	3191

THURSDAY

BUDGET AND FISCAL REVIEW		
(Every Thursday)	8:00 A.M.	4203

CLASSIFICATION OF SENATORS AS TO THEIR SENIORITY

Senate seniority is divided into 7 classes and the following list shows the classification of each Senator:

1. Perata .... (November 1998)
2. Alarcón .... (December 1998)
   Bowen .... (December 1998)
   Chesbro .... (December 1998)
   Dunn .... (December 1998)
   Escutia .... (December 1998)
   Figueroa .... (December 1998)
   Morrow .... (December 1998)
   Murray .... (December 1998)
   Ortiz .... (December 1998)
   Poochigian .... (December 1998)
   Speier .... (December 1998)
*3. Soto .... (March 2000)
4. Ackerman .... (December 2000)
   Battin .... (December 2000)
   Kuehl .... (December 2000)
   Machado .... (December 2000)
   Margett .... (December 2000)
   McClintock .... (December 2000)
   Scott .... (December 2000)
   Torlakson .... (December 2000)
   Vincent .... (December 2000)
*5. Romero (Special Election) .... (March 2001)
6. Aanestad .... (December 2002)
   Ashburn .... (December 2002)
   Cedillo .... (December 2002)
   Denham .... (December 2002)
   Moreno Ducheny .... (December 2002)
   Florez .... (December 2002)
   Hollingsworth .... (December 2002)
7. Alquist .... (December 2004)
   Campbell .... (December 2004)
   Cox .... (December 2004)
   Dutton .... (December 2004)
   Kehoe .... (December 2004)
   Maldonado .... (December 2004)
   Migden .... (December 2004)
   Lowenthal .... (December 2004)
   Runner .... (December 2004)
   Simitian .... (December 2004)

* Elected to fill unexpired term—oath of office in year designated.

OFFICES OF THE SENATE
Sacramento Address: State Capitol, Sacramento, CA 95814

PRESIDENT PRO TEMPORE—
State Capitol, Room 205
651-4009
ERIN NIEMELA, *Chief Assistant to the pro Tempore*
DAVE SEBECK, *Press Secretary*
GARETH ELLIOTT, *Legislative Director*
DIANE CUMMINS, *Chief Fiscal Policy Advisor*
NANCY LYNOTT, *Special Assistant to the pro Tempore*

RULES COMMITTEE—
State Capitol, Room 400
651-4120
CYNTHIA LAVAGETTO, *Deputy Executive Officer*
KEITH FELTE, *Deputy Executive Officer*
MIKE WARD, *Fiscal Officer*
LINDA STARR, *Accounting Officer*
DINA HIDALGO, *Personnel Officer*
SANDY KENYON, *Bill Referral*
PAT WEBB, *Committee Assistant*

SECRETARY OF THE SENATE—
State Capitol, Room 3044
651-4171
GREGORY SCHMIDT, *Secretary of the Senate*
DAVID VALVERDE, *Chief Assistant Secretary*
SUSAN DeLaFUENTE, *Assistant to Secretary*
MARIE HARLAN, *Engrossing and Enrolling Clerk*
MARLISSA HERNANDEZ, *File Clerk*
HOLLY DAWN HUMMELT, *Amending Clerk*
DAVID H. KNEALE, *History Clerk*
BERNADETTE McNULTY, *Assistant Secretary*
KIPCHOGE RANDALL, *Reading Clerk*
PAULA ROSSETO, *Journal Clerk*
JAMIE TAYLOR, *Assistant File Clerk*
ZACHARY L. TWILLA, *Assistant Amending Clerk*

OFFICES OF THE SENATE—Continued

OFFICE OF FLOOR ANALYSIS—
    1020 N St., Room 524
    651-1520
    DAVID WILKENING, *Director*
    NORA CROWLEY
    ROBERT GRAHAM
    TIM MELLO
    NANCY LAMBROS
    MELISSA YOCCA
    JONAS AUSTIN
    ALICIA BELMANTES
    DENISE OSEGUDEA
    CHRIS WHITE

SERGEANT AT ARMS—
    STATE CAPITOL, ROOM 3030
    651-4184
    TONY BEARD, JR., *Sergeant at Arms*
    DEBBIE MANNING, *Chief Deputy*
    MELINDA PICKEREL, *Executive Assistant*
    FRANCES STIZZO, *Executive Assistant*

OFFICE OF RESEARCH—
    1020 N St., Room 200
    651-1500
    DON MOULDS, *Director*

MAJORITY FLOOR LEADER—
    STATE CAPITOL, ROOM 313
    651-4024
    RICHARD ZEIGER, *Chief of Staff*
    MARGARET PENA, *Legislative Director*
    LAURA SOTELO, *Executive Assistant*

DEMOCRATIC CAUCUS—
    1020 N St., Room 250
    651-1502
    JOE CAMICIA, *Director*
    CATHLEEN GARDELLA, *Deputy Director*
    LORIE SHELLEY, *Consultant*
    SONIA VALVERDE, *Consultant*
    TIAVA LEE, *Secretarial Staff*
    JOHN MANN, *Consultant*
    BENETIA RAPTAKIS, *Consultant*
    DREW MENDELSON, *Consultant*
    ROSALIND ESCOBAR, *Consultant*
    AARON BLOOM, *Consultant*
    JOHN HOOPER, *Consultant*

OFFICES OF THE SENATE—Continued

MINORITY FLOOR LEADER—
   State Capitol, Room 305
   651-4033
   Dan Chick, *Chief of Staff*

REPUBLICAN CAUCUS—
   1020 N St., Room 536
   651-1521

   PUBLIC AFFAIRS—
   Matt Ross, *Director*

   POLICY—
   1020 N St., Room 234
   Mike Pettingale, *Director*

   FISCAL—
   1020 N St., Room 234
   Jeff Bell, *Director*

REPROGRAPHICS—
   1020 N St., Room B-7
   651-1510
   Luis Salinas Jr., *Manager*

VOTE FOR MEMBERS OF THE SENATE
Primary Election March 2, 2004

First Senatorial District

County	Kristine Lang McDonald (D)	Allan L. Dollison (D)	Dave Cox (R)	Chris Schneider (R)	Roberto Leibman (Lib)
Alpine	120	35	117	81	0
Amador	2,134	1,461	3,995	1,671	52
Calaveras	2,712	2,000	4,488	2,318	138
El Dorado	9,581	4,373	17,693	6,256	187
Lassen	1,162	952	2,375	993	19
Modoc	472	394	1,008	556	13
Mono	604	295	769	468	14
Nevada	1,236	480	1,238	524	28
Placer	11,073	5,313	21,799	7,142	158
Plumas	1,307	909	1,991	1,058	29
Sacramento	19,636	10,506	40,595	9,837	297
Sierra	251	135	389	183	15
Totals	50,288	26,853	96,457	31,087	950

Third Senatorial District

County	Carole Migden (D)	Davy Jones (D)	Andrew D. Felder (R)	David Rhodes (Lib)	Ian J. Grimes (PF)
Marin	37,431	6,606	16,184	260	58
San Francisco	58,639	7,952	6,419	369	204
Sonoma	19,822	6,127	11,969	184	63
Totals	115,892	20,685	34,572	813	325

Fifth Senatorial District

County	Michael J. Machado (D)	Gary A. Podesto (R)
Sacramento	3,143	2,759
San Joaquin	30,132	22,987
Solano	16,583	12,834
Yolo	19,397	11,285
Totals	69,255	49,865

Seventh Senatorial District

County	Tom Torlakson (D)
Contra Costa	107,011

Ninth Senatorial District

County	Don Perata (D)	Patricia Deutsche (R)	Peter Von Pinnon (Lib)	Tom Condit (PF)
Alameda	105,675	21,042	518	261
Contra Costa	8,957	928	28	20
Totals	114,632	21,970	546	281

Eleventh Senatorial District

County	Ted Lempert (D)	Joe Simitian (D)	Jon Zellhoefer (R)	Allen M. Rice (Lib)
San Mateo	14,082	12,086	9,515	188
Santa Clara	22,985	36,604	27,249	531
Santa Cruz	11,450	16,907	6,168	343
Totals	48,517	65,597	42,932	1,062

Thirteenth Senatorial District

County	Elaine Alquist (D)	Manny Diaz (D)	Jose Medeiros (D)	Andrew Abe Diaz (R)	Shane Patrick Connolly (R)	John Webster (Lib)	Michael Laursen (Lib)
Santa Clara	34,982	32,094	2,864	3,584	21,205	284	286

Fifteenth Senatorial District

County	Peg Pinard (D)	Abel Maldonado (R)	Brook Madsen (Grn)
Monterey	15,592	12,969	308
San Luis Obispo	23,292	34,876	588
Santa Barbara	6,211	10,061	45
Santa Clara	15,247	16,042	155
Santa Cruz	11,010	6,514	305
Totals	71,352	80,462	1,401

Seventeenth Senatorial District

County	Jonathan Daniel Kraut (D)	George C. Runner (R)	John S. Ballard (Lib)
Kern	1	5	0
Los Angeles	25,232	40,676	338
San Bernardino	9,603	21,172	173
Ventura	3,348	2,642	37
Totals	38,184	64,495	548

Nineteenth Senatorial District

County	Paul Graber (D)	Tom McClintock (R)
Los Angeles	2,928	6,194
Santa Barbara	28,900	29,782
Ventura	38,636	63,325
Totals	70,464	99,301

Twenty-first Senatorial District

County	Jack Scott (D)	Bob New (Lib)
Los Angeles	62,295	505

Twenty-third Senatorial District

County	Sheila James Kuehl (D)	Leonard Michael Lanzi (R)	Colin Goldman (Lib)
Los Angeles	77,097	30,159	443
Ventura	10,806	6,780	81
Totals	87,903	36,939	524

Twenty-fifth Senatorial District

County	Edward Vincent (D)	Brenda Carol Green (R)	James Arlandus Spencer (R)	Ernest L. Woods (R)	Dale F. Ogden (Lib)
Los Angeles	48,962	7,127	9,062	3,071	199

Twenty-seventh Senatorial District

County	Alan S. Lowenthal (D)	Michael Jackson (R)	Cesar Navarro Castellanos (R)
Los Angeles	45,082	14,874	16,626

Twenty-ninth Senatorial District

County	Rufino Mallari Bautista, Jr. (D)	Bob Margett (R)	Dan Fernandes (Lib)
Los Angeles	24,574	39,395	265
Orange	10,814	25,714	133
San Bernardino	5,002	8,540	53
Totals	40,390	73,649	451

Thirty-first Senatorial District

County	Marjorie Musser Mikels (D)	Bob Dutton (R)
Riverside	19,155	22,091
San Bernardino	21,808	42,758
Totals	40,963	64,849

Thirty-third Senatorial District

County	Randall Daugherty (D)	Dick Ackerman (R)
Orange	45,563	104,828

Thirty-fifth Senatorial District

	Rita B. Siebert (D)	Ken Maddox (R)	Joe Snyder (R)	John Campbell (R)	Timothy Johnson (Lib)
County Orange	51,364	33,484	10,335	66,939	981

Thirty-seventh Senatorial District

	Pat Johansen (D)	Jim Battin (R)
County Riverside	49,699	77,096

Thirty-ninth Senatorial District

County	Christine Kehoe (D)	Ken Bourke (R)	Ralph Denney (R)	Jim Galley (R)	Larry Stirling (R)	John Murphy (Lib)
San Diego	82,055	6,793	6,000	3,391	45,536	1,040

General Election November 2, 2004

First Senatorial District

County	Kristine Lang McDonald (D)	Dave Cox (R)	Roberto Leibman (Lib)
Alpine	332	309	27
Amador	5,804	10,511	652
Calaveras	7,351	12,992	970
El Dorado	27,578	50,428	2,843
Lassen	2,992	7,548	345
Modoc	1,100	3,000	147
Mono	2,057	2,722	201
Nevada	4,253	4,196	424
Placer	30,157	57,044	2,916
Plumas	3,601	6,621	384
Sacramento	55,651	104,638	4,289
Sierra	586	1,198	94
Totals	141,462	261,207	13,292

Third Senatorial District

County	Carole Migden (D)	Andrew D. Felder (R)	David Rhodes (Lib)	Ian J. Grimes (PF)
Marin	72,892	45,049	2,974	3,524
San Francisco	141,612	25,601	5,366	6,180
Sonoma	43,662	27,682	1,894	2,309
Totals	258,166	98,332	10,234	12,013

Fifth Senatorial District

County	Michael J. Machado (D)	Gary A. Podesto (R)
Sacramento	8,733	8,621
San Joaquin	64,740	64,569
Solano	39,922	40,986
Yolo	41,124	27,363
Totals	154,519	141,539

Seventh Senatorial District

County	Tom Torlakson (D)
Contra Costa	282,714

Ninth Senatorial District

County	Don Perata (D)	Patricia Deutsche (R)	Peter Von Pinnon (Lib)	Tom Condit (PF)
Alameda	229,283	47,796	6,039	16,598
Contra Costa	19,331	2,314	344	814
Totals	248,614	50,110	6,383	17,412

Eleventh Senatorial District

County	Joe Simitian (D)	Jon Zellhoefer (R)	Allen M. Rice (Lib)
San Mateo	53,779	22,232	2,518
Santa Clara	124,931	65,426	7,876
Santa Cruz	51,774	14,229	3,686
Totals	230,484	101,887	14,080

Thirteenth Senatorial District

County	Elaine Alquist (D)	Shane Patrick Connolly (R)	Michael Laursen (Lib)	John H. Webster (Wif)
Santa Clara	156,321	62,157	9,585	28

Fifteenth Senatorial District

County	Peg Pinard (D)	Abel Maldonado (R)	Brook Madsen (Grn)
Monterey	36,394	37,153	3,969
San Luis Obispo	46,572	72,301	6,216
Santa Barbara	12,535	19,997	1,407
Santa Clara	38,744	46,288	2,709
Santa Cruz	23,311	18,935	2,343
Totals	157,556	194,674	16,644

Seventeenth Senatorial District

County	Jonathan Daniel Kraut (D)	George C. Runner (R)	John S. Ballard (Lib)
Kern	1	2	1
Los Angeles	76,835	122,171	8,638
San Bernardino	24,216	51,819	3,240
Ventura	7,985	6,000	600
Totals	109,037	179,992	12,479

Nineteenth Senatorial District

County	Paul Graber (D)	Tom McClintock (R)
Los Angeles	8,979	18,595
Santa Barbara	60,199	66,699
Ventura	81,907	148,071
Totals	151,085	233,365

Twenty-first Senatorial District

County	Jack Scott (D)	Bob New (Lib)
Los Angeles	217,515	61,160

Twenty-third Senatorial District

County	Sheila James Kuehl (D)	Leonard Michael Lanzi (R)	Colin Goldman (Lib)
Los Angeles	199,271	86,415	16,245
Ventura	30,050	15,233	1,923
Totals	229,321	101,648	18,168

Twenty-fifth Senatorial District

County	Edward Vincent (D)	James Arlandus Spencer (R)	Dale F. Ogden (Lib)
Los Angeles	165,479	52,485	6,683

Twenty-seventh Senatorial District

County	Alan S. Lowenthal (D)	Cesar Navarro Castellanos (R)
Los Angeles	150,289	87,319

Twenty-ninth Senatorial District

County	Rufino Mallari Bautista, Jr. (D)	Bob Margett (R)	Dan Fernandes (Lib)
Los Angeles	62,016	103,566	10,778
Orange	23,278	61,052	4,453
San Bernardino	16,056	25,547	1,813
Totals	101,350	190,165	17,044

Thirty-first Senatorial District

County	Marjorie Musser Mikels (D)	Bob Dutton (R)
Riverside	48,350	54,017
San Bernardino	67,962	116,883
Totals	116,312	170,900

Thirty-third Senatorial District

County	Randall Daugherty (D)	Dick Ackerman (R)
Orange	110,313	245,116

Thirty-fifth Senatorial District

County	Rita B. Siebert (D)	John Campbell (R)	Timothy Johnson (Lib)
Orange	114,126	230,220	16,561

Thirty-seventh Senatorial District

County	Pat Johansen (D)	Jim Battin (R)
Riverside	123,602	182,578

Thirty-ninth Senatorial District

County	Christine Kehoe (D)	Larry Stirling (R)	John Murphy (Lib)
San Diego	200,737	118,417	15,552

Special Primary Election, March 8, 2005
Fifth Congressional District

County	Doris Matsui* (D)	Julie Padilla (D)	Charles "Carlos", Pineda, Jr. (D)	Serge A. Chernay (R)	John Thomas Flynn (R)	Michael O'Brien (R)	Shane Singh (R)
Sacramento	56,175	7,158	659	3,742	6,559	2,591	1,753

	Bruce Robert Stevens (R)	Pat Driscoll (Grn)	Gale Morgan (Lib)	John C. Reiger (PF)	Leonard Padilla (I)	Laura Shapiro (W/I)	
	1,124	976	451	286	916	6	

* Elected
Vacancy resulting from the death of Robert Matsui.

STANDING RULES

OF THE SENATE

2005–06 Regular Session

Senate Resolution No. 4 (Ashburn)

(Adopted December 6, 2004, Senate Journal, p. 8; as amended by Senate Resolution No. 10 (Perata), adopted March 17, 2005; Senate Journal, p. 323)

STANDING RULES OF THE SENATE

CONVENING AND SESSIONS

Hours of Meeting

1. The Senate shall meet at 9:00 a.m. daily, except Saturdays and Sundays, unless otherwise ordered by the Senate.

Calling to Order

2. The President pro Tempore, Assistant President pro Tempore, Vice Chair of the Committee on Rules, or senior member present shall call the Senate to order at the hour stated and, if a quorum is present, shall proceed with the order of business.

Attendance of Senators

3. No Senator may absent himself or herself from attendance upon the Senate without first obtaining leave. A lesser number than a quorum of the Senate is authorized to send the Sergeant at Arms for any and all absent Senators at the expense of the absent Senators, unless an excuse for nonattendance made to the Senate when a quorum is present shall be judged sufficient, and in that case the expense shall be paid out of the Senate Operating Fund. The President pro Tempore or Assistant President pro Tempore, or less than a quorum present, shall have the power to issue process directly to the Sergeant at Arms to compel the attendance of Senators absent without leave. Any Senator who refuses to obey that process, unless sick or unable to attend, shall be deemed guilty of contempt of the Senate, and the Sergeant at Arms shall have power to use force as may be necessary to compel the attendance of the absent Senator, and for this purpose he or she may command the force of the county, or of any county in the state.

Order of Business

4. The order of business shall be as follows:
    (1) Rollcall.
    (2) Prayer by the Chaplain.
    (3) Pledge of Allegiance.
    (4) Privileges of the Floor.
    (5) Communications and Petitions.
    (6) Messages from the Governor.
    (7) Messages from the Assembly.
    (8) Reports of Committees.
    (9) Motions, Resolutions and Notices.
    (10) Introduction and First Reading of Bills.
    (11) Consideration of Daily File:
        (a) Second Reading.
        (b) Special Orders.
        (c) Unfinished Business.
        (d) Third Reading.
    (12) Announcement of Committee Meetings.
    (13) Leaves of Absence.
    (14) Adjournment.

Executive Sessions

5. When a motion is adopted to close the doors of the Senate, on the discussion of any business that may require an executive session, he or she who is presiding shall require all persons, except the Senators, Secretary, Minute Clerk, and Sergeant at Arms, to withdraw, and during the discussion of that business the doors shall remain closed. Every Senator and officer present shall keep secret all matters and proceedings concerning which secrecy shall be enjoined by order of the Senate.

OFFICERS OF THE SENATE

The President

6. The President may preside upon invitation of the Senate.

The President pro Tempore

7. The President pro Tempore shall take the Chair and call the Senate to order at the hour of the meetings

of the Senate. The President pro Tempore is the Presiding Officer of the Senate.

It shall be the particular responsibility of the President pro Tempore to secure the prompt and businesslike disposition of bills and other business before the Senate. He or she shall maintain order in the Senate Chamber and, in case of a disturbance or disorderly conduct outside the bar or in the gallery, he or she shall have the power to order the same cleared.

The President pro Tempore shall serve ex officio as a member of all Senate and joint committees of which he or she is not a regular member, with all of the rights and privileges of that membership except the right to vote. In counting a quorum of any of these committees, the President pro Tempore may not be counted as a member.

The Assistant President pro Tempore or the Vice Chair of the Committee on Rules shall, in the absence of the President pro Tempore, perform the duties, and have all powers and authority, of the President pro Tempore.

The Assistant President pro Tempore

8. The President pro Tempore of the Senate may name a Senator to perform the duties of the Chair in his or her absence. The Senator so named shall be vested, during that time on the floor, with all the powers of the President pro Tempore, and the Senator who performs these duties shall be known as the Assistant President pro Tempore.

In the absence of the President pro Tempore, the Assistant President pro Tempore, or the Vice Chair of the Committee on Rules, any Senator may perform the duties of the Chair.

Secretary of the Senate

9. It shall be the duty of the Secretary of the Senate to attend every session, call the roll, and read all bills, amendments, and resolutions, and all papers ordered read by the Senate or the Presiding Officer.

The Secretary of the Senate shall superintend all printing to be done for the Senate.

The Secretary of the Senate shall certify to, and transmit to, the Assembly all bills, joint and concurrent resolutions, constitutional amendments, and papers requiring the concurrence of the Assembly, immediately after their passage or adoption by the Senate.

The Secretary of the Senate shall also keep a correct Journal of the proceedings of the Senate, and shall notify the Assembly of the action by the Senate on all matters originating in the Assembly and requiring action on the part of the Senate.

The Secretary of the Senate shall have custody of all bills, documents, papers, and records of the Senate and may not permit any of the bills, documents, records, or papers to be taken from the Desk or out of his or her custody by any person, except in the regular course of the business of the Senate.

The Secretary of the Senate is the Executive Officer of the Committee on Rules and shall act as its authorized representative in all matters delegated to him or her by the committee.

Initiative measures received by the Secretary of the Senate in accordance with Section 9034 of the Elections Code shall be transmitted to the Committee on Rules and referred by the Committee on Rules to the appropriate committee.

Sergeant at Arms of the Senate

10.   The Sergeant at Arms shall attend the Senate during all of its sittings, and shall execute the commands of the Senate from time to time, together with all process issued by its authority, as shall be directed to him or her by the President. The Sergeant at Arms is authorized to arrest for contempt all persons outside the bar, or in the gallery, found in loud conversation or otherwise making a noise to the disturbance of the Senate. The actual expenses for the Sergeant at Arms for every arrest and for each day's custody and release, and his or her traveling expenses, shall be paid out of the Senate Operating Fund.

The Sergeant at Arms shall place copies of all bills, joint and concurrent resolutions, constitutional amendments, Journals, Histories, and Files, when printed, on the desks of Senators, at least one hour previous to the opening of the session.

Elected and Appointed Officers

10.5. On the first day of each session, the President pro Tempore, members of the Committee on Rules, Secretary of the Senate, and Sergeant at Arms shall be elected by a majority vote of the duly elected and qualified Members of the Senate and shall serve until their successors are elected and qualify. The Committee on Rules shall appoint an Assistant Secretary, a Minute Clerk, a Chaplain, and other employees with such duties as the committee requires.

Officers and Employees Compensation: Approval

10.6. The Controller is hereby authorized and directed to draw his or her warrants in favor of officers and employees who render services to the Senate, as certified by the Committee on Rules or by its authorized representative, from the fund set aside for the pay of officers and employees of the Senate at the rate of compensation certified by the committee or its representative, and the Treasurer is hereby directed to pay the same.

COMMITTEES OF THE SENATE

Appointment of Committees

11. The Committee on Rules shall consist of the President pro Tempore of the Senate, who shall be the chair of the committee, and four other Members of the Senate to be elected by the Senate. There is a vacancy on the committee in the event a member ceases to be a Member of the Senate or resigns from the Committee on Rules. Any vacancy occurring during a summer, interim study, or final recess, except in the case of the President pro Tempore, shall be filled by the remaining members of the Committee on Rules. A vacancy occurring at any other time shall be filled by election by the Senate.

The Committee on Rules shall appoint all other committees of the Senate and shall designate a chair and vice chair of each committee.

In making committee appointments, the Committee on Rules shall give consideration to seniority, preference, and experience. However, in making committee appointments, the Committee on Rules shall, as far as practicable, give equal representation to all parts of the state.

Standing Committees

12. The standing committees of the Senate and subjects to be referred to each are set out below. The provisions set forth below as to the assignment of bills are intended as a guide to the Committee on Rules, but are not binding upon the committee.

(1) Agriculture, 9 members. Bills relating to agriculture.

(2) Appropriations, 13 members. Bills that are subject to Joint Rule 10.5 and are not referred to the Budget and Fiscal Review Committee. Bills that constitute a state-mandated local program.

(3) Banking, Finance and Insurance, 11 members. Bills relating to financial institutions, corporations, and retail credit interest rates. Bills relating to insurance, managed care, indemnity, surety, and warranty agreements.

(4) Budget and Fiscal Review, 17 members. The Budget Bill and bills implementing the Budget. Bills that directly affect the State Budget, including deficiencies and reappropriations.

(5) Business, Professions and Economic Development, 7 members. Bills relating to business and professional practices, licensing, and regulations other than bills relating to horse racing, alcoholic beverages, oil, mining, geothermal, and forestry industries. Bills relating to economic development, commerce and international trade.

(6) Education, 12 members. Bills relating to education, higher education, and certificated educational personnel.

(7) Elections, Reapportionment, and Constitutional Amendments, 6 members. Bills relating to elections and reapportionment. Bills relating to constitutional amendments, when favorably reported out of the standing committee having jurisdiction of the subject matter.

(8) Energy, Utilities, and Communications, 11 members. Bills relating to public utilities and carriers, energy companies, alternative energy development and conservation, and communications development and technology.

(9) Environmental Quality, 9 members. Bills relating to environmental quality, air quality, water quality, integrated waste management, recycling, toxics, and hazardous waste.

(10) Government Modernization, Efficiency and Accountability, 10 members. Bills relating to state government organization and the efficient delivery of state government services. Bills that have been considered by other committees having jurisdiction of the appropriate subject, for consideration of any question relating to state government.

(11) Governmental Organization, 11 members. Bills relating to horse racing, public gaming, and alcoholic beverages, bills related to the management of public safety emergencies and disaster response, and bills regarding the use of state-controlled lands and buildings, state publishing, seals, bonds, and interstate compacts.

(12) Health, 11 members. Bills relating to public health, alcohol and drug abuse, mental health, managed care, and related institutions.

(13) Human Services, 7 members. Bills relating to welfare, social programs and services, and related institutions.

(14) Judiciary, 7 members. Bills amending the following:

(a) Civil Code, except measures related to retail credit interest rates.

(b) Code of Civil Procedure.

(c) Evidence Code, except matters relating to criminal procedure.

(d) Family Code.

(e) Probate Code.

(f) Bills relating to municipal and state court judgeships, court attachés, and personnel. Bills relating to liens, claims, and unclaimed property, collections, and franchises.

(15) Labor and Industrial Relations, 8 members. Bills relating to labor, industrial safety, unemployment, workers' compensation and insurance, and noncertificated public school employees.

(16) Local Government, 7 members. Bills relating to local governmental procedure and organization. Bills relating to land use. Bills that have been considered by other committees having jurisdiction of the appropriate subject, for consideration of any questions relating to local government administration.

(17) Natural Resources and Water, 11 members. Bills relating to conservation and the management of public resources, fish and wildlife, regulation of oil, mining, geothermal development, acid deposition, wetlands and lakes, global atmospheric effects, ocean and bay pollution, coastal resources, forestry practices, recreation, parks, and historical resources. Bills relating to water supply management.

(18) Public Employment and Retirement, 5 members. Bills relating to state and local nonschool public employees and public employee retirement.

(19) Public Safety, 7 members. Bills amending the following:

(a) Evidence Code, relating to criminal procedure.

(b) Penal Code.

(c) Statutes of a penal nature not related closely to a subject included in another subdivision of this rule.

(d) Bills relating to the Youth and Adult Corrections Agency.

(20) Revenue and Taxation, 8 members. Bills relating to state and local revenues and taxation, except bills described in subdivision (a) of Rule 28.9.

(21) Rules, 5 members. Proposed amendments to the rules and other matters relating to the business of the Legislature.

(22) Transportation and Housing, 14 members. Bills relating to the operation, safety, equipment, transfer of

ownership, licensing, and registration of vehicles, aircraft, and vessels. Bills relating to the Department of Transportation and the Department of Motor Vehicles. Bills relating to waterways, harbors, highways, public transportation systems, and airports. Bills relating to housing and community redevelopment.

(23) Veterans Affairs, 5 members. Bills relating to veterans, military affairs, and armories. Bills amending the Military and Veterans Code.

The standing committees of any regular session shall be the standing committees of concurrent special or extraordinary sessions unless otherwise ordered by the Senate.

Committee on Legislative Ethics

12.3. (a) (1) The Committee on Legislative Ethics is hereby created. The committee shall be appointed by the Committee on Rules and shall consist of six Senators, at least two of whom are members of the political party having the greatest number of members in the Senate and at least two of whom are members of the political party having the second greatest number of members in the Senate. The members of the committee shall serve two-year terms. The President pro Tempore and the Minority Floor Leader shall serve as ex officio, nonvoting members of the committee.

(2) The Committee on Rules shall select a Chair and a Vice Chair, who may not be members of the same political party. The Chair may not serve more than two consecutive two-year terms, and the Committee on Rules shall select a successor who is not a member of the same political party as the immediately previous Chair.

(3) Vacancies in the committee shall be filled within 30 days by the Committee on Rules for the remainder of a term.

(4) If a complaint is filed against a member of the committee, the Committee on Rules shall temporarily replace the member with a Senator of the same political party, who shall serve until the complaint is dismissed by the committee or the Senate takes action as it deems appropriate, whichever occurs earlier.

(5) The Committee on Rules, upon the recommendation of the Committee on Legislative Ethics, shall appoint a Chief Counsel to assist the committee in carrying out its functions. The staff of the committee shall be considered permanent and professional, and shall perform their duties in a nonpartisan manner. No staff of the committee may engage in partisan activities regarding a Senate election campaign. The committee may retain independent counsel when necessary for specific investigations.

(b) The committee shall do all of the following:

(1) The committee shall formulate and recommend, for adoption by the Senate, standards of conduct for Senators and officers and employees of the Senate in the performance of their legislative responsibilities. The Ethics Manual for Members, Officers, and Employees of the United States House of Representatives, as prepared by the Staff of the Committee on Standards of Official Conduct, 102nd Congress Second Session (United States Government Printing Office, Washington, 1992), the Code of Ethics (Article 2 (commencing with Section 8920) of Chapter 1 of Part 1 of Division 2 of Title 2 of the Government Code), and Joint Rule 44 shall serve as guides in the formulation of the standards of conduct.

(2) At the request of any Senator or officer or employee of the Senate, the committee shall provide an advisory opinion with respect to the standards of conduct of the Senate on the general propriety of past, current, or anticipated conduct of that Senator, officer, or employee. The opinion shall be rendered within 21 days unless the Chair and Vice Chair agree otherwise. The committee may, with appropriate deletions to ensure the privacy of the individuals concerned, publish the advisory opinions for the guidance of other Senators, officers, or employees.

(3) The committee shall develop, issue, and annually update a clear, informative, and usable manual for the Senate based on the standards of conduct adopted by the Senate, including any advisory opinions published pursuant to paragraph (2).

(4) The committee shall conduct periodic workshops, at least once each calendar year, for Senators and officers and employees of the Senate, including workshops specifically designed for newly elected Senators and newly appointed officers and employees. At least once in each biennial session, each Senator, and each officer or employee of the Senate who is a designated employee under the Senate Conflict of Interest Code, shall attend one of these workshops. The workshops shall include, but not be limited to, a comprehensive review of all applicable statutes and Senate rules.

(5) After adoption by the Senate of the standards of conduct, the committee shall receive and review complaints alleging violations of the standards of conduct by Senators, or officers or employees of the Senate, in accordance with the procedures specified in subdivisions (c) to (s), inclusive.

(6) The committee shall maintain a record of its investigations, hearings, and other proceedings. All records, complaints, documents, and reports filed with, submitted to, or made by the committee, and all records and transcripts of any investigations or hearings of the committee shall be confidential and may not be open to inspection by any person other than a member of the committee or the staff of the committee, except as otherwise specifically provided in this rule. Any member of the committee or any person on the staff of the committee who discloses any record, complaint, document, report, or transcript that is confidential shall be subject to discipline. The committee may, by a majority vote of the membership of the committee, authorize the release of any records, complaints, documents, reports, and transcripts in its possession to the appropriate enforcement agency if the committee determines that there is probable cause to believe that the violation or violations alleged in the complaint would constitute a felony or if the committee determines that the information is material to any matter pending before the enforcement agency.

(c) (1) Any person may file a complaint with the committee that alleges a violation of the standards of conduct.

(2) Except as provided in paragraphs (3) and (4), a complaint may not be filed more than 18 months after the date that the alleged violation occurred.

(3) If the committee determines that the person filing the complaint did not know, or through the exercise of reasonable diligence could not have known, of the alleged violation within 18 months after the date that the alleged violation occurred, the complaint may be filed within three years after the date that the alleged violation occurred.

(4) If a complaint is filed within 60 days prior to an election at which a Senator or officer or employee is a candidate for elective office, the complaint shall be returned to the person filing the complaint, and the person shall be informed that the complaint may be filed with an appropriate enforcement agency and may be refiled with the committee after the election. The period of time for filing the complaint shall be extended for 60 days.

(5) A complaint may not be filed if it alleges a violation that occurred prior to the adoption of the standards of conduct.

(d) A complaint shall satisfy all of the following requirements:

(1) It shall be in writing.

(2) It shall state the name of the person filing the complaint.

(3) It shall state the name of Senator, or the name and position or title of the officer or employee of the Senate, who is alleged to have committed a violation of the standards of conduct.

(4) It shall set forth allegations that, if true, would constitute a violation of the standards of conduct. The allegations shall be stated with sufficient clarity and detail to enable the committee to make a finding pursuant to subdivision (h).

(5) It shall state the date of the alleged violation.

(6) It shall include a statement that the allegations are true of the person's own knowledge or that the person believes them to be true, and shall be signed by the person under penalty of perjury.

(e) The committee, on its own motion, two-thirds of the membership concurring, may initiate a proceeding by filing a complaint that complies with paragraphs (1) to (5), inclusive, of subdivision (d).

(f) The committee shall promptly send a copy of a complaint to the Senator, or officer or employee of the Senate, alleged to have committed the violation, who shall thereafter be designated as the respondent.

(g) If a complaint is filed by a person other than the committee, the Chair and Vice Chair of the committee shall examine the complaint to determine whether it was filed in accordance with this rule and any rules of the committee. Within 15 days after the complaint is filed, the Chair and Vice Chair shall provide to the committee a copy of the complaint and their opinion as to whether the allegations in the complaint, if true, would constitute a violation of the standards of conduct. If the committee, by a two-thirds vote of its membership, finds that the allegations, if true, would constitute a violation of the standards of conduct, the committee shall hold a hearing within 30 days to conduct a preliminary inquiry. If two-thirds of the membership of the committee fails to find that the allegations, if true, would constitute a violation of the standards of conduct, it shall dismiss the complaint and so notify the person who filed the complaint and the respondent, and the complaint shall not be made public.

(h) At the preliminary inquiry, the respondent may respond to the allegations in the complaint by written statement or oral testimony. If two-thirds of the membership of the committee finds that probable cause exists for believing that the respondent committed a violation of the standards of conduct, the committee shall issue a count-by-count statement of alleged violations. If two-thirds of the membership of the committee fails to find that probable cause exists, the committee shall dismiss the complaint. In either event, the committee shall immediately notify the respondent and the person who filed the complaint of its action. If the committee finds that probable cause exists, the statement of alleged violations shall be made public within seven days.

(i) Within 21 days after the issuance of the statement of alleged violations, the respondent may file an answer that admits or denies each count. Upon request of the respondent, the committee may grant the respondent an additional 21 days to respond.

(j) Within 60 days after the issuance of the statement of alleged violations, the committee shall hold a disciplinary hearing. If a majority of the membership of each party on the committee fails to find that the respondent committed a violation of the standards of conduct, the committee shall dismiss the complaint. If a majority of the membership of each party on the committee finds by clear and convincing evidence that the respondent committed a violation of the standards of conduct, the committee shall take the following action:

(1) If the respondent is a Senator, it shall hold a hearing to determine an appropriate sanction.

(2) If the respondent is an officer or employee, it shall transmit its findings to the Committee on Rules for appropriate action.

(k) (1) At the hearing to determine an appropriate sanction, two-thirds of the membership of the committee shall determine whether the violation is serious or minor.

(2) If the committee determines that a violation is minor or fails to determine that a violation is serious, two-thirds of the membership of the committee (A) shall, if it determines that the violation bears upon the exercise of a right or privilege, recommend that the Committee on Rules deny or limit that right or privilege and shall transmit its findings and recommendation to the Committee on Rules, or (B) shall impose any lesser sanction. Within 15 days after the imposition of a lesser sanction, the respondent may appeal the sanction imposed to the Committee on Rules.

(3) If the committee determines that a violation is serious, two-thirds of the membership of the committee shall recommend that the Senate take one or more of the

following actions and shall transmit its findings and recommendation to the Senate:

(A) The denial or limitation of any right or privilege, if the violation bears upon the exercise of that right or privilege.

(B) A reprimand for a serious violation.

(C) A censure for a more serious violation.

(D) An expulsion for a most serious violation.

(*l*) The Senate shall, within 15 legislative days after receiving the findings and recommendation, vote on the recommendation of the committee. The Senate, by 21 votes, may deny or limit any right or privilege of, reprimand, or censure the Senator or, by 27 votes, may expel the Senator.

(m) The committee or Senate may defer any action required by this rule if other proceedings have been commenced on the same matter.

(n) (1) At all hearings, the Chief Counsel of the committee shall present the case. All relevant and probative evidence is admissible unless it is privileged. Witnesses may be called and cross-examined by the committee and the respondent, and exhibits and other documents may be entered into the record. The respondent has the right to be represented by legal counsel or any other person of his or her choosing.

(2) If the committee receives, at any time, any exculpatory information relating to the alleged violation, the committee shall make the information available to the respondent.

(o) If the committee determines that the complaint was filed with malicious intent, it may request that the Committee on Rules reimburse the expenses incurred by the respondent.

(p) At any time during the proceedings, the respondent may admit that he or she committed a violation of the standards of conduct. If the respondent admits some but not all of the violations alleged in the complaint or the counts set forth in the statement of alleged violations, the committee shall find that the admitted violations constituted a violation of the standards of conduct and may continue the proceedings to determine whether the other alleged violations constituted violations of the standards of conduct. If the respondent admits to all alleged violations, the committee shall find that the admitted violations constituted a violation of the standards of conduct, terminate the preliminary inquiry or disciplinary hearing, and take the action required by paragraph (1) or (2) of subdivision (j).

(q) Meetings of the committee may not be open to the public until the committee finds that probable cause exists for believing that the respondent committed a violation of the standards of conduct. Subsequent meetings of the committee or Senate shall be public, and notice of any meeting shall be published in the Senate File for four calendar days prior to the meeting.

(r) If the committee finds that probable cause exists for believing that the respondent committed a violation of the standards of conduct, the transcript of any testimony given, or any documents admitted into evidence, at a public hearing and any report prepared by the committee subsequent to that finding that states a final finding or recommendation shall be open to public inspection.

(s) Upon request of the respondent, the committee may permit the respondent to inspect, copy, or photograph books, papers, documents, photographs, or other tangible objects that relate to the allegations in the complaint. If the committee finds that probable cause exists for believing that the respondent committed a violation of the standards of conduct, the committee shall permit the respondent to inspect, copy, or photograph books, papers, documents, photographs, or other tangible objects that relate to the statement of alleged violations.

(t) (1) A Senator or officer or employee of the Senate may not directly or indirectly use or attempt to use his or her official authority or influence to intimidate, threaten, coerce, command, or attempt to intimidate, threaten, coerce, or command any person for the purpose of interfering with the right of that person to file a complaint with the committee, testify before, or in any way cooperate with, the committee or any panel.

(2) For the purpose of paragraph (1), "use of official authority or influence" includes promising to confer, or

conferring, any benefit; effecting, or threatening to effect, any reprisal; or taking, or directing others to take, or recommending, processing, or approving, any personnel action, including, but not limited to, appointment, promotion, transfer, assignment, performance evaluation, suspension, or other disciplinary action.

(3) Nothing in this subdivision may be construed to authorize any person to disclose information the disclosure of which is otherwise prohibited by law.

(u) The committee may adopt rules governing its proceedings not inconsistent with this rule. The provisions of Joint Rule 36 relating to investigating committees apply to the committee to the extent those provisions are consistent with this rule.

(v) The powers and procedures set forth in subdivisions (b) to (u), inclusive, confer independent authority and may not be limited or altered by Joint Rule 45.

General Research Committee

12.5.   The General Research Committee is hereby created pursuant to Section 11 of Article IV of the California Constitution, which relates to legislative committees. The committee consists of the 40 Senators, and the President pro Tempore is its chair. The committee is allocated all subjects within the scope of legislative regulation and control, but may not undertake any investigation that another committee has been specifically requested or directed to undertake. The General Research Committee may act through subcommittees appointed by the Senate Committee on Rules, and each of the subcommittees may act only on the particular study or investigation assigned by the Committee on Rules to that subcommittee. Each member of the General Research Committee is authorized and directed to receive and investigate requests for legislative action made by individuals or groups and to report thereon to the full committee.

The committee and its members shall have and exercise all of the rights, duties, and powers conferred upon investigating committees and their members by the Senate Rules and the Joint Rules of the Senate and Assembly. However, neither the committee nor its members may issue a subpoena without the prior approval of the Committee on Rules. The committee has the following additional powers and duties:

(a) To contract with other agencies, public or private, for the rendition and affording of services, facilities, studies, and reports to the committee as the committee deems necessary to assist it to carry out the purposes for which it is created.

(b) To cooperate with and secure the cooperation of county, city, city and county, and other local law enforcement agencies in investigating any matter within the scope established by this rule, and to direct the sheriff of any county to serve subpoenas, orders, and other process issued by the committee.

(c) To meet and act at any place within the State of California and, when authorized in writing by the Committee on Rules to do so, to meet and act outside the state to carry out its duties.

(d) To report its findings and recommendations to the Legislature and the people from time to time.

(e) To act during sessions of the Legislature, including any recess.

(f) To do any and all other things necessary or convenient to enable it fully and adequately to exercise its powers, perform its duties, and accomplish the objects and purposes of this rule.

The Committee on Rules may allocate, from time to time, to the General Research Committee from the Senate Operating Fund those sums that are necessary to permit the General Research Committee and the members thereof to carry out the duties imposed on them. In addition, the Committee on Rules may allocate to any subcommittee from the Senate Operating Fund those sums that the Committee on Rules deems necessary to complete the investigation or study conferred upon that subcommittee.

Additional Committee on Rules Powers

12.7.   In addition to other rights, duties and powers vested in the Committee on Rules, the committee and the members thereof shall have and exercise all of the rights, duties, and powers of the General Research

Committee and the members thereof, as provided in Rule 12.5, with authority to act on any subject allocated by Rule 12.5 to the General Research Committee.

Committee on Rules

13. (a) The Committee on Rules is charged with the general responsibility for the administrative functioning of the Senate. The committee has general charge of the books, documents, and other papers and property of the Senate and shall see that the same are properly kept, cared for, filed, or otherwise disposed of in accordance with applicable law and rules. The committee also has the duties of making studies and recommendations designed to promote, improve, and expedite the business and procedure of the Senate and its committees, including investigating committees consisting wholly or in part of Members of the Senate, and of proposing any amendments to the rules deemed necessary to accomplish those purposes.

(b) The Committee on Rules shall continue in existence during any recess of the Legislature until the convening of the next regular session, and shall have the same powers and duties as while the Senate is in session. The committee has the authority to fill vacancies in any Senate committee or in the Senate membership of any joint committee.

(c) The committee and its members shall have and exercise all of the rights, duties, and powers conferred upon investigating committees and their members by the Joint Rules of the Senate and Assembly as they are adopted and amended from time to time, which provisions are incorporated herein and made applicable to the Committee on Rules and its members.

(d) The committee may make available to any Senate or joint committee, or any Member of the Senate, assistance in connection with the duties of the committee or other legislative matters as the personnel resources under the direction of the committee or its other facilities permit.

(e) All employees on the payroll of the Senate are employees of the Senate and not of individual members, and they are under the direct control of the Committee on Rules. The Committee on Rules has general supervision over all employees of the Senate and the powers and duties to suspend, discipline, or discharge any employees when necessary. Any insubordination or inefficiency on the part of any employee shall be reported to the Committee on Rules.

(f) The committee shall make available and furnish to the Members of the Senate, and the Senate committees, personnel resources as may be reasonably necessary for the Members and the committees to carry out their duties.

(g) The Committee on Rules constitutes the Committee on Introduction of Bills and has charge of the engrossment and enrollment of bills, the contingent expenses of the Senate, and legislative printing, except insofar as these functions are delegated to the Secretary of the Senate.

(h) The rooms, passages, and buildings set apart for the use of the Senate are under the direction of the Committee on Rules, and the committee may assign the press desks in the Senate Chamber to accredited newspaper representatives.

(i) Executive communication of nominations sent by the Governor to the Senate for confirmation shall be referred to the Committee on Rules, unless otherwise ordered by the Senate, without debate.

(j) The Committee on Rules shall, at each regular session, appoint a Member of the Senate to serve on the Judicial Council and has the authority during any joint recess to fill any vacancy in that position that occurs during the recess.

(k) When a report of a joint legislative committee is delivered to the Senate Desk, the Committee on Rules shall refer it to a standing committee for review and appropriate action.

Expenses of Senate Committees

13.1. All claims for expenses incurred by investigating committees of the Senate, the Secretary of the Senate, and the Sergeant at Arms shall be approved by the Committee on Rules or its authorized representative before the claims are presented to the Controller.

All proposed expenditures, including furniture, equipment, and other property, but not including stationery supplies, shall be approved by the Committee on Rules or its authorized representatives before the expenses are incurred, unless the expenditure is specifically exempted from the provisions of this rule by the resolution authorizing it.

A warrant may not be drawn in payment of any claim for expenses until the approval of the Committee on Rules, or its authorized representative, has been obtained in accordance with this rule.

The Committee on Rules may adopt rules and regulations limiting the amount, time, and place of expenses and allowances to be paid to employees of Senate investigating committees and regulating the terms and conditions of employment of their employees. Copies of all rules and regulations adopted pursuant to this rule shall be distributed to the chair of every investigating committee.

Alteration, Repair, Improvement to Senate

13.2. The Committee on Rules is authorized and directed to incur and pay expenses of the Senate not otherwise provided for as the committee determines are reasonably necessary, including the repair, alteration, improvement, and equipping of the Senate Chamber and the offices provided for the Senate in the State Capitol.

In order to avoid unanticipated reversions of appropriations for contingent expenses, the Committee on Rules may designate the appropriation from which payment shall be made pursuant to allocations to committees or for other purposes. If insufficient money is available in any appropriation to pay all claims pursuant to allocations charged against it, the committee shall designate another appropriation from which the allocations shall be paid.

Rooms and Property of Senate

13.3. The Committee on Rules is responsible for the safekeeping of Senate property. The Director of General Services is directed to maintain the Senate

Chamber and all the committee rooms and other rooms used by the Senators and officers of the Senate in a condition that they will be available for the use of the Senate at any time. It is further directed that no persons other than the Members, officers, and employees of the Senate may occupy or use the offices, committee rooms, or other rooms now occupied by the Senate without permission as hereinafter provided, that the desks, furniture, and other equipment of the Senate shall be at the disposal of the Committee on Rules, and that no person except Members of the Senate may occupy any of the Senate's offices or make use of Senate equipment without permission of the committee or its authorized representative.

Inventory of Senate Property

13.4.   The Committee on Rules is authorized and directed, through its authorized representative, to make and maintain a complete inventory of all property of the Senate, including all property in the possession or control of any Senate committee. The Committee on Rules has custody and control of all property of the Senate and shall adopt rules or orders as it may determine are necessary relating to the purchase, care, custody, and use or disposal thereof.

Status of Standing Rules for Regular Session

13.5.   The adoption of the Standing Rules for any special session are not to be construed as modifying or rescinding the Standing Rules of the Senate for a regular session.

Operating Expense Fund

13.6.   The Committee on Rules is the committee identified in Section 9126 of the Government Code. The balance of all money in the Senate Operating Fund, including money now or hereafter appropriated by the Legislature, except sums that are made available specifically for purposes other than the expenses of designated committees, is hereby made available to the Committee on Rules for any charges or claims it may incur in carrying out the duties imposed upon it by these rules or by Senate or concurrent resolution.

Rules Committee Appointees

13.8. The Committee on Rules shall review its nonlegislator appointees every two years. That review shall be completed not later than the 120th calendar day of the regular session in which the review is undertaken.

Schedule of Committee Meetings

14. The Committee on Rules shall propose to the Senate such schedules for regular meetings of the standing committees as will permit all members of each committee to attend without a conflict of committee engagements.

The committee may also propose such special committee meetings or special schedules of committee meetings as will facilitate the business of the Senate. Those schedules may provide a special schedule of committee meetings upon certain days of the week or to meet any special condition that may arise.

Powers of Standing Committees

16. Each standing committee of the Senate to which a proposed law or bill is assigned has full power and authority during the session of the Legislature, or any recess thereof, to make an investigation and study concerning any proposed law or bill as the committee shall determine necessary to enable it to properly act thereon.

In the exercise of the power granted by this rule, each committee may appoint a secretary and employ clerical, legal, and technical assistants as may appear necessary when money has been made available therefor by the Senate.

Each standing committee is authorized and empowered to summon and subpoena witnesses, to require the production of papers, books, accounts, reports, documents, records, and papers of every kind and description, to issue subpoenas, and to take all necessary means to compel the attendance of witnesses and to procure testimony, oral and documentary. However, no committee may issue a subpoena, nor may a committee require testimony under oath, without the prior approval of the Committee on Rules.

The Sergeant at Arms, or other person designated by the Sergeant at Arms or by the committee, shall serve any and all subpoenas, orders, and other process that may be issued by the committee, when directed to do so upon a vote of the majority of the membership of the committee.

Each of the members of the standing committees is authorized and empowered to administer oaths, and all of the provisions of Chapter 4 (commencing with Section 9400) of Part 1 of Division 2 of Title 2 of the Government Code, relating to the attendance and examination of witnesses before the Legislature and the committees thereof, apply to the committees.

All officers of this state, including the head of each department, agency, and subdivision thereof, all employees of the departments, agencies, and subdivisions of the state, the Legislative Counsel, and all other persons, whether connected with the state government or not, shall give and furnish to these committees upon request such information, records, and documents as the committees deem necessary or proper for the achievement of the purposes for which each standing committee was created.

Each standing committee may meet at the State Capitol and do any and all things necessary or convenient to enable it to exercise the powers and perform the duties herein granted to it, and may expend such money as may be made available by the Senate for that purpose, except that no committee may incur any indebtedness unless money has been first made available therefor.

Funerals

17.5.   The Chair or Vice Chair of the Committee on Rules may designate any one or more of the Members of the Senate as a Senate committee to attend funerals in appropriate circumstances. The Members so designated may receive expenses as provided in Joint Rule 35.

The Chair or Vice Chair of the Committee on Rules, or any Member of the Senate designated by either of these officers, may incur such expense as may be necessary for the purchase on behalf of the Senate of suitable floral pieces for the funeral.

All expenses incurred pursuant to this rule shall be paid out of the money allocated from the Senate Operating Fund to the Committee on Rules and disbursed, after certification by the Chair or Vice Chair of the committee or by the committee's disbursing officer appointed and designated therefor by the committee, upon warrants drawn by the Controller upon the Treasury.

Expenditures

18.   A member of a committee may not incur any expense chargeable to the Senate unless authorized by resolution of the Senate.

The Committee on Rules shall provide, by rules and regulations, for the manner of authorizing expenditures by Members, committees, and officers and employees of the Senate that are not otherwise authorized by law, these rules, or the Joint Rules of the Senate and Assembly, and for the payment of the expenditures from the Senate Operating Fund upon certification of claims therefor to the Controller by the Committee on Rules or its authorized representative.

Printing of Reports

18.5.   All requests for the printing of reports of Senate committees shall be made to the Committee on Rules.

The Committee on Rules shall determine if the report is to be printed, the number of copies needed, and whether or not the report shall be printed in the Journal.

If the report is to be printed by the Office of State Publishing, it shall hold the type for each Senate committee report for a period of 90 days from the date of the first printing or for such other time as the Committee on Rules deems necessary.

PROCEDURES AND RULES

Joint and Concurrent Resolutions and Constitutional Amendments

19.   Joint and concurrent resolutions and constitutional amendments shall be treated the same as bills under these rules, except that they shall have only one official reading, which reading shall occur after they have been reported by committee.

Parliamentary Rules

20.   In all cases not provided for by the Constitution, these rules, the Joint Rules of the Senate and Assembly, or statute, the authority shall be the latest edition of Mason's Manual or the custom and usage of the Senate.

Suspension of Rules or Amending of Rules

21.   A standing rule of the Senate may not be adopted, amended, or repealed except upon an affirmative vote of a majority of the membership of the Senate, one day's notice being given, except that any rule not requiring more than a majority vote may be temporarily suspended without that notice by a vote of a majority of the membership of the Senate. A rule requiring a two-thirds vote on any question may be amended only by a two-thirds vote on one day's notice, except that a rule requiring a two-thirds vote may be temporarily suspended without that notice by a two-thirds vote.

All proposed amendments to these rules shall, upon presentation, be referred to the Committee on Rules without debate.

Suspension of the Joint Rules

21.1.   Pursuant to Joint Rule 33, a joint rule may not be suspended by the Senate except with the concurrence of 27 Members unless a lower vote is prescribed by these rules or the Joint Rules of the Senate and the Assembly.

Permission of Committee on Rules

21.2.   Notwithstanding Rule 21 or 21.1, a Senate or Joint Rule may not be suspended unless the Committee on Rules determines that an extraordinary circumstance exists that justifies the suspension.

Rules Governing Standing Committees

21.5.   Except as otherwise provided in these rules, standing committees of the Senate shall be governed as follows:

(a) The officers of each Senate committee shall be a chair, vice chair, and secretary.

(b) The chair shall preside at meetings when present except when the committee is considering a bill of which he or she is the sole author or the lead author. Whenever the chair is not presiding, the vice chair shall assume the duties of the chair. In the absence of both, a member designated by the chair shall preside.

(c) The secretary shall keep a complete record of the meetings and actions taken by the committee. Bills and other measures favorably acted upon shall be reported to the Senate as expeditiously as the reports can be prepared.

(d) The committee shall meet in regular session on the day and hour designated by the Committee on Rules. Adjourned meetings or special meetings shall be held at the time fixed in the adjourning motion, or, for a special meeting, on the call of the chair.

(e) A special meeting may be called by the chair, with the approval of the Committee on Rules, by giving reasonable notice to all members of the committee, either in writing or by telephone, specifying the purpose of the meeting, the time and place thereof, and the matters to be considered at the meeting. Notice of hearing of bills as required by subdivision (a) of Joint Rule 62 may also be given in the Daily File. A matter may not be considered at the special meeting unless specified in the notice.

A special meeting shall be scheduled so as to permit all members of the committee to attend without conflict with other scheduled committee meetings.

(f) A majority of the membership of the committee shall constitute a quorum. A vote of a majority of the membership of the committee shall be required to table a bill, remove it from the table, or reconsider a vote on a bill.

(g) Action may not be taken on any measure outside of a duly constituted committee meeting.

(h) The chair shall set the hearings of bills and arrange the calendar for committee hearings. Notice of hearing of any bill shall be given to the author and other persons requiring notice. A bill may not be considered in the absence of the author without his or her consent, except that a bill may be presented by the author's representative who is authorized in writing.

(i) A committee or a subcommittee thereof, by a majority vote of the membership of the committee, may meet in executive session for any purpose authorized by Section 9029 of the Government Code. Otherwise, all meetings shall be open and public.

(j) The chair shall direct the order of presentation of the arguments for and against matters for consideration by the committee, and shall permit questions to be asked by members of the committee in an orderly fashion and in keeping with proper decorum.

(k) Further consideration of a bill that has been voted out of a committee or defeated shall be by reconsideration only, as follows:

(1) A motion to reconsider a vote by which a bill is voted out shall be in order, and shall be voted upon at the same meeting. If the motion is carried by a vote of a majority of the membership of the committee, the bill may be considered at that meeting, provided the author is present, or at a subsequent meeting.

(2) The procedure for reconsideration of a bill that has been defeated shall conform to the requirements of subdivision (a) of Joint Rule 62. Any bill as to which reconsideration has been granted pursuant to this paragraph may not be heard again until a subsequent meeting of the committee, after being calendared in the Daily File.

(*l*) Any bill that has been laid on the table and is removed from the table at a later meeting may not be heard again until a subsequent meeting of the committee, after being calendared in the Daily File and after notice.

(m) When a committee adopts proposed amendments to a bill, the bill may be taken up for vote at that meeting or, if the committee or author requests, sent out to print before final action. If the amendments are not in proper form, they shall be prepared and submitted to the chair for approval before being reported to the Desk. Amendments submitted by the author that, in the opinion of the committee chair, are major or substantial shall be submitted to the committee at least two legislative days before the bill is scheduled for hearing.

(n) A bill may not be set for hearing, nor may any notice thereof be published, by a Senate committee until the bill has been referred to the committee by the Committee on Rules.

(o) The chair may appoint, with the permission of the Committee on Rules, subcommittees of one or more members to consider and recommend to the full committee action on matters as may be assigned to the subcommittee for consideration from time to time by the chair. The chair may assign and reassign members of, and matters to, the various subcommittees. The recommendation of a subcommittee may be accepted by a vote of a majority of the members of the committee.

(p) In all cases not provided for by this rule, the Senate Rules, the Joint Rules of the Senate and Assembly, or statute, the authority shall be the latest edition of Mason's Manual.

Additional Rules

21.6. Committees may adopt additional rules that are not in conflict with Rule 21.5 or other rules.

Reporting Measures Out of Committee

21.7. The vote of a majority of the membership of a standing committee shall be required to report a bill, constitutional amendment, concurrent resolution, or joint resolution out of committee.

A vote of a majority of all members of a standing committee who are present and voting shall be required to report a Senate resolution out of committee.

Press Participation

21.8.   Accredited press representatives may not be excluded from any public legislative meeting or hearing, and may not be prohibited from taking photographs of, televising, or recording the committee or house hearings, subject to the following conditions:

(1) This rule extends to all public legislative meetings.

(2) Lights may be used only when cameras are filming and, when possible, proceedings in hearing rooms and the chamber shall be filmed without lights.

(3) Every effort should be made to set up filming equipment before hearings or sessions begin.

(4) The committee chair or the Committee on Rules shall be notified, as far in advance of the proceedings as possible, that recordings and television cameras will be present and filming.

(5) To the extent practical, flash cameras shall not be used.

(6) Photographs shall be taken in an orderly and expeditious manner so as to cause the least possible inconvenience to the committee or to the Members in the chamber.

However, the chair of a committee may request any person to relocate or remove any object, or discontinue the use of any equipment, that is situated or used in a manner so as to disrupt the proceedings or to create a potential danger to, or substantially obstruct the view of, members of the committee or the public.

In case any person fails to respond to a request of the chair to relocate, remove, or discontinue the use of the objects or equipment, the committee may, by majority vote, require it.

INTRODUCTION AND REFERENCE OF MEASURES

Introduction, First Reading, and Reference of Measures

22. Any Senator desiring to introduce a bill, constitutional amendment, concurrent resolution, joint resolution, or Senate resolution shall send it to the Senate Desk.

When received at the Secretary's desk, a bill shall, under the proper order of business, be numbered, read, printed, and referred by the Committee on Rules to a standing committee. The Committee on Rules shall check all Assembly measures before reference to committee and shall designate the committee to which they shall be referred.

All joint resolutions, concurrent resolutions, and Senate resolutions shall be automatically referred to the Committee on Rules upon introduction, and may be rereferred to any other standing committee upon the vote of a majority of the membership of the Committee on Rules.

Unless otherwise ordered by the Senate without debate, the assignment of the measure shall then be complete and, after printing, the Secretary shall deliver the measure to the committee designated by the Committee on Rules.

Under the order of Messages from the Assembly, the Secretary shall read each Assembly bill the first time and shall read the name of the committee to which the bill has been assigned by the Committee on Rules. Unless otherwise ordered by the Senate without debate the assignment of the bill shall then be complete, and the Secretary shall deliver the bill to the committee so designated.

Bill Introduction Limitation

22.5. (a) A Member of the Senate may introduce or subsequently author not more than 50 bills in the regular session.

(b) This rule may be suspended with respect to a particular bill by approval of the Committee on Rules.

(c) This rule does not apply to a constitutional amendment, any type of resolution, or a bill introduced by a committee.

Short Title

22.6.   A bill may not add a short title that names a current or former Member of the Legislature.

Introduction of Bills by a Committee

23.   (a) A standing committee may introduce a bill germane to any subject within the proper consideration of the committee in the same manner as any Member. A committee bill shall contain the signatures of all of the members of the committee.

(b) A committee may amend into a bill related provisions germane to the subject and embraced within the title and, with the consent of the author, may constitute that bill a committee bill.

Bill Introduction Deadline

23.5.   The Senate Desk shall remain open for the introduction of bills from 9:00 a.m. to 5:00 p.m. on the days designated in subdivision (a) of Joint Rule 54 as the deadlines for the introduction of bills in the first and second years of the regular session.

Introduction of Bills and Resolutions at Special Sessions

24.   Whenever, at any special session, a bill or resolution is received at the Desk, under the order of Introduction of Bills, it shall be referred to the Committee on Rules, which shall decide whether or not the bill or resolution can properly be considered at the session. If, in the judgment of the Committee on Rules, the bill or resolution can be considered, the committee shall report the bill or resolution back and designate the committee to which it shall be assigned. Thereafter

the bill or resolution shall be assigned a number by the Secretary, read the first time, and referred to the committee recommended by the Committee on Rules unless otherwise referred on motion without debate.

Resolutions

24.5. A Senate concurrent resolution or Senate resolution may be introduced relating to a present or former state or federal elected official or a member of his or her immediate family. Other resolutions for the purpose of commendation or congratulation of any person, group, or organization, or for the purpose of expressing sympathy, regret, or sorrow on the death of any person, shall be prepared as Rules Committee resolutions and presented to the Committee on Rules for appropriate action.

The Committee on Rules may approve exceptions to this rule for Senate resolutions. The Secretary may not accept for introduction any Senate resolution that is contrary to this rule unless it is accompanied by the approval of the Committee on Rules.

Senate Resolutions

25. All Senate resolutions eligible to be introduced under the rules, upon being presented, shall be given a number by the Secretary. A Senate resolution shall be printed, and indexed in the History and Journal.

Bills Authored by a Former Member

26. Whenever a bill in the Senate is authored by an individual who is no longer a Member of the Legislature, upon a request of a committee or current Member of the house in which the bill was introduced, the Senate Committee on Rules may authorize that committee or Member to be the author of that bill. Absent that authorization, action may not be taken by a committee or the Senate with respect to a bill authored by a former Member.

BILLS IN COMMITTEE

Author's Amendments

27. Upon request of the author of a bill, the chair of the committee to which the bill has been referred may, by his or her individual action taken independently of any committee meeting, cause the bill to be reported to the Senate with the recommendation that amendments submitted by the author be adopted and the bill be reprinted as amended and rereferred to the committee.

Withdrawing a Bill From Committee

28. A bill or resolution may not be withdrawn from committee except upon written notice being first given to the Committee on Rules and by 21 votes of the Senate.

Consent Calendar

28.3. (a) If a Senate bill or Assembly bill is amended in the Senate to create a new bill or to rewrite the bill, a standing committee may not place the bill on its consent calendar, and may not report the bill out of committee with the recommendation that it be placed on the consent calendar on the floor.

(b) For purposes of this rule, an amendment creates a new bill or rewrites the bill if the amendment (1) changes the subject of the bill to a new or different subject, or (2) adds a new subject to the bill that is different from, and not related to, the contents of the bill.

Referral of Bills

28.4. (a) If a Senate bill or Assembly bill is amended in the Committee on Appropriations to create a new bill or to rewrite the bill and the chair of the committee determines pursuant to Senate Rule 28.8 that (1) any additional state costs are not significant and do not and will not require the appropriation of additional state funds, and (2) the bill will cause no significant reduction in revenues, the bill shall be reported to the Senate with the recommendation that it be placed on second reading, except that the bill first shall be referred to the Committee on Rules. Upon receipt of the bill, the Committee on Rules shall either refer the bill to an appropriate policy committee or order that the bill be placed on second reading.

(b) For purposes of this rule, an amendment creates a new bill or rewrites the bill if the amendment (1) changes the subject of the bill to a new or different subject, or (2) adds a new subject to the bill that is different from, and not related to, the contents of the bill.

Measures to be Authored

28.5. Each bill, constitutional amendment, or resolution shall be authored by a Member or committee of the Legislature before it is considered or voted on by a committee or the Senate. Each amendment to a bill, constitutional amendment, or resolution shall be signed by a Member or committee of the Legislature prior to adoption by the Senate. A bill may be authored only by a Member or committee of the house of origin. A Member other than a Member of the house of origin may be a "principal coauthor" or "coauthor."

Vote in Committee

28.7. Voting on the disposition of bills, constitutional amendments, concurrent resolutions, and joint resolutions by committees shall be by rollcall vote only. A rollcall vote shall be taken on a motion to amend only if requested by any member of the committee or the author of the measure. All rollcall votes taken in committees shall be promptly transmitted by their respective chairs to the Secretary of the Senate, who shall cause a record of the rollcall votes to be printed in the Journal, together with the text of amendments voted upon where the rollcall has been recorded and the amendments adopted.

This rule does not apply to:

(a) Procedural motions that do not have the effect of disposing of a bill.

(b) Withdrawal of a bill from a committee calendar at the request of an author.

(c) A committee's return of a bill to the Senate, if the bill has not been voted on by the committee.

(d) The assignment of bills to committee.

On a legislative day when the President pro Tempore or Minority Floor Leader is in attendance, he or she, in the absence of any objection, may instruct the committee secretary of a committee of which he or she is a member to add his or her vote to any previously announced vote that was taken while he or she was performing the responsibilities of the office of President pro Tempore or Minority Floor Leader, provided the outcome of the vote is not thereby changed. This provision does not apply to any rollcall after adjournment of the legislative day during which the rollcall in question was taken. The intent of this paragraph is to allow the President pro Tempore and the Minority Floor Leader to carry out the unique and special duties of their offices without losing the opportunity to vote on matters before the committees of which they are members.

Appropriations Committee

28.8.   Any bill referred to the Committee on Appropriations pursuant to Joint Rule 10.5 that does not appropriate money may not be set for hearing and shall, along with any nonsubstantive amendments, promptly be reported to the Senate with the recommendation it be placed on second reading if the chair of the committee determines that (a) any additional state costs are not significant and do not and will not require the appropriation of additional state funds, and (b) the bill will cause no significant reduction in revenues.

State-Mandated Local Program Bills

28.9.   (a) Any bill having a digest that, pursuant to Section 17575 of the Government Code, indicates that the bill requires state reimbursement to local agencies or school districts for costs mandated by the state shall be rereferred to the Committee on Appropriations. The bill may not be rereferred to the Committee on Revenue and Taxation.

(b) Any bill rereferred to the Committee on Appropriations pursuant to this rule that does not appropriate money and does not contain a complete disclaimer of all of the provisions of Section 905.2 of, and Part 7 (commencing with Section 17500) of Division 4 of Title 2 of, the Government Code, need not be set for hearing and may, along with any nonsubstantive amendments, be reported to the Senate with the recommendation that it be placed on second reading if the chair of the committee determines, after consideration of the analyses of local costs prepared by the Legislative Analyst and the Department of Finance, that (1) any additional local costs are not significant and (2) the bill will cause no significant reduction in local revenues.

For the purposes of this rule, "complete disclaimer" means a provision in a bill that prohibits local agencies and school districts from filing claims with the State Board of Control for reimbursement for the costs of unfunded mandated programs or services.

(c) Whenever the Assembly amends and passes a Senate bill and the Senate must concur in the amendments, upon the request of any Senator the bill shall be rereferred to the Committee on Appropriations if, based upon the Legislative Counsel's Digest of the Assembly amendments, the bill (1) imposes state-mandated local costs without providing adequate reimbursement, or (2) contains a complete disclaimer. The Committee on Appropriations shall make a recommendation to the Senate regarding whether the Senate should concur in the Assembly amendments.

(d) Any bill referred to the Committee on Appropriations solely pursuant to this rule, and that otherwise would not be rereferred to the committee pursuant to Joint Rule 10.5, is not subject to subparagraph (a)(1), (a)(6), (b)(3), or (b)(8) of Joint Rule 61.

CONSIDERATION OF BILLS

Order of Making Files

29. When bills are reported from committee they shall be placed upon the Daily File, to be kept by the Secretary as follows: All bills when reported to the

Senate by the committee shall be placed at the foot of the Second Reading Senate or Assembly File, in the order in which the reports are made and, after the second reading, shall be placed at the foot of the Senate or Assembly Third Reading File, in the order of reading. Unless otherwise ordered by the Senate the File shall be taken up in the following order: Senate Second Reading File, Assembly Second Reading File, Special Orders, Unfinished Business, Senate Third Reading File, Assembly Third Reading File. The bills upon the third reading shall be considered in the order in which they appear upon the File, unless otherwise ordered by the Senate.

A Senate bill returned from the Assembly for concurrence in Assembly amendments may not be considered until it appears under Unfinished Business on the Daily File pursuant to Joint Rule 26.5 and an analysis is provided to each Senator pursuant to Senate Rule 29.8.

An inactive file shall be kept, to which bills and resolutions may be transferred at the request of the author, or on motion. Bills shall be so transferred when they have been passed on third reading file without action three successive times. Bills and resolutions may be transferred from the inactive file to the second reading file on motion and, after being read the second time, the bills shall take their place regularly on third reading file and be available for consideration and passage.

Bills, resolutions, and other questions may be transferred from the unfinished business file to the inactive file upon request or motion and may be returned to the unfinished business file by request or on motion.

Placement of any question on the inactive file shall not prejudice the question.

Strike From File

29.2.   A motion to strike any bill, resolution, or other question from the File shall require 21 votes. That bill, resolution, or other question may not be acted upon again during the session.

Measures Amended From the Floor

29.3.   The consideration of a bill, constitutional amendment, concurrent resolution, joint resolution, or Senate resolution that has been amended by amendments offered from the floor, except committee amendments reported with measures or amendments offered with a motion to amend and rerefer to committee, is not in order until the amended measure has been in print for not less than one legislative day. Any measure so amended shall be placed on the second reading file.

Bills Approving Memoranda of Understanding

29.4.   The Senate may not pass a bill that approves a memorandum of understanding, for purposes of Section 3517.5 and following of the Government Code, until the final version of the subject memorandum of understanding is received by the Secretary of the Senate and made available for review for seven legislative days and its availability for review noted in the Senate Daily Journal for that period.

Amended Forms of Measures

29.5.   No bill, constitutional amendment, concurrent resolution, joint resolution, or Senate resolution may be considered for passage unless and until a copy of the measure as last amended is on the desk of each Member in printed or electronic form.

Conference Reports

29.6.   (a)   No conference committee on any bill, other than the Budget Bill and the budget implementation bills, may approve any substantial policy change in any bill if that substantial policy change has been defeated in a policy committee of the Senate during the current legislative session.

(b)   For purposes of subdivision (d) of Joint Rule 29.5, the term "heard" means that a printed bill with substantially similar language was before the appropriate committee and taken up at a regular or special hearing of the committee during the current legislative session, or that an amendment, which was drafted and given a request number or approved as to form by Legislative Counsel, was before the committee and taken up at a regular or special hearing of the committee.

Conference Committee Meetings

29.7.   Before the adoption of a conference report by the Senate, any Senator may raise a point of order and put the following question to the chair of the committee on conference from the Senate: "Did the Committee on Conference meet at a public meeting attended by at least two of the Assembly Members and two of the Senate Members of the Committee on Conference and adopt the conference report by an affirmative rollcall vote of not less than two of the Assembly Members and two of the Senate Members constituting the Committee on Conference?" If the chair answers this question in the negative, the conference report shall be returned to the Committee on Conference and may not be further considered by the Senate until the committee has met at a public meeting attended by at least two of the Assembly Members and two of the Senate Members of the committee, and has adopted the conference report by an affirmative rollcall vote of not less than two of the Assembly Members and two of the Senate Members constituting the committee.

Analysis of Measures, Conference Reports, and Floor Amendments

29.8.   (a) With the exception of the Budget Bill and budget implementation bills, no bill, constitutional amendment, concurrent resolution, joint resolution, Senate resolution, unfinished business item, or report of a conference committee may be considered unless and until an analysis thereof has been prepared by the Office of Senate Floor Analyses and placed upon the desks of the Senators, unless otherwise ordered by the President pro Tempore.

(b) An amendment from the floor is not in order unless and until the amendment has been reviewed by the Office of Senate Floor Analyses. Upon a request by the Chair or Vice Chair of the Committee on Rules, or by the lead author of the measure to which a substantive amendment is proposed from the floor, an analysis thereof shall be prepared by the Office of Senate Floor Analyses and placed upon the desks of the Senators.

Consideration of Conference Reports

29.9.   No conference report may be adopted by the Senate until it has been in print for two days prior to being taken up by the Senate.

Referral of Bills

29.10.   (a) If the analysis, prepared in accordance with subdivision (b) of Rule 29.8, of proposed floor amendments to a bill, other than the Budget Bill, discloses that the amendments create a new bill or rewrite the current form of the bill, the amendments shall, prior to consideration of the amendments by the Senate, be referred to the Committee on Rules. If the amendments to the bill are proposed by any Senator other than the author of the bill or the Senator present- ing the Assembly bill on the floor, action on the bill shall be deferred until after the Committee on Rules acts upon the amendments. Upon receipt of the amend- ments, the Committee on Rules by a vote of a majority of its membership may either (1) refer the amendments to an appropriate standing committee, or (2) return the amendments to the Senate floor for consideration.

If the amendments are referred to a standing com- mittee, the committee shall meet and act upon the amendments no later than the next scheduled hearing of the committee. If the amendments are referred to a standing committee during a time when standing com- mittees are not meeting, the standing committee shall meet and act upon the amendments as directed by the Committee on Rules and, in any event, within two legislative days of receipt of the amendments. Upon receipt of the amendments, the committee by a vote of a majority of the membership may do any of the following: (1) hold the amendments, (2) return the amendments to the Senate floor for consideration, or

(3) return amendments as approved by the committee to the Senate floor.

If the amendments are referred to a standing committee during the time when no committee may meet, the Committee on Rules shall grant permission to suspend the joint rule to allow the committee to meet as directed by the Committee on Rules.

If the amendments are referred to the Committee on Rules on the last legislative day preceding a joint recess, the Committee on Rules and, if the amendments are referred to a standing committee, the standing committee, shall meet and act upon the amendments before adjourning for the recess. If the amendments are referred to the Committee on Rules on any of the three legislative days preceding February 1 or September 1 of an even-numbered year, the Committee on Rules and, if the amendments are referred to a standing committee, the standing committee, shall meet and act upon the amendments on the same legislative day.

(b) If the analysis, prepared in accordance with subdivision (a) of Rule 29.8, of a bill, other than the Budget Bill, that is returned to the Senate for a vote on concurrence discloses that the Assembly amendments create a new bill or rewrite the bill as passed by the Senate, action on the bill shall be deferred until the Committee on Rules acts upon the bill. The Committee on Rules by a vote of a majority of its membership may either (1) refer the bill to an appropriate standing committee, or (2) recommend that the bill be taken up for consideration of the Assembly amendments.

If the bill is referred to a standing committee, the committee shall meet and act upon the bill no later than the next scheduled hearing of the committee. If the bill is referred to a standing committee during a time when standing committees are not meeting, the standing committee shall meet and act upon the bill as directed by the Committee on Rules and, in any event, within two legislative days of receipt of the bill. Upon receipt of the bill, the committee by a majority vote of the membership may either (1) hold the bill, or (2) return the bill to the Senate floor for consideration of the Assembly amendments.

If the bill is referred to a standing committee during the time when no committee may meet, the Committee on Rules shall grant permission to suspend the joint rule to allow the committee to meet as directed by the Committee on Rules.

If the bill is referred to the Committee on Rules on the last legislative day preceding a joint recess, the Committee on Rules and, if the bill is referred to a standing committee, the standing committee, shall meet and act upon the bill before adjourning for the recess. If the bill is referred to the Committee on Rules on any of the three legislative days preceding February 1 or September 1 of an even-numbered year, the Committee on Rules and, if the bill is referred to a standing committee, the standing committee, shall meet and act upon the bill on the same legislative day.

(c) An amendment creates a new bill or rewrites the bill if the amendment (1) changes the subject of the bill to a new or different subject, or (2) adds a new subject to the bill that is different from, and not related to, the contents of the bill.

Special Order

30. Any measure or subject may, by vote of a majority of those voting, be made a special order and, when the time fixed for its consideration arrives, he or she who is presiding shall lay it before the Senate.

Messages From the Governor or Assembly

31. Messages from the Governor or from the Assembly may be introduced at any stage of business except while a question is being put, while the ayes and noes are being called, or while a Senator is addressing the Senate.

Messages from the Governor or from the Assembly may be considered when indicated in the order of business or at any other time by unanimous consent or upon motion.

Engrossing Measures

32. All Senate bills, constitutional amendments, and joint and concurrent resolutions shall be engrossed

after each amendment and before final action is taken on them in the Senate. Engrossment shall consist of comparing the printed engrossed measure with the original measure introduced and any amendments adopted to ascertain that it is correct. When a measure is reported correctly engrossed it shall be substituted for the original measure.

Enrolling Measures

33.   All Senate measures shall be enrolled immediately following their final passage and receipt from the Assembly. An enrolled copy of every bill, constitutional amendment, or resolution shall be printed and examined to ascertain that it is a true and accurate copy of the measure as it was passed. It shall then be authenticated by the signature of the Secretary of the Senate or his or her designee, and the Chief Clerk of the Assembly or his or her designee, and transmitted to the Governor or Secretary of State, as the case may be.

Debate

Statement of Motion

34.   A motion may not be debated until it is distinctly announced by he or she who is presiding, and it shall be reduced to writing if desired by any Senator, and read by the Secretary, before it is debated.

Regulations as to Speaking

35.   (a)   When a Senator desires to address the Senate, he or she shall rise in his or her place, address he or she who is presiding, and, when recognized, proceed to speak through the public address system.

(b)   A Senator may not speak more than twice in any one debate on the same day, and at the same stage of the bill, without leave; Senators who have once spoken are not again entitled to the floor (except for explanation) so long as any Senator who has not spoken desires to speak.

(c) When two or more Senators arise at the same time to address the Senate, he or she who is presiding shall designate the Senator who is entitled to the floor.

(d) A Senator may not be interrupted when speaking, and no question may be asked of him or her except through he or she who is presiding.

(e) The author of a bill, motion, or resolution shall have the privilege of closing the debate.

Order in Debate

36.   When a Senator is called to order he or she shall sit down until he or she who is presiding has determined whether or not he or she is in order. Every question of order shall be decided by he or she who is presiding, subject to an appeal to the Senate by any Senator. If a Senator is called to order for words spoken, the objectionable language shall immediately be taken down in writing by the Secretary of the Senate.

Right to Address the Senate

37.   A person other than a Member of the Senate, may not address the Senate while it is in session, except that the Senate may resolve itself into a Committee of the Whole and, while sitting as a Committee of the Whole, may be addressed by persons other than Members.

QUESTIONS AND MOTIONS

Amendments to Measures

38.   When amendments to a measure are reported by a committee or offered from the floor, the amendments shall be submitted in writing.

Adoption of amendments to any measure in the Senate prior to third reading, other than by rollcall, shall not preclude subsequent consideration, in committee or on the third reading of the measure, of the amendments or any part thereof by the Senate.

Amendments to Be Germane

38.5. Every amendment proposed must be germane. In order to be germane, an amendment must relate to the same subject as the original bill, resolution, or other question under consideration.

A point of order may be raised that the proposed amendment or an amendment now in the bill, resolution, or other question under consideration is not germane, so long as the question is within control of the body. In that case the President pro Tempore shall decide whether the point of order is well taken. In the absence of the President pro Tempore, the Vice Chair of the Committee on Rules shall decide whether the point of order is well taken. If, in the opinion of the President pro Tempore or the Vice Chair of the Committee on Rules, the point of order is well taken, the question of germaneness shall on his or her motion be referred to the Committee on Rules for determination. The Committee on Rules shall make its determination by the following legislative day. If the point of order is raised and referral is made on the last legislative day preceding a joint recess, the Committee on Rules shall make its determination before adjourning for the recess.

The proposition shall remain on file until the determination is made. If, upon consideration of the matter, the Committee on Rules determines that the amendment is not germane, the bill, resolution, or other question shall be stricken from the file and may not be acted upon during the remainder of the session, provided that the author of a bill, resolution, or other question shall be given the opportunity to amend the bill, resolution, or other question to delete the portions that are not germane, in which case the bill, resolution, or other question may continue to be acted upon. If the Committee on Rules determines that the amendment is germane, the bill, resolution, or other question may thereafter be acted upon by the house.

Notwithstanding Rule 21, this rule may not be suspended unless the Committee on Rules determines that an extraordinary circumstance and overwhelming public interest exist that justify the suspension.

Amendments From the Floor

38.6. Amendments to a bill, constitutional amendment, concurrent resolution, joint resolution, or Senate resolution offered from the floor, except committee amendments reported with measures or amendments offered with a motion to amend and refer to committee, are not in order unless and until a copy of the proposed amendments provided by the author has been placed upon the desks of the Members.

Motion to Lay on the Table

39. When an amendment proposed to any pending measure is laid on the table, it may not carry with it or prejudice the measure.

Division of a Question

40. If a question in debate contains more than one distinct proposition, any Senator may have the same divided.

The Previous Question

41. The previous question shall be put in the following form: "Shall the question be now put?" It shall require a majority vote of the Senators present, and its effect shall be to put an end to all the debate except that the author of the bill or the amendment shall have the right to close, and the question under discussion shall thereupon be immediately put to a vote.

Call of the Senate

42. Upon a motion being carried for a call of the Senate, he or she who is presiding shall immediately order the doors to be closed, and shall direct the Secretary to call the names of the absentees as disclosed by the last previous rollcall. Thereupon, a Member may not be permitted to leave the Senate Chamber except by written permission of the President pro Tempore or, in his or her absence, of the Assistant President pro Tempore or the Vice Chair of the Committee on Rules, or, in their absence of another member of the Committee on Rules designated for that purpose by the

President pro Tempore or the Vice Chair of the Committee on Rules. Those Members who are found to be absent and for whom no excuse or insufficient excuses are made may, by order of those present, be taken into custody, as they appear, or may be sent for and then taken into custody by the Sergeant at Arms whenever found, or by special messenger to be appointed for that purpose. In the absence of a quorum, a majority of the Members present may order a rollcall of the Senate and compel the attendance of absentees in the manner above provided.

A call of the Senate may be ordered after the roll has been called and prior to the announcement of the vote. A call of the Senate may be dispensed with at any time upon a majority vote of the Senators present, that action to become effective upon completion of the rollcall and the announcement of the vote upon the matter for which the call was ordered.

A recess may not be taken during a call of the Senate. During any call, the call may be made to apply also to other items of business by a motion made and adopted by a majority vote of the Members present. Under those circumstances, when the call of the Senate is dispensed with as to any item of business, the call is deemed to be continued in effect until other items of business that have been made subject to the call by a majority of the Members present have been acted upon. When a call of the Senate is ordered, pending the announcement of the vote upon the completion of a rollcall, the pending rollcall shall become unfinished business, the consideration of which shall be continued until further proceedings under the call of the Senate are dispensed with, when it will forthwith become the order of business before the Senate.

A motion to adjourn is not in order during a call of the Senate.

Reconsideration

43. On the day on which a vote has been taken on any question, a motion to reconsider the vote may be made by any Member. Reconsideration may be granted only once.

The motion may be considered on the day made or on the succeeding legislative day, but may not be further postponed without the concurrence of 30 Members.

A vote by which a bill was passed may not be reconsidered on the last legislative day preceding the interim study joint recess or the final recess, and a vote by which the bill was passed may not be reconsidered on a Senate bill introduced during the first year of the biennium of the legislative session on January 31, or on the last legislative day immediately preceding January 31, of an even-numbered year.

When reconsideration of the vote by which any bill has passed has been demanded, the Secretary may not transmit it to the Assembly until the demand has been disposed of or the time for reconsideration has expired, but if the bill has already been transmitted to the Assembly the demand for reconsideration shall be preceded by a motion to request the Assembly to return the bill. The motion shall be put to a vote immediately without debate and, if not adopted, shall preclude a demand for reconsideration.

A demand to reconsider the vote on any debatable question opens the main question to debate, and the vote on the reconsideration shall be on the merits of the main question.

VOTING BY SENATE

Rescinding

43.5.   An action whereby a bill has been passed or defeated may not be rescinded without the concurrence of 27 Members.

Voting on Rollcall

44.   Whenever a rollcall is required by the Constitution or rules, or is ordered by the Senate or demanded by three Members, every Member within the Senate shall without debate answer "Aye" or "No" when his or her name is called.

The names of Members shall be called alphabetically.

A Senator may not vote or change his or her vote after the announcement of the vote by the presiding officer.

On a legislative day when the President pro Tempore or Minority Floor Leader is in attendance throughout a session, he or she, in the absence of any objection, may instruct the Secretary of the Senate to add his or her vote to any previously announced vote that was taken while he or she was performing the responsibilities of the office of President pro Tempore or Minority Floor Leader, provided the outcome of the vote is not thereby changed. This provision does not apply to any rollcall after adjournment of the legislative day during which the rollcall in question was taken. The intent of this paragraph is to allow the President pro Tempore and the Minority Floor Leader to carry out the unique and special duties of their offices without losing the opportunity to vote on matters before the Senate.

Excused From Voting

45.   When a Senator declines or fails to vote on call of his or her name, he or she may, after completion of the rollcall and before the announcement of the vote, be required to assign his or her reasons therefor and, the Senator having assigned them, the presiding officer shall submit the question to the Senate: "Shall the Senator, for the reasons assigned by him or her, be excused from voting?" which question shall be decided without debate. Unless the Senator is excused from voting he or she shall be required to vote.

Voting by Presiding Senator

46.   When any Member is presiding over the Senate, he or she shall vote on rollcall the same as though he or she were not presiding.

Vote Required

47.   Unless otherwise required by the Constitution, the Joint Rules of the Senate and Assembly, or these rules, any action that can be taken by the Senate requires only a majority vote of the Senate, a quorum being present.

The following actions require 32 votes:
 (1) To pass a bill amending specified provisions of the Tobacco Tax and Health Protection Act of 1988 (Prop. 99, Nov. 8, 1988; Sec. 30130, R.& T.C.).
 (2) To pass a bill amending the Clean Air and Transportation Improvement Act of 1990 (Prop. 116, June 5, 1990; Sec. 99605, P.U.C.).
 (3) To pass a bill amending the California Wildlife Protection Act of 1990 (Sec. 8, Prop. 117, June 5, 1990).

The following actions require 30 votes:
 (4) To dispense with the constitutional provision requiring a 30-calendar-day delay after introduction before a bill may be heard by any committee or acted upon by either house (Constitution, Art. IV, Sec. 8(a)).
 (5) To postpone the reconsideration of a vote beyond the first legislative day succeeding the day the motion was made.

The following actions require 27 votes:
 (6) To pass an urgency clause and urgency statute (Constitution, Art. IV, Sec. 8(d)).
 (7) To dispense with the constitutional provision requiring the reading of bills on three several days (Constitution, Art. IV, Sec. 8(b)).
 (8) To pass a bill over the Governor's veto (Constitution, Art. IV, Sec. 10).
 (9) To prescribe compensation and reimbursement for travel and living expenses of the Members of the Legislature (Constitution, Art. IV, Sec. 4).
 (10) To propose an amendment to or revision of the Constitution (Constitution, Art. XVIII, Secs. 1, 2).
 (11) To amend or withdraw a proposed legislative constitutional amendment or revision (Constitution, Art. XVIII, Sec. 1).
 (12) To classify or exempt personal property for property taxation purpose (Constitution, Art. XIII, Sec. 2).

(13) To permit an exemption of real property from taxation (Constitution, Art. XIII, Sec. 7).

(14) To remove a member of the Public Utilities Commission (Constitution, Art. XII, Sec. 1).

(15) To reconsider the vote by which a concurrent resolution proposing a constitutional amendment is defeated.

(16) To rescind the action whereby a bill has been passed or defeated.

(17) To suspend the rule against lobbying in the Senate Chamber.

(18) To concur in Assembly amendments to, or adopt a report of a committee on conference concerning, a constitutional amendment or bill that requires 27 votes for passage.

(19) To concur in Assembly amendments to, or adopt a report of a committee on conference concerning, a Senate bill that contains an item or items of appropriation subject to Section 12(d) of Article IV of the Constitution.

(20) To amend an initiative statute that permits that action and requires 27 votes for passage.

The following actions require 21 votes:

(21) To adopt, amend, or suspend the rules, except as provided in Rule 21.

(22) To pass a bill, unless under other rules a greater vote is required (Constitution, Art. IV, Sec. 8(b)).

(23) To adopt a joint or concurrent resolution.

(24) To reconsider a bill, or a joint or concurrent resolution.

(25) To confirm an appointment by the Governor unless a greater vote is required by statute, or to reconsider the same.

(26) To recall a bill from committee.

(27) To concur in Assembly amendments to, or adopt a report of a committee on conference concerning, a joint or concurrent resolution or bill that requires 21 votes for passage.

(28) To change a rate of bank and corporation taxation, or tax on insurers, for state purposes (Constitution, Art. XIII, Secs. 27, 28).

(29) To strike from file.

(30) To adopt a resolution that does not favor a Governor's Reorganization Plan (Sec. 12080.5, Gov. Code).

Actions requiring 14 votes:

(31) To reconsider a vote by which a concurrent resolution proposing a constitutional amendment was adopted.

Vote Required for Amendments

48. A constitutional amendment or bill requiring a vote of two-thirds of the Members elected to the Senate for final adoption or passage may be amended by a majority of those voting.

Contents of Senate Journal

Proceedings to Be Printed

49. The proceedings of the Senate, when not acting as a Committee of the Whole, shall be entered in the Journal as concisely as possible, care being taken to record a true and accurate account of the proceedings.

The Journal shall state the name of the Senator presenting each Assembly bill, concurrent or joint resolution, or constitutional amendment to the Senate for final action.

Every vote of the Senate shall be recorded in the Journal.

Titles of Measures to Be Printed

50. The titles of all bills, joint and concurrent resolutions, and constitutional amendments when introduced and when acted upon by the Senate, and a brief statement of the contents of each petition, memorial, or paper presented to the Senate, shall be printed in the Journal.

Other Matters to Be Printed

51. Messages from the Governor (other than annual messages and inaugural addresses) shall be printed in the Journal, unless otherwise ordered by the Senate.

Letters of transmittal presenting reports of committees and reports of state departments and agencies as shall be made to the Senate pursuant to law or resolution adopted by the Senate shall be printed in the Journal, but the reports shall be printed in the Appendix to the Journal unless otherwise directed by the Senate.

Duty of Secretary to Order Printing

52. It shall be the duty of the Secretary of the Senate, and he or she is hereby directed, to order for the Senate the necessary printing, including stationery for the Members, and to audit and approve all bills for printing to be charged to the Senate. The Secretary of the Senate shall order from the Office of State Publishing the number of copies of bills, Journals, Histories, Files, forms, and other printing as shall be necessary.

It shall further be the duty of the Secretary of the Senate to order bills and other legislative publications for which there is a demand, to be printed before the supply of same shall become exhausted.

Printing Only on Written Orders; Rush Orders

53. The Office of State Publishing may not charge any printing or other work to the Senate except as required by law unless he or she has a written order from the Secretary of the Senate prior to beginning the printing or other work. All printing orders by the Secretary of the Senate shall be delivered as directed by him or her. The Secretary of the Senate may, when necessity requires it, order from the Office of State Publishing the printing that he or she deems necessary to be printed in advance of the regular order of business, under a specially prepared written order to be known as a "Rush Order."

THE SENATE CHAMBER

Admission to the Senate Chamber

55.   (a)   Persons who are not Members, officers, or employees of the Senate may be admitted to the Senate Chamber only as follows:

 1.   The Members, officers, and assistant clerks of the Assembly.

 2.   The Legislative Counsel or his or her representatives.

 3.   The accredited press, radio, and television representatives.

 4.   Former State Senators and Assembly Members.

 5.   Visitors in the chairs reserved for that purpose, on invitation of the President or a Senator or on presentation of a pass.

 (b)   While the Senate is in session a person, except Members of the Legislature, may not engage in influencing the passage or defeat of legislation in any way in the Senate Chamber.

 (c)   A person meeting the definition of a lobbyist in Section 82039 of the Government Code may not be admitted to the Senate Chamber while the Senate is in session.

 (d)   Only Members and officers of the Senate and Assembly, former Members of the Senate, assistant clerks of the Senate and the Assembly, the Legislative Counsel or his or her representatives, Senate employees for the purpose of delivering messages, and when so directed by a Member of the Senate, and members of the press who have seats assigned to them may be permitted on the Floor of the Senate.

 (e)   The Senate Chamber is the Senate Chamber proper, the adjoining hallway, Rooms 3030, 3046, 3191, 3195, and 3196 of the Capitol Annex, and Room 215 of the Capitol.

 (f)   The Floor of the Senate is all of the Senate Chamber except the adjoining hallway and the rooms listed in subdivision (e), the visitors seating area, and the western portion of Room 3191.

(g) Notwithstanding any other provision of this rule, any person may be admitted to Room 3191 and Room 215 to attend a meeting of a Senate, Assembly, joint, or conference committee.

(h) Notwithstanding any other provision of this rule, a person may not be permitted on the Floor of the Senate while it is in session unless the person is wearing appropriate attire. Appropriate attire includes coats and ties for men. Accredited camerapersons, sound technicians, and photographers are excepted from this requirement. Floor of the Senate, for this purpose, has the same meaning set forth in subdivision (f).

(i) This rule may be suspended by a vote of two-thirds of the Members of the Senate.

INDEX TO STANDING RULES
OF THE SENATE

A

Rule

Q

R

S

V

W

Standards of Conduct
of the Senate
(adopted by the Senate May 4, 1992)

The Standards of Conduct of the Senate are as follows:

First—That each Senator and each officer and employee of the Senate has an obligation to exercise his or her independent judgment on behalf of the people of California, rather than for any personal gain or private benefit.

(a) No Senator or officer or employee of the Senate should accept anything from anyone that would interfere with the exercise of his or her independent judgment.

(b) No Senator or officer or employee of the Senate should accept outside employment that is inconsistent with the conscientious performance of his or her duties.

(c) No Senator should use the prestige of his or her office, and no Senate officer or employee of the Senate should use the status of his or her position for material or financial gain or private benefit.

Second—That each Senator has an obligation to provide energetic and diligent representation, and each officer and employee of the Senate has an obligation to provide energetic and diligent service on behalf of the Senate, with due consideration for the interests of all of the people of California.

(a) Each Senator and each officer and employee of the Senate has an obligation to be informed and prepared, recognizing all sides of an issue.

(b) Each Senator and each officer and employee of the Senate, when intervening on behalf of a constituent with any governmental agency should make every effort to ensure that decisions affecting any constituent are made on their merits and in a fair and equitable manner.

(c) Each Senator should be accessible to all constituents, making a special effort to attend to the concerns of those who might not otherwise be heard.

(d) Each Senator should fairly characterize the issues confronting the Legislature and accurately inform the public regarding the conduct of his or her office.

Third—That each Senator and each officer and employee of the Senate has an obligation to the public and to his or her colleagues to be informed about, and abide by, the rules that govern the proceedings of the Senate and the Legislature.

(a) Each Senator should perform his or her duties with courtesy and respect for both colleagues and those who may appear before them.

(b) In exercising the power of confirmation, each Senator should act with due regard for the general welfare of the people of California.

(c) Each Senator and each officer and employee of the Senate, when exercising oversight functions with respect to any governmental agency, should act in an informed fashion, with attention to the underlying policies being implemented and with due respect for the independence of the agency.

Fourth—Each Senator, when acting in a position of leadership, should exercise his or her power and carry out his or her responsibility so as to enhance reasoned and visible decisionmaking by the Senate.

Fifth—Each Senator has an obligation to treat every officer and employee of the Senate with fairness and without discrimination, and to ensure that each officer and employee performs only those tasks for which there is a legislative or governmental purpose.

Sixth—Each officer and employee of the Senate has an obligation to perform his or her properly assigned duties using his or her best judgment with diligence and a duty of loyalty to the Senate as an institution.

Seventh—Each Senator and each officer and employee of the Senate has an obligation to make proper use of public funds.

(a) No Senator and no officer or employee of the Senate may use state resources for personal or campaign purposes.

(b) Each officer and employee of the Senate is free to volunteer for, and participate in, campaign activities on his or her own time, but no officer or employee of the Senate may be intimidated, coerced, or compelled, as a condition of continued appointment or employment, to either volunteer time or contribute money to a candidate or campaign.

Eighth—Each Senator and each officer and employee of the Senate shall uphold the Constitution of California and the Constitution of the United States, and shall adhere to the spirit and the letter of the laws, rules, and regulations governing officeholder conduct.

Ninth—Each Senator and each officer and employee of the Senate shall conduct himself or herself in the performance of his or her duties in a manner that each does not discredit the Senate.

Tenth—Each Senator and each officer and employee of the Senate, is encouraged to report to the proper authority any apparent and substantial violation of these standards, or related statutes, regulations, and rules, and to consult with the Senate Committee on Legislative Ethics, or any other appropriate governmental agency, regarding the propriety of any conduct.

JOINT RULES

2005–06

REGULAR SESSION

(SCR No. 1)
Adopted by the Senate
December 6, 2004
Amended April 7, 2005

JOINT RULES OF THE
SENATE AND ASSEMBLY
(As Amended April 7, 2005)

Standing Committees

1.   Each house shall appoint standing committees as the business of the house may require, the committees, the number of members, and the manner of selection to be determined by the rules of each house.

Joint Meeting of Committees

3.   Whenever any bill has been referred by the Senate to one of its committees, and the same or a like bill has been referred by the Assembly to one of its committees, the chairmen or chairwomen of the respective committees, when in their judgment the interests of legislation or the expedition of business will be better served thereby, shall arrange for a joint meeting of their committees for the consideration of the bill.

Effect of Adoption of Joint Rules

3.5.   The adoption of the Joint Rules for any extraordinary session may not be construed as modifying or rescinding the Joint Rules of the Senate and Assembly for any previous session, nor as affecting in any way the status or powers of the committees created by those rules.

Definition of Word "Bill"

4.   Whenever the word "bill" is used in these rules, it includes any constitutional amendment, any resolution ratifying a proposed amendment to the United States Constitution, and any resolution calling for a constitutional convention.

Concurrent and Joint Resolutions

5.   Concurrent resolutions relate to matters to be treated by both houses of the Legislature. Joint resolutions relate to matters connected with the federal government.

Resolutions Treated as Bills

6. Concurrent and joint resolutions, other than resolutions ratifying proposed amendments to the United States Constitution and resolutions calling for constitutional conventions, shall be treated in all respects as bills except as follows:

(a) They shall be given only one formal reading in each house.

(b) They may not be deemed bills within the meaning of subdivision (a) of Section 8 of Article IV of the California Constitution.

(c) They may not be deemed bills for the purposes of Rules 10.8, 53, 55, 56, and 61, and subdivisions (a) and (c) of Rule 54 and subdivisions (a) and (b) of Rule 62.

(d) They may not, except for those relating to voting procedures on the floor or in committee, be deemed bills for the purposes of subdivision (c) of Rule 62.

PREPARATION AND INTRODUCTION OF BILLS

Title of Bill

7. The title of every bill introduced shall convey an accurate idea of the contents of the bill and shall indicate the scope of the act and the object to be accomplished. In amending a code section, the mere reference to the section by number is not deemed sufficient.

Division of Bill Into Sections

8. A bill amending more than one section of an existing law shall contain a separate section for each section amended.

Bills that are not amendatory of existing laws shall be divided into short sections, where this can be done without destroying the sense of any particular section, to the end that future amendments may be made without the necessity of setting forth and repeating sections of unnecessary length.

Digest of Bills Introduced

8.5. A bill may not be introduced unless it is contained in a cover attached by the Legislative Counsel and it is accompanied by a digest, prepared and attached to the bill by the Legislative Counsel, showing the changes in the existing law that are proposed by the bill. A bill may not be printed where the body of the bill or the Legislative Counsel's Digest has been altered, unless the alteration has been approved by the Legislative Counsel. If any bill is presented to the Secretary of the Senate or Chief Clerk of the Assembly for introduction, that does not comply with the foregoing requirements of this rule, the Secretary or Chief Clerk shall return it to the member who presented it. The digest shall be printed on the bill as introduced, commencing on the first page thereof.

Digest of Bills Amended

8.6. Whenever a bill is amended in either house, the Secretary of the Senate or the Chief Clerk of the Assembly, as the case may be, shall request the Legislative Counsel to prepare an amended digest and cause it to be printed on the first page of the bill as amended. The digest shall be amended to show changes in the existing law that are proposed by the bill as amended, with any material changes in the digest indicated by the use of appropriate type.

Errors in Digest

8.7. If a material error in a printed digest referred to in Rule 8.5 or 8.6 is brought to the attention of the Legislative Counsel, he or she shall prepare a corrected digest that shows the changes made in the digest as provided in Rule 10 for amendments to bills. He or she shall deliver the corrected digest to the Secretary of the Senate or the Chief Clerk of the Assembly, as the case may be. If the correction so warrants in the opinion of the President pro Tempore of the Senate or the Speaker of the Assembly, a corrected print of the bill as introduced shall be ordered with the corrected digest printed thereon.

Bills Amending Title 9 of the Government Code

8.8.   A member who is the first-named author of a bill, that would amend, add, or repeal any provision of Title 9 (commencing with Section 81000) of the Government Code, upon introduction or amendment of the bill in either house shall notify the Chief Clerk of the Assembly or the Secretary of the Senate, as the case may be, of the nature of the bill. Thereafter, the Chief Clerk of the Assembly or the Secretary of the Senate shall deliver a copy of the bill as introduced or amended to the Fair Political Practices Commission pursuant to Section 81012 of the Government Code.

Restrictions as to Amendments

9.   A substitute or amendment must relate to the same subject as the original bill, constitutional amendment, or resolution under consideration. An amendment is not in order when all that would be done to the bill is the addition of a coauthor or coauthors, unless the Committee on Rules of the house in which the amendment is to be offered grants prior approval.

Changes in Existing Law to Be Marked by Author

10.   In a bill amending or repealing a code section or a general law, any new matter shall be underlined, and any matter to be omitted shall be in type bearing a horizontal line through the center and commonly known as "strikeout" type. When printed the new matter shall be printed in italics, and the matter to be omitted shall be printed in "strikeout" type.

In an amendment to a bill that sets out for the first time a section being amended or repealed, any new matter to be added and any matter to be omitted shall be indicated by the author and shall be printed in the same manner as though the section as amended or repealed was a part of the original bill and was being printed for the first time.

When an entire code is repealed as part of a codification or recodification, or when an entire title, part, division, chapter, or article of a code is repealed, the sections comprising the code, title, part, division, chapter, or article shall not be set forth in the bill or amendment in strikeout type.

Rereferral to Fiscal and Rules Committees

10.5. A bill shall be rereferred to the fiscal committee of each house when it would do any of the following:

(1) Appropriate money.

(2) Result in substantial expenditure of state money by: (a) imposing new responsibilities on the state, (b) imposing new or additional duties on a state agency, or (c) liberalizing any state program, function, or responsibility.

(3) Result in a substantial loss of revenue to the state.

(4) Result in substantial reduction of expenditures of state money by reducing, transferring, or eliminating any existing responsibilities of any state agency, program, or function. Concurrent and joint resolutions shall be rereferred to the fiscal committee of each house when they contemplate any action that would involve any of the following:

(1) Any substantial expenditure of state money.

(2) Any substantial loss of revenue to the state.

The above requirements do not apply to bills or concurrent resolutions that contemplate the expenditure or allocation of operating funds.

A bill that assigns a study to the Joint Legislative Budget Committee or to the Legislative Analyst shall be rereferred to the respective rules committees. Before the committee may act upon the bill, it shall obtain from the Joint Legislative Budget Committee an estimate of the amount required to be expended to make the study.

This rule may be suspended in either house as to any particular bill by approval of the Committee on Rules of the house and two-thirds vote of the membership of the house.

Short Title

10.6. A bill may not add a short title that names a current or former Member of the Legislature.

Heading of Bills

10.7. A bill or resolution may be authored only by a member or committee of the house of origin. Members or committees that are not of the house of origin may be "principal coauthors" or "coauthors." A bill may not indicate in its heading or elsewhere that it was introduced at the request of a state agency or officer or any other person. A bill may not contain the words "By request" or words of similar import.

Consideration of Bills

10.8. The limitation contained in subdivision (a) of Section 8 of Article IV of the Constitution may be dispensed with as follows:

(a) A written request for dispensation entitled "Request to Consider and Act on Bill Within 30 Calendar Days" shall be filed with the Chief Clerk of the Assembly or the Secretary of the Senate, as the case may be, and transmitted to the Committee on Rules of the appropriate house.

(b) The Committee on Rules of the Assembly or Senate, as the case may be, shall determine whether there exists an urgent need for dispensing with the 30-calendar-day waiting period following the bill's introduction.

(c) If the Committee on Rules recommends that the waiting period be dispensed with, the member may offer a resolution, without further reference thereof to committee, authorizing hearing and action upon the bill before the 30 calendar days have elapsed. The adoption of the resolution requires an affirmative recorded vote of three-fourths of the elected members of the house in which the resolution is presented.

Printing of Amendments

11. (a) Any bill amended by either house shall be immediately reprinted. Except as otherwise provided in

subdivision (b), if new matter is added by the amendment, the new matter shall be printed in italics in the printed bill; if matter is omitted, the matter to be omitted shall be printed in strikeout type. When a bill is amended in either house, the first or previous markings shall be omitted.

(b) If amendments to a bill, including the report of a committee on conference, are adopted that omit the entire contents of the bill, the matter omitted need not be reprinted in the amended version of the bill. Instead, the Secretary of the Senate or the Chief Clerk of the Assembly, as the case may be, may select the amended bill and cause to be printed a brief statement to appear after the last line of the amended bill identifying which previously printed version of the bill contains the complete text of the omitted matter.

Manner of Printing Bills

12. The State Printer shall observe the directions of the Joint Rules Committee in printing all bills, constitutional amendments, and concurrent and joint resolutions.

Distribution of Legislative Publications

13. The Secretary of the Senate and the Chief Clerk of the Assembly shall order a sufficient number of bills and legislative publications as may be necessary for legislative requirements.

A complete list of bills may not be delivered except upon payment therefor of the amount fixed by the Joint Rules Committee for any regular or extraordinary session. No more than one copy of any bill or other legislative publication, nor more than a total of 100 bills or other legislative publications during a session, may be distributed free to any person, office, or organization. The limitations imposed by this paragraph do not apply to Members of the Legislature, the President of the Senate, the Secretary of the Senate, or the Chief Clerk of the Assembly for the proper functioning of their respective houses; the Legislative Counsel Bureau; the Attorney General's office; the Secretary of State's office; the Controller's office; the Governor's office; the Clerk of the Supreme Court; the clerk of the court of appeal for each district; the Judicial Council; the California Law Revision Commission; the State Library; the Library of Congress; the libraries of the University of California at Berkeley and at Los Angeles; or accredited members of the press.

The State Printer shall fix the cost of the bills and publications, including postage, and moneys as may be received by him or her shall, after deducting the cost of handling and mailing, be remitted on the first day of each month, one-half each to the Secretary of the Senate and the Chief Clerk of the Assembly for credit to legislative printing. Legislative publications heretofore distributed through the Bureau of Documents shall be distributed through the Bill Room. Unless otherwise provided for, the total number of each bill to be printed may not exceed 2,500.

Legislative Index

13.1. The Legislative Counsel shall provide for the periodic publication of a cumulative Legislative Index, which shall include tables of sections affected by pending legislation. The State Printer shall print the Legislative Index in the quantities, and at the times, determined by the Secretary of the Senate and the Chief Clerk of the Assembly. The costs of that printing shall be paid from the legislative printing appropriation.

Summary Digest

13.3. The Legislative Counsel shall compile and prepare for publication a summary digest of legislation passed at each regular and extraordinary session, which digest shall be prepared in a form suitable for inclusion in the publication of statutes. The digest shall be printed as a separate legislative publication on the order of the Joint Rules Committee, and may be made available to the public in the quantities, and at the prices, determined by the Joint Rules Committee.

Statutory Record

13.5. The Legislative Counsel shall prepare for publication from time to time a cumulative statutory record. The statutory record shall be printed as a legislative publication on the order of the Secretary of the Senate or the Chief Clerk of the Assembly.

OTHER LEGISLATIVE PRINTING

Printing of the Daily Journal

14. The State Printer shall print, in the quantities directed by the Secretary of the Senate and the Chief Clerk of the Assembly, copies of the Daily Journal of each day's proceedings of each house. At the end of the session he or she shall also print, as directed by the Secretary of the Senate and the Chief Clerk of the Assembly, a sufficient number of copies properly paged after being corrected and indexed by the Secretary of the Senate and the Chief Clerk of the Assembly, to bind in book form as the Daily Journal of the respective houses of the Legislature.

What Shall Be Printed in the Daily Journal

15. The following shall be printed in the Daily Journal of each house:

(a) Messages from the Governor and messages from the other house, and the titles of all bills, joint and concurrent resolutions, and constitutional amendments when introduced in, offered to, or acted upon by, the house.

(b) Every vote taken in the house, and a statement of the contents of each petition, memorial, or paper presented to the house.

(c) A true and accurate account of the proceedings of the house, when not acting as a Committee of the Whole.

Printing of the Daily File

16. A Daily File of bills ready for consideration shall be printed each day for each house when the Legislature is not in joint recess, except days when a house does not meet.

Printing of History

17. Each house shall cause to be printed, once each week, a complete Weekly History of all bills, constitutional amendments, and concurrent, joint, and house resolutions originating in, considered by, or acted upon by, the respective houses and committees thereof. A regular form shall be prescribed by the Secretary of the Senate and the Chief Clerk of the Assembly. The Weekly History shall show the action taken upon each measure up to and including the legislative day preceding its issuance. Except for periods when the houses are in joint recess, for each day intervening there shall be printed a Daily History showing the consideration given to or action taken upon any measure since the issuance of the complete Weekly History.

Authority for Printing Orders

18. The State Printer may not print for use of either house, nor charge to legislative printing, any matter other than provided by law or by the rules, except upon a written order signed by the Secretary of the Senate, on behalf of the Senate, or the Chief Clerk of the Assembly or other person authorized by the Assembly, on behalf of the Assembly. Persons authorized to order printing under this rule may, when necessity requires it, order certain matter printed in advance of the regular order, by the issuance of a rush order.

The Secretary of the Senate, on behalf of the Senate, and the Chief Clerk of the Assembly or other person authorized by the Assembly, on behalf of the Assembly, are hereby authorized and directed to order and distribute for the members stationery and legislative publications for which there is a demand, and, subject to the rules of their respective houses, to approve the bills covering those orders. All bills for printing must be presented by the State Printer within 30 days after the completion of the printing.

RECORD OF BILLS

Secretary and Chief Clerk to Keep Records

19. The Secretary of the Senate and the Chief Clerk of the Assembly shall keep a complete and accurate record of every action taken by the Senate and Assembly on every bill.

Secretary and Chief Clerk Shall Endorse Bills

20. The Secretary of the Senate and the Chief Clerk of the Assembly shall endorse on every original or engrossed bill a statement of any action taken by the Senate or Assembly concerning the bill.

ACTION IN ONE HOUSE ON BILL TRANSMITTED FROM THE OTHER

After a Bill Has Been Passed by the Senate or Assembly

21. When a bill has been passed by either house it shall be transmitted promptly to the other, unless a motion to reconsider or a notice of motion to reconsider has been made or it is held pursuant to some rule or order of the house.

The procedure of referring bills to committees shall be determined by the respective houses.

Messages to Be in Writing Under Proper Signatures

22. Notice of the action of either house to the other shall be in writing and under the signature of the Secretary of the Senate or the Chief Clerk of the Assembly, as the case may be. A receipt shall be taken from the officer to whom the message is delivered.

Consent Calendar: Uncontested Bills

22.1. Each standing committee may report an uncontested bill out of committee with the recommendation that it be placed on the Consent Calendar. The Secretary of the Senate and the Chief Clerk of the Assembly shall provide to each committee chairman or chairwoman appropriate forms for that report. As used in this rule, "uncontested bill" means a bill that (a) receives a do-pass or do-pass-as-amended recommendation from the committee to which it is referred, by unanimous vote of the members present provided a quorum is present, (b) has no opposition expressed by any person present at the committee meeting with respect to the final version of the bill as approved by the committee, and (c) prior to final action by the committee, has been requested by the author to be placed on the Consent Calendar.

Consent Calendar

22.2. Following its second reading and the adoption of any committee amendments thereto, any bill certified by the committee chairman or chairwoman as an uncontested bill shall be placed by the Secretary of the Senate or the Chief Clerk of the Assembly on the Consent Calendar, and shall be known as a "Consent Calendar bill." Any Consent Calendar bill that is amended from the floor shall cease to be a Consent Calendar bill and shall be returned to the Third Reading File. Upon objection of any member to the placement or retention of any bill on the Consent Calendar, the bill shall cease to be a Consent Calendar bill and shall be returned to the Third Reading File. No Consent Calendar bill may be considered for adoption until the second legislative day following the day of its placement on the Consent Calendar.

Consideration of Bills on Consent Calendar

22.3. A bill on the Consent Calendar is not debatable, except that the President of the Senate or the Speaker of the Assembly shall allow a reasonable time for questions from the floor and shall permit a proponent of the bill to answer the questions. Immediately prior to voting on the first bill on the Consent Calendar, the President of the Senate or the Speaker of the Assembly shall call to the attention of the members the fact that the next rollcall will be the rollcall on the first bill on the Consent Calendar.

The Consent Calendar shall be considered as the last order of business on the Daily File.

PASSAGE AND ENROLLING OF BILL

Procedure on Defeat of More Than Majority Bill

23.5. Whenever a bill containing a section or sections requiring for passage an affirmative recorded vote of more than 21 votes in the Senate and more than 41 votes in the Assembly is being considered for passage, and the urgency clause, if the bill is an urgency bill, or the bill, in any case, fails to receive the necessary votes to make all sections effective, further action may not be taken on the bill, except that an amendment to remove all sections requiring the higher vote for passage from the bill shall be in order prior to consideration of further business. If the amendment is adopted, the bill shall be reprinted to reflect the amendment. When the bill is reprinted, it shall be returned to the same place on the file that it occupied when it failed to receive the necessary votes.

Enrollment of Bill After Passage

24. After a bill has passed both houses it shall be printed in enrolled form, omitting symbols indicating amendments, and shall be compared by the Engrossing and Enrolling Clerk and the proper committee of the house where it originated to determine that it is in the form approved by the houses. The enrolled bill shall thereupon be signed by the Secretary of the Senate and Chief Clerk of the Assembly and, except as otherwise provided by these rules, presented without delay to the Governor. The committee shall report the time of presentation of the bill to the Governor to the house and the record shall be entered in the Daily Journal. After enrollment and signature by the officers of the Legislature, constitutional amendments, and concurrent and joint resolutions, shall be filed without delay in the office of the Secretary of State and the time of filing shall be reported to the house and the record entered in the Daily Journal.

AMENDMENTS AND CONFERENCES

Amendments to Amended Bills
Must Be Attached

25. Whenever a bill or resolution that has been passed in one house is amended in the other, it shall immediately be reprinted as amended by the house making the amendment or amendments. One copy of the amendment or amendments shall be attached to the bill or resolution so amended, and endorsed "adopted"; the amendment or amendments, if concurred in by the house in which the bill or resolution originated, shall be endorsed "concurred in"; and the endorsement shall be signed by the Secretary or Assistant Secretary of the Senate, or the Chief Clerk or Assistant Clerk of the Assembly, as the case may be. However, an amendment to the title of a bill adopted after the passage of the bill does not necessitate reprinting, but the amendment must be concurred in by the house in which the bill originated.

Amendments to Concurrent and
Joint Resolutions

25.5. When a concurrent or joint resolution is amended, and the only effect of the amendments is to add coauthors, the joint or concurrent resolution may not be reprinted unless specifically requested by one of the added coauthors, but a list of the coauthors shall appear in the Daily Journal and History.

To Concur or Refuse to Concur
in Amendments

26. If the Senate amends and passes an Assembly bill, or the Assembly amends and passes a Senate bill, the Senate (if it is a Senate bill) or the Assembly (if it is an Assembly bill) must either "concur" or "refuse to concur" in the amendments. If the Senate concurs (if it is a Senate bill), or the Assembly concurs (if it is an Assembly bill), the Secretary of the Senate or Chief

Clerk of the Assembly shall so notify the house making the amendments, and the bill shall be ordered to enrollment.

Reference to Committee

26.5. Pursuant to Rule 26, whenever a bill is returned to its house of origin for a vote on concurrence in an amendment made in the other house, the Legislative Counsel shall promptly prepare and transmit to the Chief Clerk of the Assembly and the Speaker of the Assembly in the case of an Assembly bill, or to the Secretary of the Senate and Chair of the Senate Committee on Rules in the case of a Senate bill, a brief digest summarizing the effect of the amendment made in the other house. The Secretary or Chief Clerk shall, upon receipt from the Legislative Counsel, cause the digest to be printed in the Daily File immediately following any reference to the bill covered by the digest. A motion to concur or refuse to concur in the amendment is not in order until the Legislative Counsel's Digest has appeared in the Daily File or an analysis of the bill has been prepared and distributed pursuant to Senate Rule 29.8 or Assembly Rule 77.

If the digest discloses that the amendment of the other house has made a substantial substantive change in the bill as first passed by the house of origin, the bill, if it is a Senate bill, shall, on motion of the Chair of the Senate Committee on Rules, be referred to the Senate Committee on Rules for reference to an appropriate standing committee. If the bill is an Assembly bill it shall be referred by the Speaker to the appropriate committee.

Upon receipt of the bill, the committee may, by a vote of a majority of its membership, recommend concurrence or nonconcurrence in the amendment or hold the bill in committee. The committee shall be subject to all the requirements for procedure provided under Rule 62 for committees, other than committees of first referral, and shall be subject to other requirements for normal committee procedure as the Assembly or Senate may separately provide in the standing rules of their respective houses.

Any of the provisions of this rule may be dispensed with regard to a particular bill in its house of origin upon an affirmative vote of a majority of the members of that house.

Concurring in Amendments Adding Urgency Section

27. When a bill that has been passed in one house is amended in the other by the addition of a section providing that the act shall take effect immediately as an urgency statute, and is returned to the house in which it originated for concurrence in the amendment or amendments thereto, the procedure and vote thereon shall be as follows:

The presiding officer shall first direct that the urgency section be read and put to a vote. If two-thirds of the membership of the house vote in the affirmative, the presiding officer shall then direct that the question of whether the house shall concur in the amendment or amendments shall be put to a vote. If two-thirds of the membership of the house vote in the affirmative, concurrence in the amendments shall be effective.

If the affirmative vote on either of the questions is less than two-thirds of the membership of the house, the effect is a refusal to concur in the amendment or amendments, and the procedure thereupon shall be as provided in Rule 28.

When Senate or Assembly Refuses to Concur

28. If the Senate (if it is a Senate bill) or the Assembly (if it is an Assembly bill) refuses to concur in amendments to the bill made by the other house, and the other house has been notified of the refusal to concur, a conference committee shall be appointed for each house in the manner prescribed by these rules. The Senate Committee on Rules, on behalf of the Senate, and the Speaker of the Assembly, on behalf of the Assembly, shall each appoint a committee of three on conference, and the Secretary of the Senate or the Chief Clerk of the Assembly shall immediately notify the other house of the action taken.

Committee on Conference

28.1. (a) The Senate Committee on Rules and the Speaker of the Assembly, in appointing a committee on conference, shall each select two members from those voting with the majority on the point about which the difference has arisen, and the other member from the minority, in the event there is a minority vote.

Whether a member has voted with the majority or minority on the point about which the difference has arisen is determined by his or her vote on the appropriate rollcall, as follows:

(1) In the Assembly—

(A) The rollcall on the question of final passage of a Senate bill amended in the Assembly when the Senate has refused to concur with the Assembly amendments.

(B) The rollcall on the question of concurrence with Senate amendments to an Assembly bill.

(2) In the Senate—

(A) The rollcall on the question of final passage of an Assembly bill amended in the Senate when the Assembly has refused to concur with the Senate amendments.

(B) The rollcall on the question of concurrence with Assembly amendments to a Senate bill.

(b) Either house may suspend this rule by a two-thirds vote of the membership of the house.

Meetings and Reports of Committees on Conference

29. The first Senator named on the conference committee shall act as chairman or chairwoman of the committee from the Senate, and the first Member of the Assembly named on the committee shall act as chairman or chairwoman of the committee from the Assembly. The chairman or chairwoman of the committee on conference for the house of origin of the bill shall arrange the time and place of meeting of the conference committee, and shall prepare or direct the preparation of reports. It shall require an affirmative vote of not less than two of the Assembly Members and two of the Senate Members constituting the committee on confer-

ence to agree upon a report, and the report shall be
submitted to both the Senate and the Assembly. The
committee on conference shall report to both the Senate
and the Assembly. The report is not subject to amendment. If either house refuses to adopt the report, the
conferees shall be discharged and other conferees
appointed, except that no more than three different
conference committees may be appointed on any one
bill. A member who has served on a committee on
conference may not be appointed a member of another
committee on conference on the same bill. It shall
require the same affirmative recorded vote to adopt any
conference report as required by the California Constitution upon the final passage of the bill affected by the
report. It shall require an affirmative recorded vote of
two-thirds of the entire elected membership of each
house to adopt any conference report affecting any bill
that contains an item or items of appropriation that are
subject to subdivision (d) of Section 12 of Article IV of
the California Constitution. The report of a conference
committee shall be in writing, and shall have affixed
thereto the signatures of each Senator and each Member
of the Assembly consenting to the report. Space shall
also be provided where a member of a conference
committee may indicate his or her dissent in the
committee's findings. Any dissenting member may
have attached to a conference committee report a
dissenting report which shall not exceed, in length, the
majority committee report. A copy of any amendments
proposed in the majority report shall be placed on the
desk of each member of the house before it is acted
upon by the house.

The vote on concurrence or upon the adoption of the
conference report shall be deemed the vote upon final
passage of the bill.

Conference Committees

29.5. (a) All meetings of any conference committee on the Budget Bill shall be open and readily
accessible to the public.

A conference committee on any bill may not meet,
consider, or act on the subject matter of the bill except

in a meeting that is open and readily accessible to the public, unless the action is on a report determined by the Legislative Counsel to be nonsubstantive. The Legislative Counsel shall examine each proposed report and shall note upon the face of the report that the amendments proposed are "substantive" or "nonsubstantive" as the case may be.

The chairman or chairwoman of the conference committee of each house shall give notice to the File Clerk of their respective houses of the time and place of the meeting. Notice of each public meeting shall be published in the Daily File of each house one calendar day prior to the meeting, except that the notice is not required for a meeting of a conference committee on the Budget Bill. When this subdivision is waived with respect to a meeting of any public conference committee, or when there is a meeting of a conference committee on the Budget Bill, every effort shall be made to inform the public that a meeting has been called. When this subdivision has been waived with respect to the meeting of any public conference committee, the chairman or chairwoman of the conference committee of each house shall immediately notify the chairman or chairwoman of the policy committee of their respective houses that considered the bill in question of the waiver, and of the time and place of the meeting.

(b) The first committee on conference of the Budget Bill, if a committee is appointed, shall submit its report to each house no later than 15 days after the Budget Bill has been passed by both houses. If the report is not submitted by that date, the conference committee shall be deemed to have reached no agreement and shall so inform each house pursuant to Rule 30.7.

(c) A committee on conference of the Budget Bill may consider only differences between the Assembly version of the Budget Bill as passed by the Assembly and the Senate version of the Budget Bill as passed by the Senate, and may not approve any item of expenditure or control that exceeds that contained in one of the two versions before the conference committee.

(d) A conference committee on any bill, other than the Budget Bill, may not approve any substantial financial provision in any bill if the financial provision has not been heard by the fiscal committee of each house, nor may any conference committee approve substantial policy changes that have not been heard by the policy committee of each house.

(e) A waiver of the one-calendar-day Daily File notice requirement of subdivision (a) is not effective for longer than three calendar days.

Conference Committee Reports

30. Upon submission of any report of a committee on conference recommending that the bill be further amended, the bill shall be reprinted incorporating the amendments recommended by the conference committee. The consideration of the report of a committee on conference is not in order until the bill, in the form recommended by the report of the committee on conference, has both been in print and been noticed in the Daily File for not less than one legislative day.

If the conference committee's report recommends only that the amendments of the Senate or the Assembly "be concurred in," consideration of the report shall be in order at any time, and reprinting of the bill is not required, but notice shall appear in the Daily File for not less than one legislative day.

A conference committee report is not in order unless it has been received by the Secretary of the Senate and the Chief Clerk of the Assembly at least three calendar days preceding the scheduled commencement of the summer, interim, or final recess of the Legislature.

This rule may be suspended as to any particular conference committee report by a two-thirds vote of the membership of either house.

This rule does not apply to a report of a committee on conference on the Budget Bill.

Conference Committee Reports on Urgency Statutes

30.5. When the report of a committee on conference recommends the amendment of a bill by the addition of a section providing that the act shall take effect immediately as an urgency statute, the procedure and the vote thereon shall be as follows:

The presiding officer shall first direct that the urgency section be read and put to a vote. If two-thirds of the members elected to the house vote in the affirmative, the presiding officer shall then direct that the question of whether the house shall adopt the report of the committee on conference shall be put to a vote. If two-thirds of the members elected to the house vote in the affirmative, the adoption of the report and the amendments proposed thereby shall be effective.

If the affirmative vote on either of the questions is less than two-thirds of the members elected to the house, the effect is a refusal to adopt the report of the committee on conference.

Failure to Agree on Report

30.7.   A conference committee may find and determine that it is unable to submit a report to the respective houses, upon the affirmative vote to that effect of not less than two of the Assembly Members and not less than two of the Senate Members constituting the committee. That finding may be submitted to the Chief Clerk of the Assembly and the Secretary of the Senate in the form of a letter from the chairman or chairwoman of the committee on conference for the house of origin of the bill, containing the signatures of the members of the committee consenting to the finding and determination that the committee is unable to submit a report. The Chief Clerk of the Assembly and the Secretary of the Senate, upon being notified that a conference committee is unable to submit a report, shall so inform each house, whereupon the conferees shall be discharged and other conferees appointed, in accordance with Rule 29.

MISCELLANEOUS PROVISIONS

Authority When Rules Do Not Govern

31. All relations between the houses that are not covered by these rules shall be governed by Mason's Manual.

Press Rules

32. (a) Any person desiring privileges of an accredited press representative shall make application to the Joint Rules Committee. The application shall constitute compliance with any provisions of the rules of the Assembly or the Senate with respect to registration of news correspondents. The application shall state in writing the name of any daily newspaper, periodic publication, news association, or radio or television station that employs the press representative, and any other occupations or employment he or she may have. The press representative shall further declare in the application that he or she is not employed, directly or indirectly, to assist in the prosecution of the legislative business of any person, corporation, or association, and will not become so employed while retaining the privilege of an accredited press representative.

(b) The application required by subdivision (a) of this rule shall be authenticated in a manner that is satisfactory to the Standing Committee of the Capitol Correspondents Association, which shall see that occupation of seats and desks in the Senate and the Assembly Chambers is confined to bona fide correspondents of reputable standing in their business, who represent daily newspapers requiring a daily file of legislative news, qualified periodic publications, or news associations requiring daily telegraphic or radio or television service on legislative news. It is the duty of the standing committee, at its discretion, to report any violation of accredited press privileges to the Speaker of the Assembly or the Senate Committee on Rules and, pending action thereon, the offending correspondent may be suspended by the standing committee.

(c) Except as otherwise provided in this subdivision, persons engaged in other occupations whose chief attention is not given to newspaper correspondence or to news associations requiring telegraphic or radio or television service are not entitled to the privileges accorded accredited press representatives. The press list in the Handbook of the California Legislature and the Senate and Assembly Histories shall be a list of only those persons authenticated by the Standing Committee of the Capitol Correspondents Association. Accreditation may be granted to any bona fide correspondent of reputable standing employed by a periodic publication of general circulation if the applicant is employed on a full-time basis in the Capitol area preparing articles dealing with state government and politics and the publication is not an organ or organization involved in legislative advocacy.

(d) The press seats and desks in the Senate and Assembly Chambers shall be under the control of the standing committee of correspondents, subject to the approval and supervision of the Speaker of the Assembly and the Senate Committee on Rules. Press cards shall be issued by the President of the Senate and the Speaker of the Assembly only to correspondents properly accredited in accordance with this rule.

(e) One or more rooms shall be assigned for the exclusive use of correspondents during the legislative session, which rooms shall be known as the Press Room. The Press Room shall be under the control of the Chief of the Office of Buildings and Grounds, provided that all rules and regulations must be approved by the Senate Committee on Rules and the Speaker of the Assembly.

(f) An accredited member of the Capitol Correspondents Association may not, for compensation, perform any service for state constitutional officers or members of their staffs, for state agencies, for the Legislature, for candidates for state office, for a state officeholder, or for any person registered or performing as a legislative advocate.

(g) An accredited member of the association who violates subdivision (a) or (f) of this rule shall be subject to the following penalties:

(1) For the first offense, the Standing Committee of the Capitol Correspondents Association shall send a letter of admonition to the offending member, his or her employer, and the Joint Rules Committee. The letter shall state the nature of the member's rule violation and shall warn of an additional penalty for a second offense.

(2) For a second offense, the Standing Committee of the Capitol Correspondents Association shall recommend to the Joint Rules Committee that the member's accreditation be suspended or revoked and that he or she lose all rights and privileges attached thereto. The Standing Committee of the Capitol Correspondents Association shall also dismiss the member from the association.

Any member of the Standing Committee of the Capitol Correspondents Association may propose that the committee make an inquiry to determine if an association member has violated subdivision (a) or (f) of this rule. Upon a majority vote of the Standing Committee of the Capitol Correspondents Association, an inquiry shall be made.

Upon receipt of a signed, written notice from any association member of his or her belief that another association member may have violated subdivision (a) or (f) of this rule, the Standing Committee of the Capitol Correspondents Association shall commence an inquiry into the possible violation.

If the Standing Committee of the Capitol Correspondents Association determines by majority vote that an association member has violated an association rule, it shall inform the member of its finding. Within two weeks of notification, the member may request a meeting of the membership. If the member makes that request, the Standing Committee of the Capitol Correspondents Association shall promptly schedule a meeting at the earliest possible time. After hearing the member and the committee review the circumstances of the alleged violation, the membership may, by majority vote, nullify the finding of the Standing Committee of the Capitol Correspondents Association. If nullification does not occur, the Standing Committee of the Capitol Correspondents Association immediately shall impose the appropriate penalty.

Dispensing With Joint Rules

33. A joint rule may not be dispensed with except by a vote of two-thirds of each house or as otherwise provided in these rules. If either house violates a joint rule, a question of order may be raised in the other house and decided in the same manner as in the case of the violation of the rules of the house. If it is decided that the joint rules have been violated, the bill involving the violation shall be returned to the house in which it originated, and the disputed matter shall be considered in like manner as in conference committee.

Dispensing with Joint Rules: Unanimous Consent

33.1. Notwithstanding any other rule, a joint rule that may be dispensed with by one house may be done so by unanimous consent if the rules committee of that house has approved.

Opinions of Legislative Counsel

34. Whenever the Legislative Counsel issues an opinion to any person other than the first-named author analyzing the constitutionality, operation, or effect of a bill or other legislative measure that is then pending before the Legislature or of any amendment made or proposed to be made to the bill or measure, he or she is authorized and instructed to deliver two copies of the opinion to the first-named author as promptly as feasible after the delivery of the original opinion and also to deliver a copy to any other author of the bill or measure who so requests. A copy of any letter prepared by the Legislative Counsel for the sole purpose of advising a member of a conflict between two or more bills as to the sections of law being amended, repealed,

or added shall be submitted to the chairman or chair-woman of the committee to which each bill has been referred.

Resolutions Prepared by Legislative Counsel

34.1.   Whenever the Legislative Counsel has been requested to draft a resolution commemorating or taking note of any event, or a resolution congratulating or expressing sympathy toward any person, and subsequently receives a similar request from another Member of the Legislature, he or she shall inform that requester and each subsequent requester that a resolution is being, or has been, prepared, and shall inform them of the name of the member for whom the resolution was, or is being, prepared.

Resolutions

34.2.   A concurrent resolution, Senate resolution, or House resolution may be introduced to memorialize the death of a present or former state or federal elected official or a member of his or her immediate family. In all other instances, a resolution other than a concurrent resolution, as specified by the Committee on Rules of each house, or as provided by the Joint Rules Committee in those cases requiring that the resolution should emanate from both houses, shall be used for the purpose of commendation, congratulation, sympathy, or regret with respect to any person, group, or organization.

A concurrent resolution requesting the Governor to issue a proclamation may not be introduced without the prior approval of the Committee on Rules of the house in which the resolution is to be introduced.

Identical Drafting Requests

34.5.   Whenever it comes to the attention of the Legislative Counsel that a member has requested the drafting of a bill that will be substantially identical to one already introduced, the Legislative Counsel shall inform the member of that fact.

Expense of Members

35. As provided in Section 8902 of the Government Code, each Member of the Legislature is entitled to reimbursement for living expenses while required to be in Sacramento to attend a session of the Legislature, while traveling to and from or in attendance at a committee meeting, or while attending to any legislative function or responsibility as authorized or directed by legislative rules or the Committee on Rules of the house of which he or she is a member, at the same rate as may be established by the State Board of Control for other elected state officers. Each member shall be reimbursed for travel expenses incurred in traveling to and from a session of the Legislature, when traveling to and from a meeting of a committee of which he or she is a member, or when traveling pursuant to any other legislative function or responsibility as authorized or directed by legislative rules or the Committee on Rules of the house of which he or she is a member, at the rate prescribed by Section 8903 of the Government Code.

Expense allowances for Members of the Senate and Assembly shall be approved and certified to the Controller by the Secretary of the Senate, on behalf of the Senate, and the Chief Clerk of the Assembly or other person authorized by the Assembly Committee on Rules, on behalf of the Assembly, weekly or as otherwise directed by either house, and upon certification the Controller shall draw his or her warrants in payment of the allowances to the respective members.

Issuance of Subpoenas

35.5. A subpoena requiring the attendance of a witness or the production of documents may be issued by the Senate Committee on Rules, the Speaker of the Assembly, or the chairman or chairwoman of a committee conducting an investigation only if permission has been secured from the rules committee of the respective house, or from the Joint Rules Committee if the subpoena is issued by the chairman or chairwoman of a joint committee.

Investigating Committees

36. In order to expedite the work of the Legislature, either house, or both houses jointly, may by resolution or statute provide for the appointment of committees to ascertain facts and to make recommendations as to any subject within the scope of legislative regulation or control.

The resolution providing for the appointment of a committee pursuant to this rule shall state the purpose of the committee and the scope of the subject concerning which it is to act, and may authorize it to act either during sessions of the Legislature or, when authorization may lawfully be made, after final adjournment.

In the exercise of the power granted by this rule, each committee may employ clerical, legal, and technical assistants as may be authorized by: (a) the Joint Rules Committee in the case of a joint committee, (b) the Senate Committee on Rules in the case of a Senate committee, or (c) the Assembly Committee on Rules in the case of an Assembly committee.

Except as otherwise provided herein for joint committees or by the rules of the Senate or the Assembly for single house committees, each committee may adopt and amend rules governing its procedure as may appear necessary and proper to carry out the powers granted and duties imposed under this rule. The rules may include provisions fixing the quorum of the committee and the number of votes necessary to take action on any matter. With respect to all joint committees, a majority of the membership from each house constitutes a quorum, and an affirmative vote of a majority of the membership from each house is necessary for the committee to take action.

Each committee is authorized and empowered to summon and subpoena witnesses, to require the production of papers, books, accounts, reports, documents, records, and papers of every kind and description, to issue subpoenas, and to take all necessary means to compel the attendance of witnesses and to procure testimony, oral and documentary. A committee's issuance of a subpoena shall comply with Rule 35.5.

Each member of the committees is authorized and empowered to administer oaths, and all of the provisions of Chapter 4 (commencing with Section 9400) of Part 1 of Division 2 of Title 2 of the Government Code, relating to the attendance and examination of witnesses before the Legislature and the committees thereof, apply to the committees. A committee may grant a witness immunity from criminal prosecution, pursuant to subdivision (a) of Section 9410 of the Government Code, only after securing permission from the rules committee of the respective house, or from the Joint Rules Committee in the case of a joint committee.

The Sergeant at Arms of the Senate or Assembly, or other person as may be designated by the chairman or chairwoman of the committee, shall serve any and all subpoenas, orders, and other process that may be issued by the committee, when directed to do so by the chairman or chairwoman, or by a majority of the membership of the committee.

Every department, commission, board, agency, officer, and employee of the state government, including the Legislative Counsel and the Attorney General and their subordinates, and of every political subdivision, county, city, or public district of or in this state, shall give and furnish to these committees and to their subcommittees upon request information, records, and documents as the committees deem necessary or proper for the achievement of the purposes for which each committee was created.

Each committee or subcommittee of either house, in accordance with the rules of that respective house, and each joint committee or subcommittee thereof, may meet at any time during the period in which it is authorized to act, either at the State Capitol or at any other place in the State of California, in public or executive session, and do any and all things necessary or convenient to enable it to exercise the powers and perform the duties herein granted to it or accomplish the objects and purposes of the resolution creating it, subject to the following exceptions:

(a) When the Legislature is in session:

(1) A committee or subcommittee of either house may not meet outside the State Capitol without the prior approval of the Senate Committee on Rules with respect to Senate committees and subcommittees, or the Speaker of the Assembly with respect to Assembly committees and subcommittees.

(2) A committee or subcommittee of either house, other than a standing committee or subcommittee thereof, may not meet unless notice of the meeting has been printed in the Daily File for four days prior thereto. This requirement may be waived by a majority vote of either house with respect to a particular bill.

(3) A joint committee or subcommittee thereof, other than the Joint Committees on Legislative Audit, Legislative Budget, and Rules, may not meet outside the State Capitol without the prior approval of the Joint Rules Committee.

(4) A joint committee or subcommittee thereof, other than the Joint Committees on Legislative Audit, Legislative Budget, and Rules, may not meet unless notice of the meeting has been printed in the Daily File for four days prior thereto.

(b) When the Legislature is in joint recess, each joint committee or subcommittee, other than the Joint Committees on Legislative Audit, Legislative Budget, and Rules, shall notify the Joint Rules Committee at least two weeks prior to a meeting.

(c) The requirements placed upon joint committees by subdivisions (a) and (b) of this rule may be waived as deemed necessary by the Joint Rules Committee.

Each committee may expend such money as is made available to it for its purpose, but a committee may not incur any indebtedness unless money has been first made available therefor.

Living expenses may not be allowed in connection with legislative business for a day on which the member receives reimbursement for expenses while required to be in Sacramento to attend a session of the Legislature. The chairman or chairwoman of each committee shall

audit and approve the expense claims of the members of
the committee, including claims for mileage in connection with attendance on committee business, or in
connection with specific assignments by the committee
chairman or chairwoman, but excluding other types of
mileage, and shall certify the amount approved to the
Controller. The Controller shall draw his or her warrants upon the certification of the chairman or chairwoman.

Subject to the rules of each house for the respective
committees of each house, or the joint rules for any
joint committee, with the permission of the appointing
authority of the respective house, or the permission of
the appointing authorities of the two houses in the case
of a joint committee, the chairman or chairwoman of
any committee may appoint subcommittees and chairmen or chairwomen thereof for the purpose of more
expeditiously handling and considering matters referred
to it, and the subcommittees and the chairmen or
chairwomen thereof shall have all the powers and
authority herein conferred upon the committee and its
chairman or chairwoman. The chairman or chairwoman
of a subcommittee shall audit the expense claims of the
members of the subcommittee, and other claims and the
expenses incurred by it, and shall certify the amount
thereof to the chairman or chairwoman of the committee, who shall, if he or she approves the same, certify
the amount thereof to the Controller; the Controller
shall draw his or her warrant therefor upon that certification, and the Treasurer shall pay the same. Any
committee or subcommittee thereof that is authorized to
leave the State of California in the performance of its
duties shall, while out of the state, have the same
authority as if it were acting and functioning within the
state, and the members thereof shall be reimbursed for
expenses.

Notwithstanding any other provision of this rule, if
the standing rules of either house require that expense
claims of committees for goods or services, pursuant to
contracts, or for expenses of employees or members of
committees be audited or approved, after approval of
the committee chairman or chairwoman, by another

agency of either house, the Controller shall draw his or her warrants only upon the certification of the other agency. All expense claims approved by the chairman or chairwoman of any joint committee, other than the Joint Legislative Budget Committee and the Joint Legislative Audit Committee, shall be approved by the Joint Rules Committee, and the Controller shall draw his or her warrants only upon the certification of the Joint Rules Committee.

Except salary claims of employees clearly subject to federal withholding taxes and the requirement as to loyalty oaths, claims presented for services or pursuant to contract shall refer to the agreement, the terms of which shall be made available to the Controller.

Expenses of Committee Employees

36.1. Unless otherwise provided by respective house or committee rule or resolution, employees of legislative committees, when entitled to traveling expenses, are entitled to allowances in lieu of actual expenses for hotel accommodations, breakfast, lunch, and dinner, at the rates fixed by the State Board of Control from time to time in limitation of reimbursement of expenses of state employees generally. However, if an allowance for hotel accommodations, breakfast, lunch, and dinner is made by a committee at a rate in excess of the rate fixed by the State Board of Control, the chairman or chairwoman of the committee shall notify the Controller of that fact in writing.

Appointment of Committees

36.5. This rule applies whenever a joint committee is created by a statute or resolution that either provides that appointments be made and vacancies be filled in the manner provided for in the Joint Rules, or makes no provision for the appointment of members or the filling of vacancies.

The Senate members of the committee shall be appointed by the Senate Committee on Rules; the Assembly members of the committee shall be appointed by the Speaker of the Assembly; and vacancies occurring in the membership of the committee shall be filled by the respective appointing powers. The members appointed shall hold over until their successors are regularly selected.

Appointment of Joint Committee Chairmen or Chairwomen

36.7. The chairman or chairwoman of each joint committee heretofore or hereafter created, except the Joint Legislative Budget Committee and the Joint Legislative Audit Committee, shall be appointed by the Joint Rules Committee from a member or members recommended by the Senate Committee on Rules and the Speaker of the Assembly.

Joint Committee Funds

36.8. Each joint committee heretofore or hereafter created, except the Joint Legislative Budget Committee and the Joint Legislative Audit Committee, shall expend the funds heretofore or hereafter made available to it in compliance with the policies set forth by the Joint Rules Committee with respect to personnel, salaries, purchasing, office space assignment, contractual services, rental or lease agreements, travel, and any and all other matters relating to the management and administration of committee affairs.

Joint Legislative Budget Committee

37. In addition to any other committee provided for by these rules, there is a joint committee to be known as the Joint Legislative Budget Committee, which is hereby declared to be a continuing body.

It is the duty of the committee to ascertain facts and make recommendations to the Legislature and to the houses thereof concerning the State Budget, the revenues and expenditures of the state, and the organization and functions of the state and its departments, subdivisions, and agencies, with a view to reducing the cost of the state government and securing greater efficiency and economy.

The committee consists of eight Members of the Senate and eight Members of the Assembly. The Senate members of the committee shall be appointed by the Senate Committee on Rules. The Assembly members of the committee shall be appointed by the Speaker of the Assembly. The committee shall select its own chairman or chairwoman.

Any vacancy occurring at any time in the Senate membership of the Joint Legislative Budget Committee shall be filled by the Senate Committee on Rules, and the Senators appointed shall hold over until their successors are regularly selected. For the purposes of this rule, a vacancy shall be deemed to exist as to a Senator whose term is expiring whenever he or she is not reelected at the general election.

Any vacancy occurring at any time in the Assembly membership of the Joint Legislative Budget Committee shall be filled by appointment by the Speaker of the Assembly, and the Members of the Assembly appointed shall hold over between regular sessions until their successors are regularly selected. For the purposes of this rule, a vacancy shall be deemed to exist as to a Member of the Assembly whose term is expiring whenever he or she is not reelected at the general election.

The committee may adopt rules to govern its own proceedings and its employees. The committee, with the permission of the appointing authorities of the two houses, may also create subcommittees from its membership, assigning to its subcommittees any study, inquiry, investigation, or hearing that the committee itself has authority to undertake or hold. A subcommittee for the purpose of this assignment has and may exercise all the powers conferred upon the committee, limited only by the express terms of any rule or resolution of the committee defining the powers and duties of the subcommittee. Those powers may be withdrawn or terminated at any time by the committee.

The Joint Legislative Budget Committee may render services to any investigating committee of the Legislature pursuant to contract between the Joint Legislative Budget Committee and the committee for which the services are to be performed. The contract may provide for payment to the Joint Legislative Budget Committee of the cost of the services from the funds appropriated to the contracting investigating committee. All legislative investigating committees are authorized to enter into those contracts with the Joint Legislative Budget Committee. Money received by the Joint Legislative Budget Committee pursuant to any agreement shall be in augmentation of the current appropriation for the support of the Joint Legislative Budget Committee.

The provisions of Rule 36 shall apply to the Joint Legislative Budget Committee, which has all the authority provided in that rule or pursuant to Section 11 of Article IV of the California Constitution.

The committee has authority to appoint a Legislative Analyst, to fix his or her compensation, to prescribe his or her duties, and to appoint any other clerical and technical employees as may appear necessary. The duties of the Legislative Analyst are as follows:

(1) To ascertain the facts and make recommendations to the Joint Legislative Budget Committee and, under its direction, to the committees of the Legislature concerning:

(a) The State Budget.

(b) The revenues and expenditures of the state.

(c) The organization and functions of the state and its departments, subdivisions, and agencies.

(2) To assist the Senate Budget and Fiscal Review Committee and the Assembly Committees on Appropriations and Budget in consideration of the Budget, all bills carrying express or implied appropriations, and all legislation affecting state departments and their efficiency; to appear before any other legislative committee; and to assist any other legislative committee upon instruction by the Joint Legislative Budget Committee.

(3) To provide all legislative committees and Members of the Legislature with information obtained under the direction of the Joint Legislative Budget Committee.

(4) To maintain a record of all work performed by the Legislative Analyst under the direction of the Joint Legislative Budget Committee, and to keep and make available all documents, data, and reports submitted to him or her by any Senate, Assembly, or joint committee.

The committee may meet either during sessions of the Legislature, any recess thereof, or after final adjournment, and may meet or conduct business at any place within the State of California.

The chairman or chairwoman of the committee or, in the event of that person's inability to act, the vice chairman or vice chairwoman, shall audit and approve the expenses of members of the committee or salaries of the employees, and all other expenses incurred in connection with the performance of its duties by the committee. The chairman or chairwoman shall certify to the Controller the expense amount approved, the Controller shall draw his or her warrants upon the certification of the chairman or chairwoman, and the Treasurer shall pay the same to the chairman or chairwoman of the committee, to be disbursed by the chairman or chairwoman.

On and after the commencement of a succeeding regular session, those members of the committee who continue to be Members of the Senate and Assembly, respectively, continue as members of the committee until their successors are appointed, and the committee continues with all its powers, duties, authority, records, papers, personnel, and staff, and all funds theretofore made available for its use.

Upon the conclusion of its work, any Assembly, Senate, or joint committee (other than a standing committee) shall deliver to the Legislative Analyst for use and custody all documents, data, reports, and other materials that have come into the possession of the committee and that are not included within the final report of the committee to the Assembly, Senate, or the Legislature, as the case may be. The documents, data, reports, and other materials shall be available, upon request, to Members of the Legislature, the Senate Office of Research, and the Assembly Office of Research.

The Legislative Analyst, with the consent of the committee, shall make available to any Member or committee of the Legislature any other reports, records, documents, or other data under his or her control, except that reports prepared by the Legislative Analyst in response to a request from a Member or committee of the Legislature may be made available only with the written permission of the member or committee who made the request.

The Legislative Analyst, upon the receipt of a request from any committee or Member of the Legislature to conduct a study or provide information that falls within the scope of his or her responsibilities and that concerns the administration of the government of the State of California, shall at once advise the Joint Legislative Budget Committee of the nature of the request without disclosing the name of the member or committee making the request.

The Legislative Analyst shall immediately undertake to provide the requesting committee or legislator with the service or information requested, and shall inform the committee or legislator of the approximate date when this information will be available. Should there be any material delay, he or she shall subsequently communicate this fact to the requester.

Neither the Committee on Rules of either house nor the Joint Rules Committee may assign any matter for study to the Joint Legislative Budget Committee or the Legislative Analyst without first obtaining from the Joint Legislative Budget Committee an estimate of the amount required to be expended by it to make the study.

Any concurrent, joint, Senate, or House resolution assigning a study to the Joint Legislative Budget Committee or to the Legislative Analyst shall be referred to the respective rules committees. Before the committees may act upon or assign the resolution, they shall obtain an estimate from the Joint Legislative Budget Committee of the amount required to be expended to make the study.

Citizen Cost Impact Report

37.1. Any Member or committee of the Legislature may recommend that the Legislative Analyst prepare a citizen cost impact analysis on proposed legislation. However, the recommendation shall first be reviewed by the Committee on Rules of the house where the recommendation originated, and this committee shall make the final determination as to which bills shall be assigned for preparation of an impact analysis. In selecting specific bills for assignment to the Legislative Analyst for preparation of citizen cost impact analyses, the Committee on Rules shall request the Legislative Analyst to present an estimate of his or her time and prospective costs for preparing the analyses. Only those bills that have a potential significant cost impact shall be assigned. Where necessary, the Committee on Rules shall provide funds to offset added costs incurred by the Legislative Analyst. The citizen cost impact analyses shall include those economic effects that the Legislative Analyst deems significant and that he or she believes will result directly from the proposed legislation. Insofar as feasible, the economic effects considered by the Legislative Analyst shall include, but not be limited to, the following:

(a) The economic effect on the public generally.

(b) Any specific economic effect on persons or businesses in the case of legislation that is regulatory.

The Legislative Analyst shall submit the citizen cost impact analyses to the committee or committees when completed, and at the time or times designated by the Committee on Rules.

The Legislative Analyst shall submit from time to time, but at least once a year, a report to the Legislature on the trends and directions of the state's economy, and shall list the alternatives and make recommendations as to legislative actions that, in his or her judgment, will insure a sound and stable state economy.

Joint Legislative Audit Committee

37.3. The Joint Legislative Audit Committee is created pursuant to the Legislature's rulemaking authority under the California Constitution, and pursuant to Chapter 4 (commencing with Section 10500) of Part 2 of Division 2 of Title 2 of the Government Code. The committee consists of seven Members of the Senate and seven Members of the Assembly, who shall be selected in the manner provided for in these rules. Notwithstanding any other provision of these rules, four members from each house constitute a quorum of the Joint Legislative Audit Committee and the number of votes necessary to take action on any matter. The Chairman or Chairwoman of the Joint Legislative Audit Committee, upon receiving a request by any Member of the Legislature or committee thereof for a copy of a report prepared or being prepared by the Bureau of State Audits, shall provide the member or committee with a copy of the report when it is, or has been, submitted by the Bureau of State Audits to the Joint Legislative Audit Committee.

Study or Audits

37.4. (a) Notwithstanding any other provision of law, the Joint Legislative Audit Committee shall establish priorities and assign all work to be done by the Bureau of State Audits.

(b) Any bill requiring action by the Bureau of State Audits shall contain an appropriation for the cost of any study or audit.

(c) Any bill or concurrent, joint, Senate, or House resolution assigning a study to the Joint Legislative Audit Committee or to the Bureau of State Audits shall be referred to the respective rules committees. Before the committees may act upon or assign the bill or resolution, they shall obtain an estimate from the Joint Legislative Audit Committee of the amount required to be expended to make the study.

Waiver

37.5. Subdivision (b) of Rule 37.4 may be waived by the Joint Legislative Audit Committee. The chairman or chairwoman of the committee shall notify the Secretary of the Senate, the Chief Clerk of the Assembly, and the Legislative Counsel in writing when subdivision (b) of Rule 37.4 has been waived. If the cost of a study or audit is less than one hundred thousand dollars ($100,000), the chairman or chairwoman of the committee may exercise the committee's authority to waive subdivision (b) of Rule 37.4.

Administrative Regulations

37.7. (a) Any Member of the Senate may request the Senate Committee on Rules, and any Member of the Assembly may request the Speaker of the Assembly, to direct a standing committee or the Office of Research of his or her respective house to study any proposed or existing regulation or group of related regulations. Upon receipt of a request, the Senate Committee on Rules or the Speaker of the Assembly shall, after review, determine whether a study shall be made. In reviewing the request, the Senate Committee on Rules or the Speaker of the Assembly shall determine:

(1) The cost of making the study.

(2) The potential public benefit to be derived from the study.

(3) The scope of the study.

(b) The study may consider, among other relevant issues, whether the proposed or existing regulation:

(1) Exceeds the agency's statutory authority.

(2) Fails to conform to the legislative intent of the enabling statute.

(3) Contradicts or duplicates other regulations adopted by federal, state, or local agencies.

(4) Involves an excessive delegation of regulatory authority to a particular state agency.

(5) Unfairly burdens particular elements of the public.

(6) Imposes social or economic costs that outweigh its intended benefits to the public.

(7) Imposes unreasonable penalties for violation.

The respective reviewing unit shall, in a timely manner, transmit its concerns, if any, to the Senate Committee on Rules or the Speaker of the Assembly, and the promulgating agency.

In the event that a state agency takes a regulatory action that the reviewing unit finds to be unacceptable, the unit shall file a report for publication in the Daily Journal of its respective house indicating the specific reasons why the regulatory action should not have been taken. The report may include a recommendation that the Legislature adopt a concurrent resolution requesting the state agency to reconsider its action or that the Legislature enact a statute to restrict the regulatory powers of the state agency taking the action.

Joint Rules Committee

40. The Joint Rules Committee is hereby created. The committee has a continuing existence and may meet, act, and conduct its business during sessions of the Legislature or any recess thereof.

The committee consists of the members of the Assembly Committee on Rules, the Assembly Majority Floor Leader, the Assembly Minority Floor Leader, the Speaker of the Assembly, four members of the Senate Committee on Rules, and as many Members of the Senate as may be required to maintain equality in the number of Assembly Members and Senators on the committee, to be appointed by the Senate Committee on Rules. Vacancies occurring in the membership shall be filled by the appointing power.

The committee and its members have and may exercise all of the rights, duties, and powers conferred upon investigating committees and their members by the Joint Rules of the Senate and Assembly as they are adopted and amended from time to time, which provisions are incorporated herein and made applicable to this committee and its members.

The committee shall ascertain facts and make recommendations to the Legislature and to the houses thereof concerning:

(a) The relationship between the two houses and procedures calculated to expedite the affairs of the Legislature by improving that relationship.

(b) The legislative branch of the state government and any defects or deficiencies in the law governing that branch.

(c) Methods whereby legislation is proposed, considered, and acted upon.

(d) The operation of the Legislature and the committees thereof, and the means of coordinating the work thereof and avoiding duplication of effort.

(e) Aids to the Legislature.

(f) Information and statistics for the use of the Legislature, the respective houses thereof, and the members.

Any matter of business of either house, the transaction of which would affect the interests of the other house, may be referred to the committee for action if the Legislature is not in recess, and shall be referred to the committee for action if the Legislature is in recess.

The committee has the following additional powers and duties:

(a) To select a chairman or chairwoman from its membership. The vice chairman or vice chairwoman of the committee shall be one of the Senate members of the committee, to be selected by the Senate Committee on Rules.

(b) To allocate space in the State Capitol Building and all annexes and additions thereto as provided by law.

(c) To approve, as provided by law, the appearance of the Legislative Counsel in litigation.

(d) To contract with other agencies, public or private, for the rendition and affording of services, facilities, studies, and reports to the committee as the committee deems necessary to assist it to carry out the purposes for which it is created.

(e) To cooperate with and secure the cooperation of county, city, city and county, and other local law enforcement agencies in investigating any matter within the scope of this rule, and to direct the sheriff of any county to serve subpoenas, orders, and other process issued by the committee.

(f) To report its findings and recommendations, including recommendations for the needed revision of any and all laws and constitutional provisions relating to the Legislature, to the Legislature and to the people from time to time.

(g) The committee, and any subcommittee when so authorized by the committee, may meet and act without as well as within the State of California, and are authorized to leave the state in the performance of their duties.

(h) To expend funds as may be made available to it to carry out the functions and activities related to the legislative affairs of the Senate and Assembly.

(i) To appoint a chief administrative officer of the committee, who shall have duties relating to the administrative, fiscal, and business affairs of the committee as the committee shall prescribe. The committee may terminate the services of the chief administrative officer at any time.

(j) To employ persons as may be necessary to assist all other joint committees, except the Joint Legislative Budget Committee and the Joint Legislative Audit Committee, in the exercise of their powers and performance of their duties. In accordance with Rule 36.8, the committee shall govern and administer the expenditure of funds by other joint committees, requiring that the claims of joint committees be approved by the Joint Rules Committee or its designee. All expenses of the committee and of all other joint committees may be paid from the Operating Funds of the Assembly and Senate.

(k) To appoint the chairmen or chairwomen of joint committees, as authorized by Rule 36.7.

(*l*) To do any and all other things necessary or convenient to enable it fully and adequately to exercise its powers, perform its duties, and accomplish the objects and purposes of this rule.

The members of the Joint Rules Committee from the Senate may meet separately as a unit, and the members of the Joint Rules Committee from the Assembly may meet separately as a unit, and consider any action that is required to be taken by the Joint Rules Committee. If the majority of members of the Joint Rules Committee of each house at the separate meetings vote in favor of that action, the action shall be deemed to be action taken by the Joint Rules Committee.

The Joint Rules Committee shall meet not less than biweekly during a session of the Legislature, other than during a joint recess, at a regularly scheduled time and place. If the full committee fails to so meet, the members of the committee from the Senate shall meet separately as a unit and the members of the committee from the Assembly shall meet separately as a unit within five days of the regularly scheduled meeting date.

The committee succeeds to, and is vested with, all of the powers and duties of the Joint Committee on Legislative Organization, the State Capitol Committee, the Joint Committee on Interhouse Cooperation, the Joint Legislative Committee for School Visitations, and the Joint Standing Committee on the Joint Rules of the Senate and the Assembly.

Review of Administrative Regulations

40.1. The Joint Rules Committee, with regard to joint committees, and the respective rules committee of each house, with regard to standing and select committees of the house, shall approve any request for a priority review made by a committee pursuant to Section 11349.7 of the Government Code and shall submit approved requests to the Office of Administrative Law. The Joint Rules Committee or the respective rules committee, and the committee initiating the request, shall each receive a copy of the priority review.

Subcommittee on Legislative Space and Facilities

40.3. (a) A subcommittee of the Joint Rules Committee is hereby created, to be known as the Subcommittee on Legislative Space and Facilities. The subcommittee consists of three Members of the Senate and three Members of the Assembly, appointed by the Chairman or Chairwoman of the Joint Rules Committee, and the chairman or chairwoman of the fiscal committee of each house who shall have full voting rights on the subcommittee. The chairman or chairwoman of the subcommittee shall be appointed by the members thereof. For purposes of this subcommittee, the chairmen or chairwomen of the fiscal committees are ex officio members of the Joint Rules Committee, but do not have voting rights on that committee, nor may they be counted in determining a quorum. The subcommittee shall consider the housing of the Legislature and legislative facilities.

(b) The subcommittee and its members have and may exercise all of the rights, duties, and powers conferred upon investigating committees and their members by the Joint Rules of the Senate and Assembly as they are adopted and amended from time to time, which provisions are incorporated herein and made applicable to this subcommittee and its members.

(c) The subcommittee has the following additional powers and duties:

(1) To contract with other agencies, public or private, for the rendition and affording of services, facilities, studies, and reports to the subcommittee as the committee deems necessary to assist it to carry out the purposes for which it is created.

(2) To cooperate with and secure the cooperation of county, city, city and county, and other local law enforcement agencies in investigating any matter within the scope of this rule, and to direct the sheriff of any county to serve subpoenas, orders, and other process issued by the subcommittee.

(3) To report its findings and recommendations to the Legislature and to the people from time to time.

(4) To do any and all other things necessary or convenient to enable it fully and adequately to exercise its powers, perform its duties, and accomplish the objects and purposes of this rule.

(d) The subcommittee is authorized to leave the State of California in the performance of its duties.

Claims for Workers' Compensation

41. The Chairman or Chairwoman of the Committee on Rules of each house, or a designated representative, shall sign any required worker's compensation report regarding injuries or death arising out of and within the course of employment suffered by any member, officer, or employee of the house, or any employee of a standing or investigating committee thereof. In the case of a joint committee, the Chairman or Chairwoman of the Committee on Rules of either house, or a designated representative, may sign any report with respect to a member or employee of a joint committee.

Information Concerning Committees

42. The Committee on Rules of each house shall provide for a continuous cumulation of information concerning the membership, organization, meetings, and studies of legislative investigating committees. Each Committee on Rules shall be responsible for information concerning the investigating committees of its own house, and concerning joint investigating committees under a chairman or chairwoman who is a member of that house. To the extent possible, each Committee on Rules shall seek to insure that the investigating committees for which it has responsibility under this rule have organized, including the organization of any subcommittees, and have had all topics for study assigned to them within a reasonable period of time.

The information thus cumulated shall be made available to the public by the Committee on Rules of each house and shall be published periodically under their joint direction.

Joint Committees

43. Any concurrent resolution creating a joint committee of the Legislature and any concurrent resolution allocating moneys from the Operating Funds of the Assembly and Senate to the committee shall be referred to the Committee on Rules of the respective houses.

Conflict of Interest

44. (a) A Member of the Legislature may not, while serving, have any interest, financial or otherwise, direct or indirect, engage in any business or transaction or professional activity, or incur any obligation of any nature, that is in substantial conflict with the proper discharge of his or her duties in the public interest and of his or her responsibilities as prescribed by the laws of this state.

(b) A Member of the Legislature may not, during the term for which he or she was elected:

(1) Accept other employment that he or she has reason to believe will either impair his or her indepen-

dence of judgment as to his or her official duties, or require him or her, or induce him or her, to disclose confidential information acquired by him or her in the course of and by reason of his or her official duties.

(2) Willfully and knowingly disclose, for pecuniary gain, to any other person, confidential information acquired by him or her in the course of and by reason of his or her official duties, or use the information for the purpose of pecuniary gain.

(3) Accept or agree to accept, or be in partnership with any person who accepts or agrees to accept, any employment, fee, or other thing of value, or portion thereof, in consideration of his or her appearance, agreeing to appear, or taking of any other action on behalf of another person regarding a licensing or regulatory matter, before any state board or agency that is established by law for the primary purpose of licensing or regulating the professional activity of persons licensed, pursuant to state law.

This rule does not prohibit a member who is an attorney at law from practicing in that capacity before the Workers' Compensation Appeals Board or the Commissioner of Corporations, and receiving compensation therefor, or from practicing for compensation before any state board or agency in connection with, or in any matter related to, any case, action, or proceeding filed and pending in any state or federal court. This rule does not prohibit a member from making inquiry for information on behalf of a constituent before a state board or agency, if no fee or reward is given or promised in consequence thereof. The prohibition contained in this rule does not apply to a partnership in which a Member of the Legislature is a member if the Member of the Legislature does not share directly or indirectly in the fee resulting from the transaction, nor does it apply in connection with any matter pending before any state board or agency on the operative date of this rule if the affected Member of the Legislature is attorney of record or representative in the matter prior to the operative date.

(4) Receive or agree to receive, directly or indirectly, any compensation, reward, or gift from any source

except the State of California for any service, advice, assistance, or other matter related to the legislative process, except fees for speeches or published works on legislative subjects and except, in connection therewith, the reimbursement of expenses for actual expenditures for travel and reasonable subsistence for which no payment or reimbursement is made by the State of California.

(5) Participate, by voting or any other action, on the floor of either house, or in committee or elsewhere, in the enactment or defeat of legislation in which he or she has a personal interest, except as follows:

(i) If, on the vote for final passage, by the house of which he or she is a member, of the legislation in which he or she has a personal interest, he or she first files a statement (which shall be entered verbatim in the Daily Journal) stating in substance that he or she has a personal interest in the legislation to be voted on and that, notwithstanding that interest, he or she is able to cast a fair and objective vote on the legislation, he or she may cast his or her vote without violating any provision of this rule.

(ii) If the member believes that, because of his or her personal interest, he or she should abstain from participating in the vote on the legislation, he or she shall so advise the presiding officer prior to the commencement of the vote and shall be excused from voting on the legislation without any entry in the Daily Journal of the fact of his or her personal interest. In the event that a rule of the house requiring that each member who is present vote aye or nay is invoked, the presiding officer shall order the member excused from compliance and shall order entered in the Daily Journal a simple statement that the member was excused from voting on the legislation pursuant to law.

(c) A person subject to this rule has an interest that is in substantial conflict with the proper discharge of his or her duties in the public interest and of his or her responsibilities as prescribed by the laws of this state, or a personal interest, arising from any situation, within the scope of this rule, if he or she has reason to believe or expect that he or she will derive a direct monetary gain or suffer a direct monetary loss, as the case may be, by reason of his or her official activity. He or she does not have an interest that is in substantial conflict with the proper discharge of his or her duties in the public interest and of his or her responsibilities as prescribed by the laws of this state, or a personal interest, arising from any situation, within the scope of this rule, if any benefit or detriment accrues to him or her as a member of a business, profession, occupation, or group to no greater extent than any other member of the business, profession, occupation, or group.

(d) A person who is subject to this rule may not be deemed to be engaged in any activity that is in substantial conflict with the proper discharge of his or her duties in the public interest and of his or her responsibilities as prescribed by the laws of this state, or to have a personal interest, arising from any situation, within the scope of this rule, solely by reason of any of the following:

(1) His or her relationship to any potential beneficiary of any situation is one that is defined as a remote interest by Section 1091 of the Government Code or is otherwise not deemed to be a prohibited interest under Section 1091.1 or 1091.5 of the Government Code.

(2) Receipt of a campaign contribution that is regulated, received, reported, and accounted for pursuant to Chapter 4 (commencing with Section 84100) of Title 9 of the Government Code, so long as the contribution is not made on the understanding or agreement, in violation of law, that the person's vote, opinion, judgment, or action will be influenced thereby.

(e) The enumeration in this rule of specific situations or conditions that are deemed not to result in substantial conflict with the proper discharge of the duties and responsibilities of a legislator or legislative employee, or in a personal interest, may not be construed as exclusive.

The Legislature, in adopting this rule, recognizes that Members of the Legislature and legislative employees may need to engage in employment, professional, or business activities other than legislative activities in order to maintain a continuity of professional or business activity, or may need to maintain investments, which activities or investments do not conflict with specific provisions of this rule. However, in construing and administering this rule, weight should be given to any coincidence of income, employment, investment, or other profit from sources that may be identified with the interests represented by those sources that are seeking action of any character on matters then pending before the Legislature.

(f) An employee of either house of the Legislature may not, during the time he or she is so employed, commit any act or engage in any activity prohibited by any part of this rule.

(g) A person may not induce or seek to induce any Member of the Legislature to violate any part of this rule.

(h) A violation of any part of this rule is punishable as provided in Section 8926 of the Government Code.

Ethics Committees

45. The Senate Committee on Legislative Ethics and the Assembly Legislative Ethics Committee, respectively, shall receive complaints concerning members of their respective houses, and may investigate and make findings and recommendations concerning violations by members of their respective houses of Article 2 (commencing with Section 8920) of Chapter 1 of Part 1 of Division 2 of Title 2 of the Government Code. Each house shall adopt rules governing the establishment and procedures of the committee of that house.

Designating Legislative Sessions

50. Regular sessions shall be identified with the odd-numbered year subsequent to each general election, followed by a hyphen, and then the last two digits of the following even-numbered year. For example: 2003–04 Regular Session.

Designating Extraordinary Sessions

50.3. All extraordinary sessions shall be designated in numerical order by the session in which convened.

Days and Dates

50.5. (a) As used in these rules, "day" means a calendar day, unless otherwise specified.

(b) When the date of a deadline, recess requirement, or circumstance falls on a Saturday, Sunday, or Monday that is a holiday, the date shall be deemed to refer to the preceding Friday. When the date falls on a holiday on a weekday other than a Monday, the date shall be deemed to refer to the preceding day.

Legislative Calendar

51. (a) The Legislature shall observe the following calendar during the first year of the regular session:

(1) Organizational Recess—The Legislature shall meet on the first Monday in December following the general election to organize. Thereafter, each house shall be in recess from the time it determines until the first Monday in January, except when the first Monday is January 1 or January 1 is a Sunday, in which case, the following Wednesday.

(2) Spring Recess—The Legislature shall be in recess from the 10th day prior to Easter until the Monday after Easter.

(3) Summer Recess—The Legislature shall be in recess from July 15 until August 15. This recess shall not commence until the Budget Bill is passed.

(4) Interim Study Recess—The Legislature shall be in recess from September 9 until the first Monday in January, except when the first Monday is January 1 or January 1 is a Sunday, in which case, the following Wednesday.

(b) The Legislature shall observe the following calendar for the remainder of the legislative session:

(1) Spring Recess—The Legislature shall be in recess from the 10th day prior to Easter until the Monday after Easter.

(2) Summer Recess—The Legislature shall be in recess from July 7 until August 7. This recess may not commence until the Budget Bill is passed.

(3) Final Recess—The Legislature shall be in recess on September 1 until adjournment sine die on November 30.

(c) Recesses shall be from the hour of adjournment on the day specified, reconvening at the time designated by the respective houses.

(d) The recesses specified by this rule shall be designated as joint recesses.

Recall From Recess

52. Notwithstanding the power of the Governor to call a special session, the Legislature may be recalled from joint recess and reconvene in regular session by any of the following means:

(a) It may be recalled by joint proclamation, which shall be entered in the Daily Journal, of the Senate Committee on Rules and the Speaker of the Assembly or, in his or her absence from the state, the Assembly Committee on Rules.

(b) Ten or more Members of the Legislature may present a request for recall from joint recess to the Chief Clerk of the Assembly and the Secretary of the Senate. The request immediately shall be printed in the Daily Journal. Within 10 days thereafter, the Speaker of the Assembly or, if the Speaker is absent from the state, the Assembly Committee on Rules, and the Senate Committee on Rules shall act upon the request. If they concur in desiring to recall the Legislature from joint recess, they shall issue their joint proclamation to that effect entered in the Daily Journal no later than 20 days after publication of the request in the Daily Journal.

(c) If either or both of the parties specified in subdivision (b) does not concur, 10 or more Members of the Legislature may request the Chief Clerk of the Assembly or the Secretary of the Senate to petition the membership of the respective house. The petition shall be entered in the Daily Journal and shall contain a specified reconvening date commencing not later than 20 days after the date of the petition. If two-thirds of the members of the house or each of the two houses concur, the Legislature shall reconvene on the date specified.

The necessary concurrences must be received at least 10 days prior to the date specified for reconvening.

Procedure on Suspending Rules by Single House

53. Whenever these rules authorize suspension of the Joint Rules as to a particular bill by action of a single house after approval by the Committee on Rules of that house, the following procedure shall be followed:

(a) A written request to suspend the joint rule shall be filed with the Chief Clerk of the Assembly or the Secretary of the Senate, as the case may be, and shall be transmitted to the Committee on Rules of the appropriate house.

(b) The Assembly Committee on Rules or the Senate Committee on Rules, as the case may be, shall determine whether there exists an urgent need for the suspension of the joint rule with regard to the bill.

(c) If the appropriate rules committee recommends that the suspension be permitted, the member may offer a resolution, without further reference thereto to committee, granting permission to suspend the joint rule. The adoption of the resolution granting permission shall require an affirmative recorded vote of the elected members of the house in which the request is made.

Introduction of Bills

54. (a) A bill may not be introduced in the first year of the regular session after February 18 and a bill may not be introduced in the second year of the regular session after February 24. These deadlines do not apply to constitutional amendments, committee bills introduced pursuant to Assembly Rule 47 or Senate Rule 23, bills introduced in the Assembly with the permission of the Speaker of the Assembly, or bills introduced in the Senate with the permission of the Senate Committee on Rules. Subject to these deadlines, a bill may be introduced at any time except when the houses are in joint summer, interim, or final recess. Each house may provide for introduction of bills during a recess other

than a joint recess. Bills shall be numbered consecutively during the regular session.

(b) The Desks of the Senate and Assembly shall remain open during a joint recess, other than a joint spring, summer, interim, or final recess, for the introduction of bills during business hours on Monday through Friday, inclusive, except holidays. Bills received at the Senate Desk during these periods shall be numbered and printed. After printing, the bills shall be delivered to the Secretary of the Senate and referred by the Senate Committee on Rules to a standing committee. Bills received at the Assembly Desk during these periods shall be numbered, printed, and referred to a committee by the Assembly Committee on Rules. After printing, the bills shall be delivered to the Chief Clerk of the Assembly. On the reconvening of each house, the bills shall be read the first time, and shall be delivered to the committee to which they were referred.

(c) A member may not author a bill during a session that would have substantially the same effect as a bill he or she previously authored during that session. This restriction does not apply in cases where the previously authored bill was vetoed by the Governor or its provisions were "chaptered out" by a later chaptered bill pursuant to Section 9605 of the Government Code. An objection based on this restriction may be raised only while the bill is being considered by the house in which it is introduced. The objection shall be referred to the Committee on Rules of the house for a determination. The bill shall remain on the Daily File or with a committee, as the case may be, until a determination is made. If, upon consideration of the objection, the Committee on Rules determines that the bill objected to would have substantially the same effect as another bill previously authored during the session by the author, the bill objected to shall be stricken from the Daily File or returned to the desk by the committee, as the case may be, and may not be acted upon during the remainder of the session. If the Committee on Rules determines that the bill objected to would not have substantially the same effect as a bill previously authored during the session by the author, the bill may thereafter be acted upon by the committee or the house, as the case may be. The Committee on Rules may obtain assistance as it may desire from the Legislative Counsel as to the similarity of a bill or amendments to a prior bill.

This joint rule may be suspended by approval of the Committee on Rules and three-fourths vote of the membership of the house.

(d) During a joint recess, the Chief Clerk of the Assembly or Secretary of the Senate shall order the preparation of preprint bills when so ordered by any of the following:

(1) The Speaker of the Assembly.

(2) The Committee on Rules of the respective house.

(3) A committee, with respect to bills within the subject matter jurisdiction of the committee.

Preprint bills shall be designated and shall be printed in the order received and numbered in the order printed. To facilitate subsequent amendment, a preprint bill shall be so prepared that, when introduced as a bill, the page and the line numbers will not change. The Chief Clerk of the Assembly and Secretary of the Senate shall publish a list periodically of preprint bills showing the preprint bill number, the title, and the Legislative Counsel's Digest. The Speaker of the Assembly and Senate Committee on Rules may refer any preprint bill to committee for study.

30-Day Waiting Period

55. A bill other than the Budget Bill may not be heard or acted upon by committee or either house until the bill has been in print for 30 days. The date a bill is returned from the printer shall be entered in the Daily History. This rule may be suspended concurrently with the suspension of the requirement of Section 8 of Article IV of the Constitution or, if that period has expired, this rule may be suspended by approval of the Committee on Rules and two-thirds vote of the house in which the bill is being considered.

Return of Bills

56. Bills introduced in the first year of the regular session and passed by the house of origin on or before the January 31st constitutional deadline are "carryover bills." Immediately after January 31, bills introduced in the first year of the regular session that do not become "carryover bills" shall be returned to the Chief Clerk of the Assembly or Secretary of the Senate, respectively. Notwithstanding Rule 4, as used in this rule "bills" does not include constitutional amendments.

Appropriation Bills

57. Appropriation bills that may not be sent to the Governor shall be held, after enrollment, by the Chief Clerk of the Assembly or Secretary of the Senate, respectively. The bills shall be sent to the Governor immediately after the Budget Bill has been passed.

Urgency Clauses

58. An amendment to add a section to a bill to provide that the act shall take effect immediately as an urgency statute may not be adopted unless the author of the amendment has first secured the approval of the Committee on Rules of the house in which the amendments are offered.

Vetoes

58.5. The Legislature may consider a Governor's veto for only 60 days, not counting days when the Legislature is in joint recess.

Publications

59. During periods of joint recess, weekly, if necessary, the following documents shall be published: Daily Files, Histories, and Daily Journals.

Committee Hearings

60. (a) A standing committee or subcommittee thereof may not take action on a bill at any hearing held outside of the State Capitol.

(b) A committee may hear the subject matter of a bill or convene for an informational hearing during a period of recess. Four days' notice in the Daily File is required prior to the hearing.

(c) A bill may not be acted upon by a committee during a joint recess.

Deadlines

61. The deadlines set forth in this rule shall be observed by the Senate and Assembly. After each deadline, the Secretary of the Senate and the Chief Clerk of the Assembly may not accept committee reports from their respective committees except as otherwise provided in this rule:

(a) Odd-numbered year:

(1) Feb. 18—Last day for bills to be introduced.

(2) April 29—Last day for policy committees to hear and report to fiscal committees fiscal bills introduced in their house.

(3) May 6—Last day for policy committees to hear and report to the floor nonfiscal bills introduced in their house.

(4) May 20—Last day for policy committees to meet prior to June 6.

(5) May 27—Last day for fiscal committees to hear and report to the floor bills introduced in their house.

(6) May 27—Last day for fiscal committees to meet prior to June 6.

(7) May 31–June 3—Floor session only. No committee may meet for any purpose.

(8) June 3—Last day for each house to pass bills introduced in that house.

(9) June 6—Committee meetings may resume.

(10) July 8—Last day for policy committees to meet and report bills.

(11) The Legislature shall be in summer recess from July 15 until August 15. This recess shall not commence until the Budget Bill is passed.

(12) Aug. 26—Last day for fiscal committees to meet and report bills.

(13) Aug. 29–Sept. 9—Floor session only. No committee may meet for any purpose.

(14) Sept. 2—Last day to amend on the floor.

(15) Sept. 9—Last day for each house to pass bills.

(b) Even-numbered year:

(1) Jan. 13—Last day for policy committees to hear and report to fiscal committees fiscal bills introduced in their house in the odd-numbered year.

(2) Jan. 20—Last day for any committee to hear and report to the floor bills introduced in that house in the odd-numbered year.

(3) Jan. 31—Last day for each house to pass bills introduced in that house in the odd-numbered year.

(4) Feb. 24—Last day for bills to be introduced.

(5) April 28—Last day for policy committees to hear and report to fiscal committees fiscal bills introduced in their house.

(6) May 12—Last day for policy committees to hear and report to the floor nonfiscal bills introduced in their house.

(7) May 19—Last day for policy committees to meet prior to June 5.

(8) May 26—Last day for fiscal committees to hear and report to the floor bills introduced in their house.

(9) May 26—Last day for fiscal committees to meet prior to June 5.

(10) May 30–June 2—Floor session only. No committee may meet for any purpose.

(11) June 2—Last day for each house to pass bills introduced in that house.

(12) June 5—Committee meetings may resume.

(13) June 30—Last day for policy committees to meet and report bills.

(14) Aug. 18—Last day for fiscal committees to meet and report bills.

(15) Aug. 21–Aug. 31—Floor session only. No committee may meet for any purpose.

(16) Aug. 25—Last day to amend on floor.

(17) Aug. 31—Last day for each house to pass bills.

(c) If a bill is acted upon in committee before the relevant deadline, and the committee votes to report the bill out with amendments that have not at the time of the vote been prepared by the Legislative Counsel, the Secretary of the Senate and the Chief Clerk of the

Assembly may subsequently receive a report recommending the bill for passage or for rereferral together with the amendments at any time within two legislative days after the deadline.

(d) Notwithstanding subdivisions (a) and (b), a policy committee may report a bill to a fiscal committee on or before the relevant deadline for reporting nonfiscal bills to the floor if, after the policy committee deadline for reporting the bill to fiscal committee, the Legislative Counsel's Digest is changed to indicate reference to fiscal committee.

(e) Any bill in the house of origin that is not acted upon during the odd-numbered year as a result of the deadlines imposed in subdivision (a) may be acted upon when the Legislature reconvenes after the interim study joint recess, or at any time the Legislature is recalled from the interim study joint recess.

(f) The deadlines imposed by this rule do not apply to the rules committees of the respective houses.

(g) The deadlines imposed by this rule do not apply in instances where a bill is referred to committee under Rule 26.5.

(h) The deadlines imposed by this rule do not apply in instances where a bill is referred to a committee under Assembly Rule 77.2.

(i) (1) Notwithstanding subdivisions (a) and (b), a policy committee or fiscal committee may meet for the purpose of hearing and reporting a constitutional amendment, or a bill that would go into immediate effect pursuant to subdivision (c) of Section 8 of Article IV of the California Constitution, at any time other than those periods when no committee may meet for any purpose.

(2) Notwithstanding subdivisions (a) and (b), either house may meet for the purpose of considering and passing a constitutional amendment, or a bill that would go into immediate effect pursuant to subdivision (c) of Section 8 of Article IV of the California Constitution, at any time during the session.

(j) This rule may be suspended as to any particular bill by approval of the Committee on Rules and two-thirds vote of the membership of the house.

Committee Procedure

62. (a) Notice of a hearing on a bill by the committee of first reference in each house, or notice of an informational hearing, shall be published in the Daily File at least four days prior to the hearing. Otherwise, notice shall be published in the Daily File two days prior to the hearing. That notice requirement may be waived by a majority vote of the house in which the bill is being considered. A bill may be set for hearing in a committee only three times. A bill is "set," for purposes of this subdivision, whenever notice of the hearing has been published in the Daily File for one or more days. If a bill is set for hearing, and the committee, on its own initiation and not the author's, postpones the hearing on the bill or adjourns the hearing while testimony is being taken, that hearing is not counted as one of the three times a bill may be set. After hearing the bill, the committee may vote on the bill. If the hearing notice in the Daily File specifically indicates that "testimony only" will be taken, that hearing is not counted as one of the three times a bill may be set. A committee may not vote on a bill so noticed until it has been heard in accordance with this rule. After a committee has voted on a bill, reconsideration may be granted only one time. Reconsideration may be granted within 15 legislative days or prior to the interim study joint recess, whichever first occurs. A vote on reconsideration may not be taken without the same notice required to set a bill unless that vote is taken at the same meeting at which the vote to be reconsidered was taken, and the author is present. When a bill fails to get the necessary votes to pass it out of committee, or upon failure to receive reconsideration, it shall be returned to the Chief Clerk of the Assembly or Secretary of the Senate of the house of the committee and may not be considered further during the session.

This subdivision may be suspended with respect to a particular bill by approval of the Committee on Rules and two-thirds vote of the members of the house.

(b) If the committee adopts amendments other than those offered by the author and orders the bill reprinted prior to its further consideration, the hearing shall not be the final time a bill may be set under subdivision (a) of this rule.

(c) When a standing committee takes action on a bill, the vote shall be by rollcall vote only. All rollcall votes taken by a standing committee shall be recorded by the committee secretary on forms provided by the Chief Clerk of the Assembly and the Secretary of the Senate. The chairman or chairwoman of each standing committee shall promptly transmit a copy of the record of the rollcall votes to the Chief Clerk of the Assembly or the Secretary of the Senate, respectively, who shall cause the votes to be published as prescribed by each house.

This subdivision also applies to action of a committee on a subcommittee report. The rules of each house shall prescribe the procedure as to rollcall votes on amendments.

Any committee may, with the unanimous consent of the members present, substitute a rollcall from a prior bill, provided that the members whose votes are substituted are present at the time of the substitution.

A bill may not be passed out by a committee without a quorum being present.

This subdivision does not apply to:

(1) Procedural motions that do not have the effect of disposing of a bill.

(2) Withdrawal of a bill from a committee calendar at the request of an author.

(3) Return of a bill to the house where the bill has not been voted on by the committee.

(4) The assignment of a bill to committee.

(d) The chairman or chairwoman of the committee hearing a bill may, at any time, order a call of the committee. Upon a request by any member of a committee or the author in person, the chairman or chairwoman shall order the call.

In the absence of a quorum, a majority of the members present may order a quorum call of the committee and compel the attendance of absentees. The chairman or chairwoman shall send the Sergeant at Arms for those members who are absent and not excused by their respective house.

When a call of a committee is ordered by the chairman or chairwoman with respect to a particular bill, he or she shall send the Sergeant at Arms, or any other person to be appointed for that purpose, for those members who have not voted on that particular bill and are not excused.

A quorum call or a call of the committee with respect to a particular bill may be dispensed with by the chairman or chairwoman without objection by any member of the committee, or by a majority of the members present.

If a motion is adopted to adjourn the committee while the committee is operating under a call, the call shall be dispensed with and any pending vote announced.

The committee secretary shall record the votes of members answering a call. The rules of each house may prescribe additional procedures for a call of a committee.

Redistricting Bills

62.5. This rule applies only to bills affecting the boundaries of legislative, congressional, or State Board of Equalization districts.

(a) Except as specifically provided in this rule, Rules 28, 28.1, 29, 29.5, 30, 30.5, 30.7, 61 (except for paragraph (12) of subdivision (a), and paragraph (15) of subdivision (b), of Rule 61), and 62 do not apply to bills affecting the boundaries of legislative, congressional, or State Board of Equalization districts.

(b) If the Senate (in the case of a Senate bill) or the Assembly (in the case of an Assembly bill) refuses to concur in amendments to a bill made by the other house, a committee on conference shall be appointed. The Speaker of the Assembly and the Senate Committee on Rules shall each appoint a committee on conference, consisting of three members, consisting of two members of the majority party and one member not of the majority party. The Secretary of the Senate and the Chief Clerk of the Assembly shall immediately notify the other house of the action taken.

(c) When a bill affecting the boundaries of legislative, congressional, or State Board of Equalization districts has been referred to a committee on conference, the chairman or chairwoman of the committee on conference shall immediately request the Senate Committee on Elections and Reapportionment and the Assembly Committee on Elections, Reapportionment, and Constitutional Amendments to hold a public hearing on the bill. The committee on conference shall also hold a public hearing on the bill. The hearings of the policy committees and the committee on conference may be noticed and held concurrently.

(d) If either or both of the policy committees hold a public hearing on a bill pursuant to the request of the chairman or chairwoman of the committee on conference, the policy committees may consider amendments to the bill, and may make recommendations on amendments to the committee on conference. A policy committee recommendation for an amendment may be adopted only by a rollcall vote of the members of the policy committee.

(e) All proposed reports of a committee on conference, all proposed amendments to a proposed report of a committee on conference, and all proposed amendments presented to a policy committee shall be accompanied by appropriate maps. A committee vote may not be taken on any proposed report of a committee on conference, any proposed amendment to a proposed report of a committee on conference, or any proposed amendment presented to a policy committee unless the proposed report or proposed amendment, with accompanying maps, has been available to the public for at least 24 hours. Notwithstanding subdivision (h), district boundaries contained in any proposed report or any proposed amendment may not be required to be prepared or approved as to form by Legislative Counsel if the accompanying maps adequately reflect the district boundaries.

(f) All hearings of the policy committees and the committee on conference shall be open and readily accessible to the public, and shall be noticed in the Daily File for not less than two calendar days.

(g) The provisions of subdivision (e) prohibiting a committee vote on any proposed report of a committee on conference, any proposed amendment to a proposed report of a committee on conference, or any proposed amendment presented to a policy committee unless the amendment, accompanied by appropriate maps, has been available to the public for at least 24 hours do not apply in any of the following situations:

(1) The amendment proposed to a policy committee or the committee on conference does not change any district boundaries.

(2) The amendment proposed to a policy committee or the committee on conference is required to correct a technical error in the bill, and the proposed amendment would shift no more than 1 percent of the population of any district to any other district or districts.

(3) The amendment is a policy committee or committee on conference amendment that is proposed in response to amendments that have been proposed to the committee.

(h) Except as provided in subdivision (i), a vote may not be taken in either house on any bill or any report of the committee on conference on that bill unless the bill or the report has been in print in Legislative Counsel form and available to the public, accompanied by appropriate maps, for at least 24 hours.

(i) If either house refuses to adopt the report of the committee on conference, the bill may be returned to the committee on conference for further consideration. If the bill is returned to the committee on conference for an amendment described in paragraph (1) or (2) of subdivision (g), the notice requirements of subdivisions (e) and (h) do not apply.

(j) Notwithstanding any other rule, this rule may be suspended upon a majority vote of the membership of each house.

Uniform Rules

63. A standing committee of either house may not adopt or apply any rule or procedure governing the voting upon bills that is not equally applicable to the bills of both houses.

Votes on Bills

64. Every meeting of each house and standing committee or subcommittee thereof where a vote is to be taken on a bill, or amendments to a bill, shall be public.

Conflicting Rules

65. The provisions of Rule 50 and following of these rules prevail over any conflicting joint rule with a lesser number.

INDEX TO THE
JOINT RULES
(Adopted by the Senate Dec. 6, 2004)
(As Amended April 7, 2005)

A

B

C

CAPITOL CORRESPONDENTS ASSOCIATION, 32(b)

CHIEF CLERK

amendments, endorsed and signed by, 25

    not printed, when, 11(b)

bills—

    actions endorsed on by, 20

    appropriation, when sent to Governor, 57

    deadlines, duties re, 61

    failure to pass, 62(a)

    introduction of, 54

    January 31st, those not "carryover bills" returned after, 56

    orders for legislature, 13

    record of action to be kept by, 19

    request to consider within 30 days transmitted to Rules Committee by, 10.8(a)

    return of, to, 54(b), 56, 62

    returns to Member if incorrectly introduced, 8.5

    signs, passed by Legislature, 24

    Title 9, Government Code, 8.8

committee rollcalls published, 62(c)

conference report, 3-day notice, 30

Consent Calendar, duties re, 22.1, 22.2

History, prescribes form of, 17

Journal, directs printing of, 14

members' expenses, certifies to Controller, 35

messages to Senate—

    of Assembly action, 22

    re concurrence in Senate amendments, 26

    re conference committee appointments, 28

    re nonconcurrence in amendments, 28

preprint bills, 54(d)

printing, authorizes for Assembly, 18

    rush order issued by, 18

publications, order by, 13, 13.1, 13.3, 13.5, 14, 18

recall from joint recess, petition, 52

reports after deadline, 61

D

E

L

The Assembly

List of

MEMBERS, OFFICERS, COMMITTEES AND THE RULES

2005–06 REGULAR SESSION

Compiled by

E. DOTSON WILSON
Chief Clerk

LAWRENCE A. MURMAN
Assistant Chief Clerk

HUGH SLAYDEN
Assistant Clerk

Date of Publication August, 2005

CONTENTS

ASSEMBLY RULES COMMITTEE

From Left to Right: Assembly Members J. Coto, J. Baca, B. Karnette, M. Dymally, Secretary A. McCabe, Chief Clerk E. D. Wilson, Chair C. Montañez, Chief Sergeant R. Pane, Chief Administrative Officer J. Waldie, Vice Chair D. Cogdill, Assembly Members J. Benoit, M. Villines.

FABIAN NUÑEZ
SPEAKER

NUÑEZ, Fabian (D) 46th District. Elected 2002. Elected Speaker of the Assembly January 8, 2004. Assumed Office of Speaker of the Assembly February 9, 2004. Full-time Legislator. Native Californian born December 27, 1966, in San Diego. Earned Bachelor of Arts degrees in Political Science and Education from Pitzer College in Claremont, California. Children: Estaban, Teresa, and Carlos. From 2000–2002, served as Government Relations Director for the Los Angeles Unified School District. In this capacity, tackled a broad range of education issues and secured millions in funding for school construction projects, children's health insurance, and low-performing schools. Served as Political Director for the Los Angeles County Federation of Labor, 1996–2000. Founder, Latino Forum. Served with the Small Business Development Center. Serves as UC Regent and CSU Trustee. Awarded University of California Students Association (UCSA) Legislator of the Year (2004); University of California Alumni Associations Legislator of the Year (2004); University of California Students Association (UCSA) Legislator of the Year (2004); Received from Equality California (EQCA), the Equality Leadership Award (2005). Personally committed to keeping the State's historic promise to expand opportunity through public education. Member, Joint Committee on Rules.

DARIO FROMMER
MAJORITY FLOOR LEADER /
MAJORITY LEADER

FROMMER, Dario (D) 43rd District. Elected 2000. Appointed Majority Floor Leader/Majority Leader February 9, 2004. Attorney/Teacher. Native Californian born October 22, 1963, in Long Beach. Married, wife Lorraine Paskett; son: Dario Antonio Paskett. Graduated Cum Laude with a B.A. in International Relations and Political Science from Colgate University in 1985; J.D., U.C. Davis Law School, served as President of the Law School. Named "Outstanding Young Californian" by the Jaycees and "Urban Park Advocate of 2001" by the Trust for Public Land; "Legislator of the Year 2002" by California Park and Recreation Society. Former Appointments Secretary to Gov. Gray Davis; Chief of Staff to Senator Art Torres. Recognized as one of the "Top 20 Lawyers Under 40 in California" by the Daily Journal. Member, Board of Advisors, YMCA Model Legislature and Court; Glendale and Burbank Chambers of Commerce. Chair, Select Committees on Runaway Production; Special Committee on Rail Safety. Member, Committees on Business and Professions; Health; Insurance; Select Committee on the Los Angeles Health Care Crisis; Joint Committee on Rules.

LELAND Y. YEE
SPEAKER PRO TEMPORE

YEE, Leland Y. (D) 12th District. Elected 2002. Appointed Speaker pro Tempore February 9, 2004; December 6, 2004. Child Psychologist. Born November 20, 1948, in China. Graduate, U.C. Berkeley; Master's, San Francisco State; Ph.D., University of Hawaii. Married, four children. Served on San Francisco Board of Education, 1988–96. Former Supervisor, San Francisco Board of Supervisors, 1996–2002. Named Public Official of the Year, 2002, by Building Owners and Managers Association of San Francisco. Recipient, 2002 Leadership Award by Golden Gate Restaurant Association. President, National Asian Pacific American Caucus of State Legislators. Co-Chair, Asian Pacific Islander Legislative Caucus. Awarded 2004 Legislator of the Year by California Psychiatric Association; Faculty Association of California Community Colleges; California School Food Service Association. Chair, Select Committee on Children's Physical and Mental Well Being in Diverse California Communities. Member, Committees on Appropriations; Business and Professions; Governmental Organization.

KEVIN MCCARTHY
REPUBLICAN LEADER

McCARTHY, Kevin (R) 32nd District. Elected 2002.
Elected Republican Leader January 5, 2004. Small Busi-
ness Owner. Native Californian born January 26, 1965, in
Bakersfield. Received B.S. and M.B.A. in Business Ad-
ministration from CSU, Bakersfield. Married, wife, Judy;
children: Connor and Meghan. Former District Director to
Congressman Bill Thomas. Past Chairman of the National
Young Republicans. Past President, Bakersfield Irish Bri-
gade; First Book Bakersfield; American Council for Young
Political Leaders. Member of Rotary. Appointed by Gov.
Pete Wilson to Board of Health Professions Education
Foundation. Served on Board of Directors for Kern County
Economic Opportunity Corporation; Head Start; Kern
County Food Bank. Delegate to Republican National
Convention in Philadelphia. Member, Joint Committee on
Rules; Joint Legislative Budget.

AGHAZARIAN, Greg (R) 26th District. Assistant Whip. Elected 2002. Small Businessman. Native Californian born September 10, 1964, in Stockton. Received B.S. in Business Admin., U.S.C.; J.D., UOP, McGeorge School of Law. Married, wife, Esther; children: Ben and Max. Member, San Joaquin and Stanislaus County Farm Bureaus; Downtown Stockton Rotary; San Joaquin A+; Stockton, Turlock, Ceres, and Modesto Chambers of Commerce. Former Member, Board of Trustees, Lincoln Unified School District. Commissioner, Stockton Parks and Recreation Commission. Vice Chair, Committee on Health. Member, Committees on Governmental Organization; Joint Legislative Audit.

ARAMBULA, Juan (D) 31st District. Elected 2004. Attorney. Born January 29, 1952, in Brownsville, Texas. Established residence in California in 1957. Received B.A. from Harvard (High Honors); Masters in Educational Administration, Stanford. J.D., U.C. Berkeley. Married, wife, Amy; four children: Joaquin, Carmen, Diego, and Miguel. Former member, Fresno Unified School Board (1987–1996); CSBA Board, Fresno County Supervisor (1997–2004); Board Chair (1998, 2003); CSAC Board (1996); Co-chair, Fresno Regional Jobs Initiative. Recipient Rose Ann Vuich Award for Ethical Leadership, 2002. Chair, Committee on Jobs, Economic Development, and the Economy. Member, Committees on Budget; Education; Human Services.

BACA, Joe Jr. (D) 62nd District. Elected 2004. Teacher. Native Californian born August 8, 1964, in Barstow. Graduate of CSU, San Bernardino with B.S. in Business Administration; Masters Degree in Public Administration. Married, wife, Jennifer Sanchez Baca; one child: Kaylie Isabella Baca. Member, NAACP; League of Women Voters; Native Sons of the Golden West; Fontana Democratic Club; San Bernardino Democratic Luncheon Club; San Bernardino Youth Accountability Board. Chair, Assembly Select Committee on Perchlorate Contamination. Member, Committees on Housing and Community Development; Jobs, Economic Development, and the Economy; Rules; Utilities and Commerce; Water, Parks and Wildlife; Joint Committee on Rules.

BASS, Karen (D) 47th District, Majority Whip. Elected 2004. Physician Assistant. Native Californian born in Los Angeles. Received Bachelor of Science Degree from Cal State Dominguez Hills; Post Baccalaureate Physician Assistant's Certificate, USC. One daughter. Founder, Executive Director, Community Coalition. Member, Los Angeles City Council Ad Hoc Committee on Gangs, Youth and Violence. Recipient, Rosa Parks Award, Southern Christian Leadership Conference; FAME Award, First African-Methodist Episcopal Church. Former Clinical Instructor, USC School of Medicine; Senior Policy Fellow, UCLA School of Public Policy. Member, Committees on Appropriations; Business and Professions; Higher Education; Human Services.

BENOIT, John J. (R) 64th District. Republican Whip. Elected 2002. Law Enforcement. Born December 27, 1951, in Kankakee, Illinois. Established residence in California in 1954. Received B.S. in Criminal Justice, CSU, Los Angeles, 1978; FBI National Academy, 1986; MPA, CSU, San Bernardino, 1993. Married, wife, Sheryl; children: Benjamin and Sarah. Former CHP Commander, Indio, 1988–2001. Member, IACP-Assn. of International Chiefs of Police. Past President, Indio Rotary Club. Past Board President and Campaign Chair, United Way of the Desert. Served on Board of Governors, Desert Sands Unified School District. Commercial, multi-engine instrument-rated pilot. Vice Chair, Committee on Insurance. Member, Committees on Budget; Rules; Joint Committee on Rules.

BERG, Patty (D) 1st District. Elected 2002. Social Worker/Legislator. Born June 6, 1942, in Seattle, Washington. Established residence in California in 1962. Received Bachelor's Degree in Sociology and Social Welfare, 1967, at CSU, Los Angeles. Two stepchildren: Gretchen and Brian Murphy. Member, Environmental Caucus; National Women's Political Caucus. Cofounder Redwood Coast Music Festivals. Founder and former Executive Director of the Area Agency on Aging serving both Humboldt and Del Norte counties. Chair, Committee on Aging and Long-Term Care; Select Committee on Sustainability. Member, Committees on Appropriations; Health; Water, Parks and Wildlife.

BERMÚDEZ, Rudy (D) 56th District. Elected 2002. Law Enforcement. Native Californian born May 1, 1958, in Los Angeles. Received B.A., Sociology, U.C.L.A.; Masters in Public Policy and Administration, CSU at Long Beach. Married, wife, Nancy; children: Rudy Jr. and Nicolas. Member, Calif. Correctional Peace Officers Assn. (CCPOA); Norwalk Knights of Columbus; Parent Teacher Association. Serves on California Commission for Economic Development; Board of Governance, Streamline Sales Tax Project; California Commission on Tax Policy in the New Economy. Former Commissioner and Member, Medical Board of California. Former Council Member, City of Norwalk, 1999–2002; Board Member, Norwalk-La Mirada Board of Education, 1991–99. Chair, Budget Subcommittee No. 4 on State Administration; Select Committee on Prison Construction and Operations. Member, Committees on Aging and Long-Term Care; Budget; Governmental Organization; Water, Parks and Wildlife.

BLAKESLEE, Sam (R) 33rd District. Elected 2004. Certified Financial Planner. Native Californian born June 25, 1955. Received B.S. and M.S. in Geophysics from U.C. Berkeley; Ph.D. in Geological Studies, U.C. Santa Barbara. Married, wife, Kara; three children. Received a patent for inventing a technique that uses cat-scan technology to create images of geological formations. Former, Cuesta Community College Trustee. Co-Chair of San Luis Obispo Housing Task Force; Treasurer for the Chamber of Commerce; authored DREAM Initiative. Recipient, San Luis Obispo Chamber of Commerce Leadership Alumni Award, 2000; Rhodes League of Women Voters Leadership Award, 2001. Vice Chair, Committee on Public Employees, Retirement and Social Security. Member, Committees on Agriculture; Budget; Utilities and Commerce.

BOGH, Russell Vincent (R) 65th District. Republican Caucus Chair. Elected in a Special Election April 3, 2001. Full-time Legislator. Native Californian born June 21, 1969, in San Bernardino. Received B.A. in Business Economics from CSU, San Bernardino in 1993. Married, wife, Sheri; children: Madison, Charlie, and Katie. Member, Moreno Valley Rotary; the Valley Group Forum. Former President, Riverside Community College Foundation. Served on Board of Directors, Moreno Valley Chamber of Commerce. Member, Mt. San Jacinto Winter Park Authority. Vice Chair, Committee on Utilities and Commerce. Member, Committees on Insurance; Transportation.

CALDERON, Ronald S. (D) 58th District. Former Assistant Majority Leader. Elected 2002. Real Estate. Native Californian born August 12, 1957, in Montebello. Married, wife, Ana; children: Jessica and Zachary. Received B.A. in Psychology from U.C.L.A.; attended Western State University of Law. Member, La Merced Elementary School PTA; Gangs Out of Downey (GOOD); Los Angeles County Economic Development Corporation (LAEDC); Northeast Community Clinic Board of Directors; Old Timers Foundation; California Center for Public Health Advocacy's Grassroots Nutrition and Physical Activity Team. Former Chief of Staff to Assembly Members Martin Gallegos and Ed Chavez. Chair, Committee on Banking and Finance. Member, Committees on Appropriations; Governmental Organization; Insurance.

CANCIAMILLA, Joseph (D) 11th District. Elected 2000. Attorney/Businessman. Native Californian born April 1955 in Pittsburg. Received B.A., St. Mary's College; J.D., John F. Kennedy University School of Law. Married, wife, Dr. Laura Stephenson-Canciamilla. Former Member Pittsburg Board of Education, 1973–88. Served as Councilmember and Mayor of Pittsburg, 1988–96; County Supervisor on Contra Costa County Board of Supervisors, 1996–2000. Former President and member, Delta Diablo Sanitation District, 1991–2000. Former member, Delta Protection Commission; Contra Costa LAFCO; Contra Costa County Transportation Authority; Bay Area Air Quality Management District Board. Convenor, Assembly Democratic Moderate Caucus. Chair, Select Committee on Growth and Infrastructure. Member, Committees on Aging and Long-Term Care; Agriculture; Jobs, Economic Development, and the Economy; Revenue and Taxation; Veterans Affairs.

CHAN, Wilma (D) 16th District. Served as Majority Leader December 5, 2002–February 9, 2004. Elected 2000. Full-time Legislator. Born October 5, 1949, in Boston, Mass. First established residence in California in 1971. Graduate Wellesley, B.A.; Stanford University, M.A. in Education Policy. Children: Jennifer and Daren. Served as Member and President Alameda County Board of Supervisors 1994 through November 2000. Former Chair, Alameda County Families and Children Commission 1999–2000. Received honors from Alameda Health Consortium; California Hunger Action Network; Chinese American Voter Education Project; Child Development Policy Advisory Committee; National Asian Women's Health Organization; Soroptimists; Alameda County Tobacco Control Coalition; American Association of University Women; Rotary International; National Association of Social Workers; California League of Women Voters. Chair, Committee on Health. Member, Committees on Budget; Labor and Employment; Transportation.

CHAVEZ, Ed (D) 57th District. Elected 2000. Full-time Legislator/Educator. Native Californian born December 9, 1963, in Los Angeles. Graduated with B.A. in Political Science, U.C.L.A., 1989. Received Long-Term Single Subject Teaching Credential from Claremont Graduate University and Designated Subjects Adult Education Teaching Credential from CSU at L.A.

Married, wife, Renee; three children: Joe, John, and Robert. Former Member and President, Board of Education for Bassett Unified School District. Served as Mayor, Mayor Pro Tem, and Councilman, La Puente City Council 1990–2000. Member, California Contract Cities Association; California League of Cities Association; San Gabriel Valley Council of Governments; Los Angeles Sanitation District. Selected 2002 Legislator of the Year by the Veterans of Foreign Wars of the United States, Department of California. Chair, Committee on Arts, Entertainment, Sports, Tourism, and Internet Media. Member, Committees on Banking and Finance; Governmental Organization; Veterans Affairs.

CHU, Judy M. (D) 49th District. Elected at a Special Election May 15, 2001. Community College Professor. Native Californian born July 7, 1953, in Los Angeles. Received B.A., U.C.L.A.; Ph.D., CA School of Professional Psychology of Los Angeles. Married, husband, Michael Eng. Founder and past President, Asian Youth Center. Found-

ing Board Member of the Greater San Gabriel Valley Community Development Corporation. Former Member, Garvey School District, 1985–88. Served on Monterey Park City Council, 1988–2001. Recipient, Public Service Award by U.C.L.A. Alumni Assn.; "Outstanding Founders Award" on National Philanthropy Day in Los Angeles. Chair, Committee on Appropriations; Select Committee on Hate Crimes. Member, Committees on Environmental Safety and Toxic Materials; Labor and Employment; Revenue and Taxation; Joint Legislative Budget.

COGDILL, David (R) 25th District. Elected 2000. Small Business Owner. Native Californian born December 31, 1950, in Long Beach. Married, wife, Stephanie; two children: David Jr. and Meghan. Served in the California Air National Guard. Designated member, (MAI-RM) Appraisal Institute. Past Master, ALTA Lodge #333 F. & A.M. Member, Modesto Chamber of Commerce Bd. of Directors; Stanislaus County YMCA Bd. of Directors; Modesto Rotary Club. Past President, Bridgeport School PTA. Completed two terms on Modesto City Council, 1991–97. Recipient, Hispanic Chamber of Commerce's "Friend of the Year" award in 1995 and Stanislaus County YMCA President's Award in 1998. Vice Chair, Committee on Rules. Co-Chair, Assembly Legislative Ethics Committee. Member, Committees on Agriculture; Budget; Joint Committee on Rules.

COHN, Rebecca (D) 24th District. Assistant Majority Floor Leader. Elected 2000. Business Consultant. Native Californian born March 30, 1954, in Vallejo. Received B.S., University of Texas at Galveston—Medical Branch, 1976. Married, husband, Ron; one son: Andrew. Member, AIPAC; DAWN; Board of Directors, Support Network for Battered Women. Appointee of Santa Clara County Board of Supervisors to the Domestic Violence Council. In 1992 appointed by the Legislature to the California Industrial Medical Council. Former Member and Chair, American Physical Therapy Association's Advisory Panel on Women. Former participant, Diversity Task Force Joint Venture Silicon Valley. Chair, Select Committee on Domestic Violence. Member, Committees on Arts, Entertainment, Sports, Tourism, and Internet Media; Health; Public Safety; Utilities and Commerce.

COTO, Joe (D) 23rd District. Elected 2004. Educator/School Superintendent. Born in Miami, Arizona. Established residence in California in 1957. Received B.A., Teaching Credential, California Western University; Administrative Credential, CSU Hayward; M.A., University of Phoenix. Married, wife, Camille; children: Sylvia and Lisa Marie. Served as Chair, Mexican Plaza Cultural Art Centers in San Jose; President, Latino Democratic Forum. Member, Joint Venture Silicon Valley; Lucille Packard Children's Hospital. Former Council Member, City of Oakland. Served as Superintendent, Oakland Unified; East Side Union High School District in San Jose. Chair, Select Committee on Urban Education in California. Member, Committees on Budget; Education; Governmental Organization; Human Services; Rules; Joint Committee on Rules.

DAUCHER, Lynn (R) 72nd District. Elected 2000. Teacher/Legislator. Born September 20, 1946, in Washington D.C. Established residence in California in 1971. Received B.S., University of Rochester. Married, husband, Don; four children: Brian, Jill, Carl, and Kelly. Member, various local Chambers of Commerce; Kiwanis; Republican Women Federated. Served on Brea Olinda Unified Board of Education, 1981–94; Brea City Council, 1994–2000. Former Board Member, Orange Sanitation Board. Former Commissioner, Orange County Integrated Waste Management Board. Chair, Select Committee on Olmstead Implementation. Vice Chair, Aging and Long-Term Care. Member, Committees on Budget; Water, Parks and Wildlife.

DE LA TORRE, Hector (D) 50th District. Assistant Whip. Elected 2004. Full-time Legislator. Graduated Occidental College; George Washington University's Elliot School of Internal Affairs. Married, wife, Christine; three children: Elinor, Henrik, Emilia. Served on South Gate City Council, 1997–2004, including two years as Mayor. South Gate representative to Executive Board of Gateway Cities Council of Government. Member, San Gabriel and Lower Los Angeles Mountains and River Conservancy. Former, Assistant to the Deputy Secretary of Labor in Clinton Administration; judicial administrator for Superior Court in Los Angeles County. Chair, Budget Subcommittee No. 1 on Health and Human Services. Member, Committees on Budget; Environmental Safety and Toxic Materials; Local Government; Utilities and Commerce; Joint Legislative Budget.

DE VORE, Chuck (R) 70th District. Elected 2004. Aerospace Executive. Born May 20, 1962, in Seattle, Washington. Established residence in California in 1976. Received B.A. with honors in Strategic Studies, Claremont McKenna College; Command and General Staff College, U.S. Army. Reservist in California Army National Guard since 1988. Former Commissioner, City of Irvine, 1991–96. Elected member of the Orange County Republican Party Central Committee, 1992–2002. Recipient, Claremont Institute Lincoln Fellow, 2004. Served in Reagan Administration as Special Assistant for Foreign Affairs in DOD, 1986–88. Former Senior Assistant, Congressman Chris Cox, 1988–90. Vice Chair, Committee on Veterans Affairs. Member, Committees on Budget; Revenue and Taxation.

DYMALLY, Mervyn M. (D) 52nd District. Elected 2002. Legislator/ University Professor. Born May 12, 1926, in Cedros, Trinidad and Tobago, British West Indies. Established residence in California in 1949. Received B.A., CSU, Los Angeles; M.A., CSU, Sacramento; Ph.D., USIU, San Diego. Married, wife, Alice Cueno; children: Mark and Lynn. Former Member, State Assembly 1963–66. Served as State Senator 1967–75; Lieutenant Governor, California 1975–79; U.S. Congress 1981–93. Chair, Coalition of Black Elected Officials and Retirees. Former Chair, Congressional Black Caucus; Subcommittee on Africa. Member, Caribbean American Coalition; NAACP; African American Political Institute; Consul, Republic of Benin, West Africa. Chair, Budget Subcommittee No. 2 on Education Finance; Select Committees on Critical Issues; Community Colleges. Member, Committees on Budget; Health; Public Safety; Rules; Water, Parks and Wildlife; Joint Committee on Rules.

EMMERSON, William J. (R) 63rd District. Elected 2002. Orthodontist. Born October 28, 1945, in Oakland. Received B.A. in History and Political Science, La Sierra University; D.D.S. and M.S. (Orthodontics), Loma Linda University. Married, wife, Nan; children: Kate and Caroline. Member, American Dental Association; California Dental Association; American Association of Orthodontists; Pacific Coast Society of Orthodontists; Tri-County Dental Society; Redlands Evening Kiwanis; San Bernardino County Republican Central Committee. Fellow, International College of Dentists; American College of Dentists. Vice Chair, Riverside Community College Task Force, dental hygiene credential program. Vice Chair, Committee on Local Government. Member, Committees on Appropriations; Water, Parks and Wildlife.

EVANS, Noreen (D) 7th District. Elected 2004. Attorney. Native Californian born April 22, 1955, in San Diego. Received B.A., CSU Sacramento, 1978; J.D., UOP McGeorge School of Law, 1981. Married, husband, Mark Fudem; children; Erin, Joel, Rachel. Member, Board of Directors of the Leadership Institute of Ecology and the Economy. Served on the Santa Rosa City Council, 1996–2004; Santa Rosa Planning Commission, 1993–96. Chair, Committee on Human Services; Select Committee on Wine. Member, Committees on Budget; Judiciary; Veterans Affairs.

FROMMER, Dario, Majority Floor Leader / Majority Leader of the Assembly. For biography see page 288.

GARCIA, Bonnie (R) 80th District. Elected 2002. Businesswoman. Established residence in California in 1985. Received B.S. in Workforce Education and Development, Southern Illinois University. Mother of Melissa and Javier. Served as the City of Coachella's first Director of Housing and Neighborhood Services. Legislative priorities include job creation and retention, women's health, identity theft, sexual predator tracking, and children's and disabled welfare. Chair, Assembly Republican Hispanic Woman's Caucus. Vice Chair, Committee on Housing and Community Development. Member, Committees on Governmental Organization; Jobs, Economic Development, and the Economy.

GOLDBERG, Jackie (D) 45th District. Elected 2000. Teacher/ Legislator. Native Californian born November 18, 1944 in Los Angeles. Received B.A., U.C. Berkeley; M.A.T., University of Chicago. Entered domestic partnership October 1, 1979; spouse, Sharon Stricker; one child: Brian. Member, NOW; NWPC; Advisory Com. of LACER; Advisory Board, L.A. Film School; Highland Park Ebell Club. Former Member, CFT; CTA. Served on LAUSD Board of Education, 1983–91; L.A. City Council, 1993–2000. Co-founder of "STARS," an after-school program for central city middle schools. Chair, Committee on Education. Member, Committees on Budget; Environmental Safety and Toxic Materials; Public Safety; Joint Legislative Audit Committee; Joint Legislative Budget.

GORDON, Mike (D)

53rd District.

Died in Office
June 25, 2005.

For Biography
See Page 329.

HANCOCK, Loni (D) 14th District. Elected 2002. Full-time Legislator. Born April 10, 1940, in Chicago, Illinois. Established residence in California in 1964. Received B.A., Ithaca College, New York; M. Social Psychology, Wright Institute, Berkeley. Married, husband, Tom Bates, former Assembly Member 1976–96; four children, six grandchildren. Founding Member, Bay Area Partnership; East Bay Public Safety Corridor Partnership. Former Head, Western Regional Office of the U.S. Dept. of Education, 1994–2001. Elected Mayor of Berkeley, 1986–94. Former Executive Director, Shalon Foundation, 1980–86. Served on Berkeley City Council, 1971–79. Chair, Committee on Natural Resources. Member, Committees on Budget; Education; Housing and Community Development.

HARMAN, Tom (R) 67th District. Elected 2000. Attorney. Native Californian born May 30, 1941, in Pasadena. Received B.S., Kansas State University, 1963; J.D., Loyola University of Los Angeles, 1968. Married, wife, Dianne; two children: Michael and Michelle. Veteran, U.S. Army, 1963–65. Member, Orange County Bar Association; Huntington Beach Chamber of Commerce; Huntington Beach Tomorrow; Bolsa Chica Land Trust; Sierra Club. Past President, Huntington Beach Youth Shelter; Huntington Beach Rotary Club. Served on Huntington Beach City Council, 1995–2000. Vice Chair, Committee on Judiciary. Member, Committees on Arts, Entertainment, Sports, Tourism, and Internet Media; Natural Resources.

HAYNES, Ray (R) 66th District. Assistant Leader. Elected 2002. Lawyer. Native Californian born August 26, 1954, in Merced. Former Member of the Assembly, 1992–94; State Senator, 1994–2002. Graduated California Lutheran Univ., 1976; Masters in Public Admin., 1981, Eastern Kentucky Univ.; J.D., 1980, U.S.C. Married, wife, Pam; daughters: Jennifer Salwender, Caitlin, and Sarah. Former Member, Bd. of Directors, Riverside Youth Service Center. Former Chair, Moreno Valley Comm. Assistance Prog. Former Chair, Comm. for No New Taxes; Treasurer, Citizens for Property Rights. Member, Rotary Club Planning Commissioner; Riverside and San Bernardino County Bar Assns.; Moreno Valley C. of C.; Riverside Citizens for Responsible Behavior; Western Center for Law and Religious Freedom. Former Member, Bd. of the Moreno Valley Rep. Forum; Murrieta-Temecula Rep. Assembly. Served as National Chairman, 2000 American Legislative Exchange Council; State Co-Chair of the Calif. Conference of the Family. Vice Chair, Committee on Human Services. Member, Committees on Appropriations; Judiciary.

HORTON, Jerome E. (D) 51st District. Elected 2000. Accountant/Business Tax and Real Estate Consultant. Born Sept. 14, 1956, in Pine Bluff, Arkansas. Established residence in California in 1962. Received B.A. in Finance and Accounting, California State University, Dominguez Hills. Married, wife, Yvonne; two children: Myeshia and Mathew. Board Member, Centinella Juvenile Diversion Project. Served as Councilman and Mayor pro Tempore, City of Inglewood 1977–2000. Former Legislative Deputy and Business Tax Advisor for the 3rd District of the Board of Equalization. Recipient, Outstanding Young Man of America Award, 1978; Legislator of the Year Award, African American Chamber of Commerce. Chair, Committee on Governmental Organization. Member, Committees on Arts, Entertainment, Sports, Tourism, and Internet Media; Banking and Finance; Utilities and Commerce.

HORTON, Shirley A. (R) 78th District. Elected 2002. Businesswoman. Received B.S. in Accounting, San Diego State University. Married, husband, Luther. Member, Scripps Memorial Hospital Community Advisory Board; Chamber of Commerce; South Bay Family YMCA. Served on Chula Vista City Council, 1991–94; Mayor, Chula Vista, 1994–2002. Member, SANDAG Executive Committee. Former Chair, Transportation Comm. of SANDAG. Former Member, San Diego Airport Authority. Vice Chair, Committee on Business and Professions. Member, Committees on Higher Education; Transportation.

HOUSTON, Guy Spencer (R) 15th District. Elected 2002. Mortgage Broker/Real Estate. Native Californian born October 20, 1960, in Walnut Creek. Received B.S. in Business Administration, St. Mary's College, Moraga, 1982; M.B.A., St. Mary's College, Moraga, 1987. Certified Financial Planner, (CFP), 1991. Married, wife, Ingeborg; children: Barlett, Sumner, and Glynnis. Served as Councilman, City of Dublin, 1992–94. Former Mayor of Dublin, 1994–2001. Vice Chair, Committee on Jobs, Economic Development, and the Economy. Member, Committees on Labor and Employment; Local Government.

HUFF, Bob (R) 60th District. Elected 2004. Commodity Wholesaler. Native Californian born September 9, 1953, in Calexico. Received B.A., Westmont College, Santa Barbara. Married, wife, Mei Mei; children: Adam (wife, Hope), J.J., Jessica, Jeff. Founding member of the Tres Hermanos Conservation Authority. Member, California Lincoln Club; Diamond Bar Chamber of Commerce; Walnut Valley Rotary Club; Diamond Bar Improvement Association; U.S. Pacific Rim Chamber of Commerce. Served on the Diamond Bar City Council, 1995–2004; Mayor, 1997 and 2001. Served on the Executive Boards of Alameda Corridor East (ACE) Construction Authority; San Gabriel Valley Council of Governments (SGVCOG); Foothill Transit; SGVCOG Transportation Committee. Vice Chair, Committee on Transportation. Member, Committees on Budget; Education.

JONES, Dave (D) 9th District. Elected 2004. Attorney. Graduate Depauw University; Harvard Law School; Harvard's Kennedy School of Government. Married, wife, Kim; two children: Isabelle and William. Former Council Member, Sacramento City Council. Served as Chairperson of the Sacramento Regional Transit District. Former Mem- ber, Sacramento Metropolitan Cable Commission; Sacramento Regional Transit District; Sacramento Solid Waste Authority; Sacramento Transit Authority. Former legal aid attorney, Legal Services of Northern California; Counsel to United States Attorney General Janet Reno. Awarded White House Fellowship, 1995. Chair, Committee on Judiciary. Member, Committees on Health; Public Employees, Retirement and Social Security; Revenue and Taxation.

KARNETTE, Betty (D) 54th District. Elected 2004. Teacher/Education Consultant. Former State Senator, 1996–2004. Former Member, State Assembly 1992–94. Native Kentuckian born in Paducah. Established residence in California in 1952. Graduate of CSU Long Beach with B.A. and Master's Degree. Married, husband, Richard; one daughter, Mary. Member, Board of Directors of the Long Beach Memorial Hospital Children's Clinic; Associate Board Member, Sage House in San Pedro. Chair, Select Committee on Ports. Member, Committees on Appropriations; Arts, Entertainment, Sports, Tourism, and Internet Media; Insurance; Rules; Transportation; Joint Committee on Rules.

KEENE, Rick (R) 3rd District. Assistant Leader. Elected 2002. Attorney. Native Californian born November 16, 1957, in Crescent City. Received B.A. in Psychology and Religious Studies from CSU, Chico; J.D., Cal Northern School of Law. Married, wife, Janice; children: Lucy, Caitlin, Rosie, Chris, and Erin. Founding Board Member, City Servant Ministries. Elder, Chico Neighborhood Church. Served on Chico City Planning Commission, 1992–94. Former City Councilmember and Mayor of Chico, 1994–2002. Member, Butte County LAFCO; Butte County Air Quality Board; Butte County Assn. of Government. Former Chair, Chico Finance Committee, 1998–2002. Vice Chair, Committee on Budget. Member, Committees on Natural Resources; Utilities and Commerce.

KLEHS, Johan (D) 18th District. Elected 2004. Former Member and Chair, Board of Equalization, 1994–2004; former Member, State Assembly, 1982–94. Educator. Native Californian born June 27, 1952, in Alameda. Graduate of CSU Hayward, B.A., Political Science; M.P.A., Public Administration. Board Member, East Bay Cancer Support Group; Chabot College Foundation. Former Council Member, San Leandro City Council, 1979–82. Chair, Committee on Revenue and Taxation. Member, Committees on Appropriations; Elections and Redistricting; Labor and Employment; Joint Legislative Audit Committee.

KORETZ, Paul (D) 42nd District. Elected 2000. Full-time Legislator. Native Californian born April 3, 1955, in Hollywood. Received B.A., U.C.L.A., 1979. Married, wife, Gail; one daughter: Rachel. Member, West Hollywood City Council, 1988–2000; Mayor, 1991–92, 1996–97. Member, West Hollywood Democratic Club; Sierra Club; Jewish Labor Committee; L.A. County Democratic Central Committee. First Southern California Director of the California League of Conservation Voters. Served as Administrative Director of the Ecology Center of Southern California. Founder, Cynthia Alliance Neighborhood Watch Group. Chair, Labor and Employment; Select Committee on Gun Violence Prevention. Member, Committees on Arts, Entertainment, Sports, Tourism, and Internet Media; Business and Professions; Natural Resources.

LA MALFA, Douglas Lee (R) 2nd District. Republican Whip. Elected 2002. Farmer. Native Californian born July 2, 1960, in Oroville. Received Bachelor's degree in Ag/Business, Cal-Poly, San Luis Obispo. Married, wife, Jill; children: Kyle, Allison, Sophia, and Natalie. Member, Richvale Hunting Area; Shelby Automobile Club. Served on the California Rice Commission. Recipient, "Legislator of the Year" from California Women in Timber 2003 and 2004. Vice Chair, Committee on Natural Resources. Member, Committees on Arts, Entertainment, Sports, Tourism, and Internet Media; Banking and Finance.

LA SUER, Jay (R) 77th District. Elected 2000. Law Enforcement/Legislator. Born January 24, 1940, in Hutchinson, Kansas. Established residence in California in 1940. Received B.A. in Public Administration, San Diego State University. Graduate FBI National Academy. Served in 101st Airborne Division, U.S. Army. Married, two daughters, three grandchildren. Former Councilmember, La Mesa City Council, 1990–2000. Thirty-one years of law enforcement. Appointed to Board of Directors, Metropolitan Transit Development Board, 1991. Elected to San Diego Republican Central Committee, 1998. Recipient, "Legislator of the Year" from San Diego Associated Builders and Contractors, 1994; "Member of Distinction Award," Boy Scouts of America, 1994; "Samuel Adams Award of Outstanding Leadership," 1999. Vice Chair, Committee on Public Safety. Member, Committees on Governmental Organization; Housing and Community Development.

LAIRD, John (D) 27th District. Elected 2002. Full-time Legislator. Native Californian born March 29, 1950, in Santa Rosa. Received A.B. with honors in Politics, Adlai Stevenson College, U.C. Santa Cruz, 1972. Partner, John Flores. Former Member, Santa Cruz Transportation Comm.; Santa Cruz Transit District Board. Former

President, Association of Monterey Bay Area Governments. Founding Board Member, Santa Cruz AIDS Project. Served on Santa Cruz City Council, 1981–90; Mayor, 1983–84, 1987. Former Cabrillo College Trustee, 1994–2002; Chair, 1998. Former Member Electoral College 1992, 1996, 2000. Chair, Committee on Budget. Vice Chair, Joint Legislative Budget. Member, Committees on Judiciary; Labor and Employment; Natural Resources.

LENO, Mark Richard (D) 13th District. Elected 2002. Business Owner. Born September 24, 1951, in Milwaukee, Wisconsin. Established residence in California in 1977. Received B.A., American College of Jerusalem. Two years of Rabbinical Studies, Hebrew Union College in New York. Former Board Member, LGBT Community Center Project; Haight Ash-

bury Community Services; Mobilization Against AIDS; San Francisco Chamber of Commerce. Former Member, San Francisco County Board of Supervisors, 1998–2002. Former Commissioner, San Francisco Transportation Authority. Former Director, Golden Gate Bridge Highway and Transportation District. Delegate to Democratic National Convention in Los Angeles, August 2000. Chair, Committee on Public Safety. Member, Committees on Appropriations; Elections and Redistricting; Labor and Employment.

LESLIE, Tim (R) 4th District. Elected 2000. Served as State Senator, First District, 1991–2000. Former State Assembly Member 1986–1991. Legislator/ Businessman. Born February 4, 1942, in Ashland, Oregon. First established residence in California in 1944. Graduated CSU, Long Beach, B.S., Pol. Sci.; and USC, M.S., Pub. Admin. Married to Clydene; children: Debbie and Scott; three grandchildren. Founding director of "Community Action Against Drug Abuse Task Force." Chair, International Board of Advisers For Hope Unlimited For Children. Named Legislator of the Year by the California School Boards Association; Sacramento Taxpayers' League. Authored the Brady-Jared Teen Driver Safety Act of 1997; Lake Tahoe Special License Plate Program; coauthored the Leslie-Hertzberg Witness Protection Act. Founded California Community Renewal Project. Vice Chair, Committee on Higher Education. Member, Committees on Judiciary; Joint Legislative Audit Committee.

LEVINE, Lloyd Edward (D) 40th District. Assistant Whip. Elected 2002. Full-time Legislator. Native Californian born July 3, 1969, in Burbank. Received B.A. in Studio Art, U.C. Riverside, 1992. Completed course work M.A., Public Policy and Administration, CSU, Sacramento. Member, U.C. Riverside Alumni Scholarship Review Committee; Calif. Alliance for Pride and Equality (CAPE); Sierra Club; Friends of the River; Simon Wiesenthal Museum of Tolerance; the Executives; L.A. City and San Fernando Valley, Young Democrats; Actions Democrats. Former Legislative Director for Assembly Member John Longville. Chair, Committee on Utilities and Commerce. Member, Committees on Elections and Redistricting; Governmental Organization; Judiciary.

LIEBER, Sally J. (D) 22nd District. Appointed Assistant Speaker pro Tempore February 9, 2004. Elected 2002. Full-time Legislator. Born April 24, 1961, in Detroit, Michigan. Established residence in California in 1986. Attended Stanford University. Married, husband, David Phillips. Former Mayor and Council member of Mountain
View. Former Board member of the Valley Transportation Authority. Served as Chair, Santa Clara Valley Water Commission; Santa Clara County Social Services Commission. Past President, YWCA of the Mid-Peninsula. Former Board member, League of Women Voters. Member, Sierra Club; NOW; National Women's Political Caucus; PFLAG; CEWAER. Chair, Select Committee on Mobilehomes. Member, Committees on Insurance; Judiciary; Local Government; Revenue and Taxation.

LIU, Carol (D) 44th District. Elected 2000. Educator. Native Californian born September 12, 1941, in Berkeley. Received B.A., San Jose State College, 1963; Lifetime Teaching Credential (1964); Administrative Credential (1978), U.C. Berkeley School of Education. Married, husband, Michael Peevey; three children: Jared, Maria,
and Darcie. Past Board President, Pasadena City College Foundation, 1997–99; CORO Foundation (Southern Calif.), 1994–2000. Member, U.C. Berkeley Foundation; Kiwanis Club of La Cañada; Assistance League of Flintridge. Former Member, La Cañada Flintridge City Council, 1992–2000; Mayor 1996 and 1999. Awarded NOW Legislator of the Year, 2004. Chair, Committee on Higher Education; Select Committee on Adult Education. Member, Committees on Education; Governmental Organization; Transportation.

MATTHEWS, Barbara S. (D) 17th District. Elected 2000. Government Relations Manager. Born November 26, 1939, in Port Huron, Michigan. Established residence in California in 1956. Received A.A., Chabot College. Married, husband, Barry; children: Paul and Dawn (deceased). Former Member, Tracy Planning Commission 1987–91; Tracy City Council, 1991–2000; Mayor pro Tem, 1998–2000; Delta Protection Commission, 1999–2000; San Joaquin County Integrated Waste Management Task Force, 1991–2000. Served on Tracy Economic Development Committee, 1991–2000; Tracy Investment Committee, 1998–2000. Chair, Committee on Agriculture; Select Committee on the Development of a 10th University of California, Merced Campus. Member, Committees on Arts, Entertainment, Sports, Tourism, and Internet Media; Higher Education; Water, Parks and Wildlife.

MAZE, Bill (R) 34th District. Elected 2002. Building Contractor/Farmer. Native Californian born April 9, 1946, in Woodlake. Received B.S., California Polytechnic College, San Luis Obispo, 1968. Married, wife, Rebecca; five children and four grandchildren. Veteran, U.S. Army. Former Chairman and Member of Tulare County Board of Supervisors; Economic Development Corporation and Business Incentive Zone Council. Past President of San Joaquin Valley Supervisors Association. Past Director of California State Association of Counties; Visalia Chamber of Commerce; Pro Youth Visalia, Inc.; Boys and Girls Club. Member of the Central California Resource Advisory Council for the Federal Bureau of Land Management; California Farm Bureau; Woodlake Rotary Club. Vice Chair, Committee on Agriculture. Member, Committees on Business and Professions; Water, Parks and Wildlife.

McCARTHY, Kevin, Republican Leader of the Assembly. For biography see page 290.

MONTAÑEZ, Cindy (D) 39th District. Elected 2002. Full-time Legislator. Native Californian born January 19, 1974, in Los Angeles. Attended UCLA. Member, San Fernando Valley National Women's Caucus; Sierra Club. Board Member, Project Grad. Elected to San Fernando City Council, 1999; Mayor, 2001. Appointed Cultural Arts Commissioner for the City of San Fernando. Served as legislative aide to former Los Angeles City Councilman Richard Alarcón. Named 2005 Legislator of the Year by California Parks and Recreation Society. Chair, Committee on Rules; Select Committee on Environmental Justice; Joint Committee on Rules. Member, Committees on Budget; Health; Judiciary; Utilities and Commerce.

MOUNTJOY, Dennis L. (R) 59th District. Elected 2000. Small Businessman. Native Californian born February 12, 1957, in Pasadena. Two children: Tammy and Nicholas and one grandchild, Diego. Member, Lincoln Club; California Republican Assembly. Selected American Legion (CA) "Legislator of the Year;" Mother's Against Drunk Driving 2002 award. Member, Committees on Governmental Organization; Insurance; Transportation.

MULLIN, Gene (D) 19th District. Elected 2002. Educator. Native Californian born April 21, 1937, in San Francisco. Received B.S. in Political Science, USF; Lifetime Standard Teaching Credential, USF. Married, wife, Terri; children: Jennifer and Kevin; three grandsons. Veteran, U.S. Army, 1959–60. Member, Calif. Teachers Assn.; Young Men's Institute; SSF Historical Society; United Irish Cultural Center; San Mateo County Retired Teachers Assn.; League of Women Voters. Served on South San Francisco City Council, 1995–2002; Mayor, 1998, 2001–02. Representative on Regional Planning Commission, ABAG; Executive Board, ABAG. Chair, SFO Airport Roundtable. Chair, Committee on Housing and Community Development; Chair, Select Committee on Biotechnology. Member, Committees on Budget; Education; Public Employees, Retirement and Social Security.

NAKANISHI, Alan (R) 10th District. Elected 2002. Physician. Native Californian born March 21, 1940, in Sacramento. Received B.A. Chemistry, Pacific Union College; M.C. Loma Linda University; Master Health Administration, Virginia Commonwealth University/Medical College of Virginia. Residency USC/LA County Medical Center and fellowship, Pacific Medical Center. Fellow, American College of Surgeons (F.A.C.S.). Married, wife, Sue; daughters, Pam and Jennifer; son Jon. Veteran, U.S. Army, Major. Co-founder, Delta Eye Medical Group. Member, Lodi City Council (1998–2002). Member San Joaquin Groundwater Banking Authority; San Joaquin Water Advisory Commission. Chairman San Joaquin Integrated Waste Management Task Force. Alternate San Joaquin Council of Governments. Former Mayor of Lodi, 2000–01. Member, Lodi Rotary since 1998. Vice Chair, Committee on Labor and Employment. Member, Committees on Appropriations; Health.

NATION, Joe (D) 6th District. Elected 2000. Teacher/Businessman. Born July 18, 1956, in Dallas, Texas. Established residence in California in 1982. Received B.A. from University of Colorado; M.S., Georgetown University; Ph.D., Rand Graduate School; Post-Doctoral Fellowship, Stanford University. Married, wife, Linda Nicolay-Nation; children: Kristen and Alexandra. Former Member, Marin Municipal Water District Board, 1993–2000; California Department of Education, Curriculum Development Commission. Member, Committees on Appropriations; Business and Professions; Human Services; Local Government.

NAVA, Pedro (D) 35th District. Elected 2004. Attorney. Born February 6, 1948, in Monterey, Nuevo Leon, Mexico. Received B.A. from CSU, San Bernardino; J.D., U.C. Davis, Martin Luther King School of Law. Married, wife, Susan; child: Jedd. Served in U.S. National Guard. Former Deputy District Attorney in both Fresno and Santa Barbara counties. President, Santa Barbara County Action Network. Past President, Santa Barbara Hispanic Chamber of Commerce; Santa Barbara and Ventura Colleges of Law Board of Trustees. Member, Santa Barbara County Partners in Education; Santa Barbara Public Education Foundation. Served on California Coastal Commission, 1997–2004. Chair, Subcommittee No. 5 on Information Technology/Transportation. Member, Committees on Budget; Higher Education; Insurance; Natural Resources; Joint Legislative Audit Committee.

NEGRETE McLEOD, Gloria (D) 61st District. Assistant Whip. Elected 2000. Full-time Legislator. Native Californian born September 6, 1941, in Los Angeles. Received A.A., Chaffey College. Married, husband, Gilbert; ten children, 27 grandchildren, nine great-grandchildren. Former President, Chaffey Community College Board. Former Member, Air Quality Management District Children's Air Quality Advisory Board. Served as Chair, Calif. Assn. of Latino Community College Trustees. Recipient, Latina Leadership Network, 1999 Madrina Award. Member, Commission on the Status of Women; National Women's Political Caucus of Calif.; Girl Scouts. Chair, Committee on Business and Professions; Select Committee on the Alameda Corridor East. Member, Committees on Governmental Organization; Health; Public Employees, Retirement and Social Security.

NIELLO, Roger (R) 5th District. Elected 2004, CPA/Business Owner. Native Californian born June 2, 1948, in San Francisco. Received B.S. in Accounting and Information Systems, U.C. Berkeley in 1970; M.S., Accounting and Information systems, U.C.L.A., 1971. Married, wife, Mary; five children: Matt, Eric, Kevin, Lisa, and Patrick. Member, Sacramento Rotary. Served on Sacramento County Board of Supervisors, 1999–2004. Former Chair, Sacramento Transportation Authority 2002; Sacramento Public Library Authority 2003; Sacramento Solid Waste Authority 2004. Past President, Sacramento Metropolitan Chamber of Commerce 1995. Working group member, Sacramento Regional Water Forum 1995–98. Former member, Sacramento County District Attorney's Citizen's Cabinet, 1996–98. Former Director of Valley Vision/Regional Action Partnership Board. Vice Chair, Committee on Banking and Finance. Member, Committees on Public Employees, Retirement and Social Security; Transportation.

NUÑEZ, Fabian, Speaker of the Assembly. For biography see page 287.

OROPEZA, Jenny (D) 55th District. Elected 2000. Full-time Legislator. Native Californian born September 27, 1957, in Montebello. Attended Cal State University, Long Beach. Married, husband, Tom Mullins. Served on Long Beach Unified School District Board, 1988–94; Long Beach City Council, 1994–2000. Board Member, Metropoli-

tan Transportation Authority; National League of Cities; National Association of Latino Elected Officials. President, Hispanic Local Elected Officials. Member, CA State University Board of Trustees. Founding Member, Long Beach Chapter American Diabetes Association. Chair, Committee on Transportation; Select Committee on Title IX. Member, Committees on Appropriations; Jobs, Economic Development, and the Economy; Veterans Affairs.

PARRA, Nicole M. (D) 30th District. Elected 2002. Full-time Legislator. Native Californian born February 3, 1970, in Bakersfield. Received Bachelor of Arts in Economics from UC Berkeley; Juris Doctorate from Catholic University, Columbus School of Law. Member, American Legion Ladies Auxiliary, Post 682; Hispanas Organized for Po-

litical Equality (H.O.P.E.). Served as mentor in the Puente Project in Visalia and the Hanford Joint Union High School District. Former District Director for Congressman Cal Dooley. Chair, Joint Legislative Audit Committee; Select Committee on Water, Infrastructure and the Economy. Member, Committees on Agriculture; Banking and Finance; Budget; Water, Parks and Wildlife.

PAVLEY, Fran (D) 41st District. Assistant Whip. Elected 2000. Full-time Legislator. Native Californian born November 11, 1948, in Los Angeles. Received, B.A., CSU, Fresno; M.A., CSU, Northridge. Married, husband, Andy; two children: Jennifer and David. Served as four term Mayor and Councilmember of Agoura Hills (1982–97), including first Mayor of city. Former President, L.A. County Division for the League of California Cities, 1995. Member, California Coastal Commission, 1995–2000. Taught for 28 years in California public schools. Recipient, 2002 Scientific American 50 Award for Policy Leader in Transportation; 2003 Governing Magazine Public Official Award. Chair, Budget Subcommittee No. 3 on Resources; Select Committee on Air and Water Quality. Member, Committees on Budget; Education; Transportation; Water, Parks and Wildlife.

PLESCIA, George A. (R) 75th District. Assistant Leader. Elected 2002. Full-time Legislator. Native Californian born August 19, 1966, in Sacramento. Received B.A. in Government, CSU at Sacramento. Member, Adam Smith Institute of California; San Diego County Republican Central Committee. Appointed by San Diego Mayor Dick Murphy to the Mayor's Sorrento Valley Traffic Subcommittee. Former Regional Director for State Senator Bill Morrow. Vice Chair, Committee on Governmental Organization. Member, Committees on Budget; Veterans Affairs.

RICHMAN, Keith Stuart (R) 38th District. Elected 2000. Physician. Assistant Republican Leader. Born November 21, 1953, in Syracuse, New York. Established residence in California in 1956. Attended U.C. Davis; Received M.D. and M.P.H. from U.C.L.A. Married, wife, Deborah; two daughters: Rachel and Dina. Co-founder, North San Fernando Valley Community Foundation. Founding President, American Diabetes Association, San Fernando Valley Chapter. Chairman Emeritus, Valley Community Clinic. Member, Community Advisory Board, Valley Community Clinic; Sun Valley Rotary and Rotary Foundation. Member, Committees on Education; Health.

RIDLEY-THOMAS, Mark (D) 48th District. Elected 2002. Civil rights Advocate/Educator. Democratic Caucus Chair. Native Californian born November 6, 1954, in Los Angeles. Received Bachelor's Degree in Social Relations; Master's Degree in Religious Studies from Immaculate Heart College; Ph.D. in Social Ethics, University of Southern California. Married, wife, Avis Ridley-Thomas; children: Sinclair and Sebastian (twin sons). Member, Board of United Way; Aspen Institute Domestic Strategy Group; USC School of Policy, Planning and Development Board of Councilors. Board Member, Alternate Living for the Aging. Former Executive Director, Southern Christian Leadership Conference, 1981–1991. Former Member, Los Angeles City Council, 1991–2002. Served on L.A. Coliseum Commission. Chair, Select Committee on the Los Angeles Health Care Crisis. Member, Committees on Appropriations; Health; Transportation; Utilities and Commerce.

RUNNER, Sharon (R) 36th District. Assistant Leader. Chair, Republican Women's Caucus. Elected 2002. Businesswoman. Native Californian born May 17, 1954, in Los Angeles. Attended Antelope Valley College. Married, husband, George; children: Micah and Rebekah. First husband and wife to serve in Legislature concurrently in California history. Member, Board of Directors, United Way; Antelope Valley Hospital Gift Foundation Board; Antelope Valley Crime Task Force; Healthy Homes Advisory Council Carenet Pregnancy Resource Center. Former Board Member, Antelope Valley Fair District. Vice Chair, Committee on Appropriations. Member, Committees on Veterans Affairs; Water, Parks and Wildlife.

RUSKIN, Ira (D) 21st District. Elected 2004. Marketing Communications Consultant. Born November 12, 1943, in New York City. Received B.A. History, UC Berkeley; M.A., Communications, Stanford University. Former Board Member, Redwood City Education Foundation. Member, Temple Beth Jacob; Redwood City, San Mateo County NAACP; Advisory Board, San Mateo County Organization of Chinese Americans. Served on Redwood City Council, 1995–2004; Mayor, 1999–2001. Chair, Bay Area Water Supply and Conservation Agency; San Francisco Bay Area Regional Water System Financing Authority; San Mateo County Transportation Authority; San Mateo County Criminal Justice Council. Chair, Committee on Environmental Safety and Toxic Materials; Select Committee on Nanotechnology and Emerging Technologies. Member, Committees on Banking and Finance; Higher Education.

SALDAÑA, Lori (D) 76th District. Assistant Whip. Elected 2004. Educator. Native Californian born November 7, 1958, in San Diego. Received B.A. and M.A. from San Diego State University. Member, Faculty Association of California Community Colleges; American Federation of Teachers. First Chairwoman, City of San Diego's Wet- lands Advisory Board, 1992–94; United States Chairwoman, Border Environment Cooperation Commission's Advisory Council, 2000–03. Environmental Policy Research Fellow, Center for US-Mexico Studies at the University of California San Diego, 2003. Director of Service Learning, San Diego Mesa College, 2002. Recipient of Sierra Club's Conservation Activist of the Year Award and Special Achievement Award. Chair, Select Committee on Bioethics, Medicine and Technology. Member, Committees on Appropriations; Natural Resources; Veterans Affairs; Water, Parks and Wildlife.

SALINAS, Simón (D) 28th District. Elected 2000. Teacher/Professor. Born October 8, 1955, in Slayton, Texas. Established residence in California in 1965. Received B.A., Claremont McKenna College, 1978; Bilingual Teaching Credential, San Jose State University, 1981; J.D., Santa Clara Law School, 1984. One child. Member, NACO; NALEO; LULAC #2055; Salinas Chamber of Commerce; Filipino American Community Club; Boys and Girls Club; Partners for Peace; Natividad Medical Center Citizen Advisory Bd. Former Councilmember and Mayor pro Tem, City of Salinas, 1989–93. Served as Supervisor for Monterey Cnty., 1993–99. Past President, Salinas Valley Solid Waste Authority, 1999; past Chair, Central Coast Alliance for Health, 1999. Chair, Committee on Local Government; Select Committee on Rural Economic Development. Member, Committees on Agriculture; Housing and Community Development; Transportation.

SPITZER, Todd Allan (R) 71st District. Republican Whip. Elected 2002. Attorney. Native Californian born November 26, 1960, in Whittier. Received B.A., U.C.L.A; M.A. in Public Policy, U.C. Berkeley; J.D., Hastings College of the Law. Married, wife, Jamie; son, Justin Tyler. Served ten years as LAPD Reserve Officer. Advisory Board Member, Mothers Against Drunk Driving; Board Member, Santa Ana Education Foundation. Former Orange County Supervisor. Former Chair, Orange County Transportation Authority; Orange County Fire Authority. Member, Committees on Human Services; Public Safety.

STRICKLAND, Audra (R) 37th District. Elected 2004. Teacher. Native Californian born July 10, 1974, in Newport Beach. Received B.A. in Political Science from UC Irvine. Married, husband, Tony. Former Member, Ventura County Board of Education. Appointed to Milton Marks "Little Hoover" Commission on California State Government Organization and Economy. Vice Chair, Committee on Arts, Entertainment, Sports, Tourism, and Internet Media. Member, Committees on Environmental Safety and Toxic Materials; Health.

TORRICO, Alberto (D) 20th District. Assistant Whip. Elected 2004. Attorney. Native Californian born March 18, 1969, in San Francisco. Received B.S., Political Science, Santa Clara University; J.D., Hastings College of the Law. Married, wife, Raquel Andrade-Torrico; two children: Mateo and Amy-Elyzabeth. Member, Newark Chamber

of Commerce; Kindango; Second Chance; Waste Management Authority; Alameda County Hispanic Chamber of Commerce. Chair, 20th Assembly District Democratic Committee. Former, Council Member and Vice-Mayor, City of Newark. Chair, Committee on Public Employees, Retirement and Social Security. Member, Committees on Governmental Organization; Housing and Community Development; Transportation.

TRAN, Van (R) 68th District. Elected 2004. Legislator/Attorney. Born in Saigon, Vietnam, in October, 1964. Established residence in California in 1980. Received B.A., U.C. Irvine; M.P.A., Hamline University; J.D., Hamline University School of Law. Married, wife, Cindy Tran. Member, Garden Grove Chamber of Commerce.

Life member, American Council of Young Political Leaders (ACYPL); California State Bar. Served on Garden Grove Planning Commission (1998–2000). Former Councilman and Mayor pro Tempore, City of Garden Grove (2000–04). Former staff aide to U.S. Congressman Bob Dornan and former State Senator Ed Royce. Founder, Vietnamese-American Voters Coalition (VAVOCO). Vice Chair, Orange County "El Capitan" District Boy Scouts of America. Vice Chair, Committee on Environmental Safety and Toxic Materials. Member, Committees on Banking and Finance; Business and Professions.

UMBERG, Tom (D) 69th District. Elected 2004. Former Member, State Assembly 1990–94. Military Officer/ Prosecutor. Born September 25, 1955, in Cincinnati, Ohio. Established residence in California in 1975. Attended U.C.L.A., B.A. 1977, and Hastings College of the Law, J.D., 1980; M.S., U.S. Army War College. Married, wife, Robin; children: Erin, Brett, and Tommy. Colonel, U.S. Army Reserve. Served on active duty 1981–85; 2004 (two overseas tours). Member, American Legion; Boy Scouts; Reserve Officer's Association. Former Assistant U.S. Attorney; Deputy Director White House Office of Drug Control Policy. Chair, Committee on Elections and Redistricting. Member, Committees on Arts, Entertainment, Sports, Tourism, and Internet Media; Education; Insurance.

VARGAS, Juan (D) 79th District. Elected 2000. Parliamentarian. Legislator/Attorney. Native Californian born March 7, 1961, in National City. Graduate of University of San Diego, B.A. (Magna Cum Laude); Fordham University, M.A.; Harvard University, J.D. Married August 25, 1990, wife, Adrienne; two daughters: Rosa Celina and Helena Jeanne. Served on San Diego City Council, 1993–2000; Deputy Mayor, 1995. Former Chair, City of San Diego Land Use and Housing Committee; Natural Resources and Culture Committee. Former Member, Metropolitan Transit Development Board; California Coastal Commission; Service Authority for Freeway Emergencies (SAFE) Board. Chair, Committee on Insurance; Select Committee on California Latin American Affairs. Member, Committees on Agriculture; Banking and Finance; Business and Professions.

VILLINES, Michael N. (R) 29th District. Republican Whip. Elected 2004. Public Relation/Business Owner. Native Californian born March 30, 1967, in San Jose. Received B.A., Political Science, CSU Fresno in 1990. Married, wife, Christina; three children: Conor, Allison, Joshua. Member, Peoples Church of Fresno; Public Relations Society of America. Served four years in Governor Pete Wilson's administration. Former Chief of Staff to former Assembly Member Chuck Poochigian. Former member, Rural Economic Development Commission. Volunteer, Break the Barriers; Senator Kenneth L. Maddy Institute for Leadership and Ethics at CSU Fresno; Juvenile Rheumatoid Arthritis. Chair, Rural Caucus. Vice Chair, Committee on Water, Parks and Wildlife. Member, Committees on Budget; Elections and Redistricting; Rules; Joint Committee on Rules.

WALTERS, Mimi (R) 73rd District. Republican Whip. Elected 2004. Investment Executive. Native Californian born May 14, 1962, in Pasadena. Received B.A., Political Science, U.C.L.A., 1984. Married, husband, David; children: Katherine, Caroline, David Jr., Tristan. Cofounder of the California Women's Leadership Asso- ciation. Served on the Boards of the National Association of Women Business Owners; Laguna Niguel Republican Women Federated; American Cancer Society; South Coast Medical Center Foundation. Former Council Member, Mayor, City of Laguna Niguel. Vice Chair, Committee on Revenue and Taxation. Member, Committees on Aging and Long-Term Care; Appropriations.

WOLK, Lois (D) 8th District. Elected 2002. Teacher. Born May 12, 1946, in Philadelphia, Pennsylvania. Established residence in California in 1978. Received B.A. from Antioch College in 1968, M.A. from Johns Hopkins School of Advanced International Studies in 1971. Married, husband, Bruce; children: Adam and Daniel. Member, Rotary; Soroptimist; CEWAER board. Served as charter board member of the Davis Science Center (Explorit) and the Yolo Basin Foundation. Founding organizer of the Yolo Land Trust; TREE Davis. Chair, Yolo County Children and Families First Commission. Former Member Davis City Council, 1990–98; Mayor, 1992–94. Former Board Member, Yolo County Bd. of Supervisors, 1998–2002. Named among "Freshman Elite" and awarded "Golden Pedigree" by The California Journal. Awarded "Outstanding Advocate Award 2004" from Easter Seals California. Received 100% voting record in support of environment "Freshman 100" for the 2003 Legislative Year from the California League of Conservation Voters. Named a "Champion of watersheds, wetlands and our coast" by CalCoast, Southern California Wetlands Recovery Project, and the California Watershed Networks. Chair, Water, Parks and Wildlife. Member, Committees on Budget; Local Government; Natural Resources.

WYLAND, Mark (R) 74th District. Republican Whip. Elected 2000. Businessman/Legislator. Native Californian born in 1946, in Escondido. Received B.A., Pomona College; M.A., Columbia University. Recipient Fulbright Scholarship. One daughter, Nicole. Former Member, President, Escondido Union School District. Former Director, Escondido Chamber of Commerce; Ecke Family YMCA. Serves as Trustee, Pomona College. Active participant in the San Diego Children and Families First Commission. Vice Chair, Committees on Education; Elections and Redistricting. Member, Committee on Utilities and Commerce.

YEE, Leland, Speaker pro Tempore of the Assembly. For biography see page 289.

In Memoriam

GORDON, Mike (D) 53rd District. Elected 2004. Business Owner. Native Californian born November 15, 1957, in Lynwood. Received B.S., Political Science, CSU Fullerton, 1978. Married, wife, Denise; children: Ryan, Erika, Amanda, Gordy. Member, El Segundo Kiwanis Club; South Bay and L.A. County Chapters, American Heart As- sociation; South Bay Diabetes Association; El Segundo Education Foundation; Reach Out Against Drugs Committee. Served as Mayor and Council Member, City of El Segundo, 1996–2004. Chair, Committee on Veterans Affairs; Select Committee on Aerospace. Member, Committees on Appropriations; Health; Natural Resources. Died in Office June 25, 2005.

OFFICERS OF
THE ASSEMBLY
(NONMEMBERS)

WILSON, E. Dotson Chief Clerk. Born in Berkeley, Calif., December 11, 1954. U.C.L.A., B.A.; U.C., Hastings College of the Law, J.D. Married to Jacqueline Rene; one daughter: Nicole Frances Rene. Recipient of the 2005 First Annual Jacob Soares Public Service Award by the Legislative Black Caucus Foundation. First elected Chief Clerk January 6, 1992. Reelected Chief Clerk on January 4, 1996; December 2, 1996; December 7, 1998; December 4, 2000; December 2, 2002; December 6, 2004.

PANE, Ronald E. Chief Sergeant at Arms. Born in Sacramento, California February 28, 1956. Four years college, U.S. Secret Service Dignitary Protection School, California Highway Patrol Protection of Public Officials School. Three children: Anthony, Carlo, and Angela. Served in Sergeant at Arms Office since 1979. First elected Chief Sergeant at Arms on April 22, 1996. Reelected on December 2, 1996; April 24, 2000; December 4, 2000; December 2, 2002; December 6, 2004.

PAPPADEMOS, Reverend Constantine C. Chaplain. Elected December 2, 2002; December 6, 2004. Served as Chaplain 1995–98. Pastor, Saint Katherine Church in Elk Grove since 1988. Ordained Deacon in November, 1984, and received Master of Divinity degree from Holy Cross Greek Orthodox School of Theology, Brookline, Massachusetts, 1985. Ordained to the Priesthood on June 30, 1985 in the Church of the Holy Cross, Belmont, California. Married to Presvytera Chrisoula; three children.

MEMBERS OF THE ASSEMBLY—EIGHTY ASSEMBLY MEMBERS

Hon. Fabian Núñez, Speaker, of Los Angeles

Hon. Leland Y. Yee, Speaker pro Tempore, of San Francisco

E. Dotson Wilson, Chief Clerk, of Elk Grove

Ronald E. Pane, Chief Sergeant at Arms, of Sacramento

Reverend Constantine Pappademos, Chaplain, of Elk Grove

(R, Republican; D, Democrat)

Democrat 47, Republican 32, Vacancy 1. Total 80.

Note: Assembly Members elected at General Elections prior to 1974 took office in January of the year following their election; those elected in 1974 and subsequently, took office in December of the year of their election.

Capitol Address of Assembly Members: State Capitol, P.O. Box 942849, Sacramento 94249-0001

Dist.	Name	Occupation	Party	Mailing Address	Legislative service since
	A				
26	Aghazarian, Greg	Small Businessman	R	4557 Quail Lakes, Suite C3, Stockton 95207	Dec. 2002
31	Arambula, Juan	Legislator	D	2550 Mariposa Mall, Room 5031, Fresno 93721	Dec. 2004

	B				
62	Baca, Joe, Jr.	Legislator	D	201 North "E" Street, Suite 205, San Bernardino 92401	Dec. 2004
47	Bass, Karen	Legislator	D	5750 Wilshire Boulevard, Suite 565, Los Angeles 90036	Dec. 2004
64	Benoit, John J.	Law Enforcement	R	1223 University Avenue, Suite 230, Riverside 92507	Dec. 2002
1	Berg, Patty	Social Worker/Legislator	D	50 "D" Street, Suite 450, Santa Rosa 95404	Dec. 2002
56	Bermúdez, Rudy	Law Enforcement	D	12501 E. Imperial Highway, Suite 210, Norwalk 90650	Dec. 2002
33	Blakeslee, Sam	Legislator	R	1302 Marsh Street, San Luis Obispo 93401	Dec. 2004
65	Bogh, Russ [1]	Businessman/Legislator	R	34932 Yucaipa Blvd., Yucaipa 92399	Apr. 2001

[1] Elected at Special Election April 3, 2001.

MEMBERS OF THE ASSEMBLY—EIGHTY ASSEMBLY MEMBERS

Dist.	Name	Occupation	Party	Mailing Address	Legislative service since
	C				
58	Calderon, Ronald S.	Legislator/Real Estate	D	400 North Montebello Blvd., Suite 100, Montebello 90640	Dec. 2002
11	Canciamilla, Joe	Full-time Legislator	D	815 Estudillo Street, Martinez 94553	Dec. 2000
16	Chan, Wilma	Legislator	D	1515 Clay Street, Suite 2204, Oakland 94612	Dec. 2000
57	Chavez, Ed	Full-time Legislator	D	13181 North Crossroads Pkwy., St. 160, City of Industry 91746-3497	Dec. 2000
49	Chu, Judy [2]	Full-time Legislator	D	1255 Corporate Center Dr., Suite PH.9, Monterey Park 91754	May 2001
25	Cogdill, David	Small Business Owner	R	1912 Standiford Avenue, Suite 4, Modesto 95350	Dec. 2000
24	Cohn, Rebecca	Management Consultant	D	100 Paseo De San Antonio, Suite 319, San Jose 95113	Dec. 2000
23	Coto, Joe	Legislator	D	100 Paseo De San Antonio, Suite 300, San Jose 95113	Dec. 2004

	D				
72	Daucher, Lynn	Legislator	R	210 West Birch Street, Suite 202, Brea 92821	Dec. 2000
50	De La Torre, Hector	Legislator	D	8724 Garfield Avenue, Suite 104, South Gate 90280	Dec. 2004
70	DeVore, Chuck	Legislator	R	3 Park Plaza, Suite 275, Irvine 92614	Dec. 2004
52	Dymally, Mervyn M. [3]	University Professor	D	322 W. Compton Blvd., Suite 100, Compton 90220	Dec. 2002
	E				
63	Emmerson, Bill	Legislator	R	10681 Foothill Blvd., Suite 325 Rancho Cucamonga 91730	Dec. 2004
7	Evans, Noreen	Legislator	D	50 "D" Street, Suite 301, Santa Rosa 95404	Dec. 2004
	F				
43	Frommer, Dario	Legislator/Majority Floor Leader	D	620 North Brand Blvd., Suite 403, Glendale 91203	Dec. 2000

[2] Elected at Special Election May 15, 2001.
[3] Previous Legislative Service, Dec. 1963–1966.

MEMBERS OF THE ASSEMBLY—EIGHTY ASSEMBLY MEMBERS

Dist.	Name	Occupation	Party	Mailing Address	Legislative service since
	G				
80	Garcia, Bonnie	Businesswoman	R	68-700 Avenida Lalo Guerrero, Ste. B, Cathedral City 92234	Dec. 2002
45	Goldberg, Jackie	Teacher/Legislator	D	106 North Ave. 56, Los Angeles 90042	Dec. 2000
53	Vacancy				
	H				
14	Hancock, Loni	Legislator	D	712 El Cerrito Plaza, El Cerrito 94530	Dec. 2002
67	Harman, Tom	Attorney	R	17011 Beach Boulevard, Suite 570, Huntington Beach 92647	Dec. 2000
66	Haynes, Ray [4]	Lawyer	R	27555 Ynez Rd., Suite 205, Temecula 92591	Dec. 2002
51	Horton, Jerome E.	Accountant/Business Tax Specialist	D	One Manchester Blvd., Suite 601, Inglewood 90306	Dec. 2000
78	Horton, Shirley	Businesswoman	R	7144 Broadway, Lemon Grove 91945	Dec. 2002

15	Houston, Guy S.	Mortgage Broker/Real Estate	R	1635 Chestnut Street, Suite A, Livermore 94551	Dec. 2002
60	Huff, Bob	Legislator	R	23355 E. Golden Springs Dr., Diamond Bar 91765	Dec. 2004
	J				
9	Jones, Dave	Attorney/Legislator	D	915 "L" Street, Suite 110, Sacramento 95814	Dec. 2004
	K				
54	Karnette, Betty	Legislator	D	3711 Long Beach Blvd., Suite 801, Long Beach 90807	Dec. 2004
3	Keene, Rick	Attorney	R	1550 Humboldt Road, Suite 4, Chico 95928	Dec. 2002
18	Klehs, Johan	Legislator	D	22320 Foothill Blvd., Suite 540, Hayward 94541	Dec. 2004
42	Koretz, Paul	Legislator	D	9200 Sunset Boulevard, PH 15, West Hollywood 90069	Dec. 2000
	L				
2	La Malfa, Doug	Farmer	R	2865 Churn Creek Rd., Suite B, Redding 96002	Dec. 2002

[4] Previous Legislative Service, Dec. 1992–1994.

MEMBERS OF THE ASSEMBLY—EIGHTY ASSEMBLY MEMBERS

Dist.	Name	Occupation	Party	Mailing Address	Legislative service since
77	La Suer, Jay	Legislator	R	5360 Jackson Drive, Suite 120, La Mesa 91942	Dec. 2000
27	Laird, John	Legislator	D	701 Ocean Street, Room 318-B, Santa Cruz 95060	Dec. 2002
13	Leno, Mark	Business Owner	D	455 Golden Gate Ave., Suite 14300, San Francisco 94102	Dec. 2002
4	Leslie, Tim [5]	Legislator	R	3300 Douglas Blvd., Suite 430, Roseville 95661	Dec. 2000
40	Levine, Lloyd	Legislator	D	6150 Van Nuys Blvd., Suite 300, Van Nuys 91401	Dec. 2002
22	Lieber, Sally J.	Legislator/Assistant Speaker pro Tempore	D	274 Castro St., Suite 202, Mountain View 94041	Dec. 2002
44	Liu, Carol	Educator	D	215 North Marengo Avenue, Suite 115, Pasadena 91101	Dec. 2000

	M				
17	Matthews, Barbara	Legislator	D	31 East Channel Street, Suite 306, Stockton 95202	Dec. 2000
34	Maze, Bill	Contractor/Farmer	R	5959 South Mooney, Visalia 93277	Dec. 2002
32	McCarthy, Kevin	Small Business Owner/ Republican Leader	R	4900 California Avenue, Suite 140A, Bakersfield 93309	Dec. 2002
39	Montañez, Cindy	Legislator	D	11541 Laurel Canyon Blvd., Suite C, Mission Hills 91345	Dec. 2002
59	Mountjoy, Dennis	Small Businessman	R	135 West Lemon Avenue, Suite A, Monrovia 91016	Dec. 2000
19	Mullin, Gene	Educator	D	1528 South El Camino Real, Suite 302, San Mateo 94402	Dec. 2002
	N				
10	Nakanishi, Alan	Physician	R	218 West Pine Street, Lodi 95240	Dec. 2002
6	Nation, Joe	Legislator	D	3501 Civic Center Drive, Room 412, San Rafael 94903	Dec. 2000
35	Nava, Pedro	Legislator	D	101 West Anapamu Street, Suite A, Santa Barbara 93101	Dec. 2004

[5] Previous Legislative Service, Dec. 1986–1991.

MEMBERS OF THE ASSEMBLY—EIGHTY ASSEMBLY MEMBERS

Dist.	Name	Occupation	Party	Mailing Address	Legislative service since
61	Negrete McLeod, Gloria.	Legislator	D	4959 Palo Verde Street, Suite 100B, Montclair 91763	Dec. 2000
5	Niello, Roger	Legislator	R	4811 Chippendale Drive, Suite 501, Sacramento 95841	Dec. 2004
46	Núñez, Fabian.	Legislator/Speaker of the Assembly	D	320 West 4th Street, #1050, Los Angeles 90013	Dec. 2002
	O				
55	Oropeza, Jenny	Full-time Legislator	D	One Civic Plaza, Suite 460, Carson 90745	Dec. 2000
	P				
30	Parra, Nicole	Legislator	D	601 24th Street, Suite A, Bakersfield 93301	Dec. 2002
41	Pavley, Fran	Teacher	D	6355 Topanga Canyon Blvd., Ste. 205, Woodland Hills 91367	Dec. 2000
75	Plescia, George A.	Legislator	R	9909 Mira Mesa Blvd. Suite 130, San Diego 92131	Dec. 2002

	R				
38	Richman, Keith	Physician	R	10727 White Oak Avenue, Suite 124, Granada Hills 91344	Dec. 2000
48	Ridley-Thomas, Mark	Civil Rights Advocate/ Educator	D	700 State Drive, Los Angeles 90037	Dec. 2002
36	Runner, Sharon	Businesswoman	R	747 W. Lancaster Blvd., Lancaster 93534	Dec. 2002
21	Ruskin, Ira	Legislator	D	5050 El Camino Real, Suite 117, Los Altos 94022	Dec. 2004
	S				
76	Saldaña, Lori	Legislator	D	1557 Columbia Street, San Diego 92101	Dec. 2004
28	Salinas, Simón	Teacher/Professor	D	100 West Alisal Street, Suite 134, Salinas 93901	Dec. 2000
71	Spitzer, Todd	Attorney	R	1940 North Tustin Street, Suite 102, Orange 92865	Dec. 2002
37	Strickland, Audra	Full-time Legislator	R	2659 Townsgate Road, Suite 236, Westlake Village 91361	Dec. 2004

MEMBERS OF THE ASSEMBLY—EIGHTY ASSEMBLY MEMBERS

Dist.	Name	Occupation	Party	Mailing Address	Legislative service since
	T				
20	Torrico, Alberto	Legislator	D	39510 Paseo Padre Parkway, Suite 280. Fremont 94538	Dec. 2004
68	Tran, Van	Legislator	R	1503 South Coast Drive, Suite 205, Costa Mesa 92626	Dec. 2004
	U				
69	Umberg, Thomas	Legislator	D	2400 E. Katella Ave., Suite 640, Anaheim 92806	Dec. 2004
	V				
79	Vargas, Juan	Legislator/Attorney	D	678 Third Avenue, Suite 105, Chula Vista 91910	Dec. 2000
29	Villines, Michael	Legislator	R	6245 N. Fresno St., Suite 106, Fresno 93710	Dec. 2004

W

73	Walters, Mimi	Legislator	R	30012 Ivy Glenn Drive, Suite 120, Laguna Nigel 92677	Dec. 2004
8	Wolk, Lois	Teacher	D	555 Mason Street, Suite 275, Vacaville 95688	Dec. 2002
74	Wyland, Mark	Legislator	R	1800 Thibodo Rd. Suite 300, Vista 92081	Dec. 2000

Y

| 12 | Yee, Leland Y. | Child Psychologist/ Speaker pro Tempore | D | 455 Golden Gate Avenue, Ste. 14600, San Francisco 94102 | Dec. 2002 |

MEMBERS OF THE ASSEMBLY,
COUNTY AND DISTRICT

District	Name	County or Counties
1	Patty Berg	DEL NORTE, HUMBOLDT, LAKE, MENDOCINO, Sonoma, TRINITY
2	Doug La Malfa	Butte, COLUSA, GLENN, MODOC, SHASTA, SISKIYOU, SUTTER, TEHAMA, Yolo
3	Rick Keene	Butte, LASSEN, NEVADA, Placer, PLUMAS, SIERRA, YUBA
4	Tim Leslie	ALPINE, El Dorado, Placer, Sacramento
5	Roger Niello	Placer, Sacramento
6	Joe Nation	MARIN, Sonoma
7	Noreen Evans	NAPA, Solano, Sonoma
8	Lois Wolk	Sacramento, Solano, Yolo
9	Dave Jones	Sacramento
10	Alan Nakanishi	AMADOR, El Dorado, Sacramento, San Joaquin
11	Joe Canciamilla	Contra Costa
12	Leland Yee	San Francisco, San Mateo
13	Mark Leno	San Francisco
14	Loni Hancock	Alameda, Contra Costa
15	Guy Houston	Alameda, Contra Costa, Sacramento, San Joaquin
16	Wilma Chan	Alameda
17	Barbara Matthews	MERCED, San Joaquin, Stanislaus
18	Johan Klehs	Alameda
19	Gene Mullin	San Mateo
20	Alberto Torrico	Alameda, Santa Clara
21	Ira Ruskin	San Mateo, Santa Clara
22	Sally Lieber	Santa Clara
23	Joe Coto	Santa Clara
24	Rebecca Cohn	Santa Clara
25	Dave Cogdill	CALAVERAS, Madera, MARIPOSA, MONO, Stanislaus, TUOLUMNE
26	Greg Aghazarian	San Joaquin, Stanislaus
27	John Laird	Monterey, Santa Clara, Santa Cruz
28	Simón Salinas	Monterey, SAN BENITO, Santa Clara, Santa Cruz

MEMBERS OF THE ASSEMBLY,
COUNTY AND DISTRICT—Continued

District	Name	County or Counties
29	Mike Villines	Fresno, Madera, Tulare
30	Nicole N. Parra	Fresno, Kern, KINGS, Tulare
31	Juan Arambula	Fresno, Tulare
32	Kevin McCarthy	Kern, San Bernardino
33	Sam Blakeslee	SAN LUIS OBISPO, Santa Barbara
34	Bill Maze	INYO, Kern, San Bernardino, Tulare
35	Pedro Nava	Santa Barbara, Ventura
36	Sharon Runner	Los Angeles, San Bernardino
37	Audra Strickland	Los Angeles, Ventura
38	Keith Stuart Richman	Los Angeles, Ventura
39	Cindy Montañez	Los Angeles
40	Lloyd E. Levine	Los Angeles
41	Fran Pavely	Los Angeles, Ventura
42	Paul Koretz	Los Angeles
43	Dario J. Frommer	Los Angeles
44	Carol Liu	Los Angeles
45	Jackie Goldberg	Los Angeles
46	Fabian Núñez	Los Angeles
47	Karen Bass	Los Angeles
48	Mark Ridley-Thomas	Los Angeles
49	Judy Chu	Los Angeles
50	Hector De La Torre	Los Angeles
51	Jerome Horton	Los Angeles
52	Mervyn Dymally	Los Angeles
53	Vacancy	Los Angeles
54	Betty Karnette	Los Angeles
55	Jenny Oropeza	Los Angeles
56	Rudy Bermúdez	Los Angeles, Orange
57	Edward "Ed" Chavez	Los Angeles
58	Ronald S. Calderon	Los Angeles
59	Dennis Mountjoy	Los Angeles, San Bernardino
60	Robert "Bob" Huff	Los Angeles, Orange, San Bernardino
61	Gloria Negrete McLeod	Los Angeles, San Bernardino
62	Joe Baca Jr.	San Bernardino
63	Bill Emmerson	Riverside, San Bernardino

**MEMBERS OF THE ASSEMBLY,
COUNTY AND DISTRICT—Continued**

District	Name	County or Counties
64	John Benoit	Riverside
65	Russ Bogh	Riverside, San Bernardino
66	Ray Haynes	Riverside, San Diego
67	Tom Harman	Orange
68	Van Tran	Orange
69	Tom Umberg	Orange
70	Chuck DeVore	Orange
71	Todd Spitzer	Orange, Riverside
72	Lynn Daucher	Orange
73	Mimi Walters	Orange, San Diego
74	Mark Wyland	San Diego
75	George A. Plescia	San Diego
76	Lori Saldaña	San Diego
77	Jay La Suer	San Diego
78	Shirley Horton	San Diego
79	Juan Vargas	San Diego
80	Bonnie Garcia	IMPERIAL, Riverside

NOTE: Names in CAPITALS denote counties that are wholly contained within the boundaries of the districts.

CLASSIFICATION OF ASSEMBLY MEMBERS AS TO LEGISLATIVE SERVICE

Number of years of legislative service is divided into classes. Computation of service is based upon the period of time between the first Monday in December immediately following the date of the general election at which the Member was originally elected and December 1, 2002, or from the date of the special election at which the Member was first elected and December 1, 2002.

No. 1—Twelve Years

Klehs* (1982–1994)

No. 2—Ten Years

Leslie* (1986–1991, 2000–2004)

No. 3—Six Years

Dymally* (1963–1966, 2003–2004) †

---

* Previous legislative service.
† Note: Assembly Members elected at General Elections prior to 1974 took office in January of the year following their election; those elected in 1974 and subsequently, took office in December of the year of their election.

CLASSIFICATION OF ASSEMBLY MEMBERS AS TO LEGISLATIVE SERVICE—Continued

No. 4—Four Years

Canciamilla	Haynes* (1992–94)	Negrete McLeod
Chan	2002–04)	Oropeza
Chavez	Horton, J.	Pavley
Cogdill	Koretz	Richman
Cohn	La Suer	Salinas
Daucher	Liu	Umberg* (1990–94)
Frommer	Matthews	Vargas
Goldberg	Mountjoy	Wyland
Harman	Nation	

No. 5 (Special Election, April 3, 2001)

Bogh

No. 6 (Special Election, May 15, 2001)

Chu

No. 7—Two Years

Aghazarian	Keene	Nakanishi
Benoit	La Malfa	Núñez
Berg	Laird	Parra
Bermúdez	Leno	Plescia
Calderon	Levine	Ridley-Thomas
Garcia	Lieber	Runner
Hancock	Maze	Spitzer
Horton, S.	McCarthy	Wolk
Houston	Montañez	Yee
Karnette* (1992–94)	Mullin	

No. 8—First Year

Arambula	Emmerson	Saldaña
Baca	Evans	Strickland
Bass	Huff	Torrico
Blakeslee	Jones	Tran
Coto	Nava	Villines
De La Torre	Niello	Walters
DeVore	Ruskin	

STANDING COMMITTEES
OF THE ASSEMBLY

2005–06 REGULAR SESSION

AGING AND LONG-TERM CARE (5)

Berg (Chair), Daucher (Vice Chair), Bermúdez, Canciamilla, and Walters. 1020 N Street, Room 360A. Phone 319-3990.

AGRICULTURE (8)

Matthews (Chair), Maze (Vice Chair), Blakeslee, Canciamilla, Cogdill, Parra, Salinas, and Vargas. 1020 N Street, Room 362. Phone 319-2084.

APPROPRIATIONS (18)

Chu (Chair), Runner (Vice Chair), Bass, Berg, Calderon, Emmerson, Haynes, Karnette, Klehs, Leno, Nakanishi, Nation, Oropeza, Ridley-Thomas, Saldaña, Walters, Yee, and vacancy. Room 2114. Phone 319-2081.

ARTS, ENTERTAINMENT, SPORTS, TOURISM, AND INTERNET MEDIA (10)

Chavez (Chair), Strickland (Vice Chair), Cohn, Harman, J. Horton, Karnette, Koretz, La Malfa, Matthews, and Umberg. 1020 N Street, Room 365. Phone 319-3450.

BANKING AND FINANCE (9)

Calderon (Chair), Niello (Vice Chair), Chavez, J. Horton, La Malfa, Parra, Ruskin, Tran, and Vargas. 1020 N Street, Room 360B. Phone 319-3081.

BUDGET (25)

Laird (Chair), Keene (Vice Chair), Arambula, Benoit, Bermúdez, Blakeslee, Chan, Cogdill, Coto, Daucher, De La Torre, DeVore, Dymally, Evans, Goldberg, Hancock, Huff, Montáñez, Mullin, Nava, Parra, Pavley, Plescia, Villines, and Wolk. Room 6026. Phone 319-2099.

**STANDING COMMITTEES OF THE
ASSEMBLY—Continued**

BUSINESS AND PROFESSIONS (10)

Negrete McLeod (Chair), S. Horton (Vice Chair), Bass, Frommer, Koretz, Maze, Nation, Tran, Vargas, and Yee. 1020 N Street, Room 124. Phone 319-3301.

EDUCATION (11)

Goldberg (Chair), Wyland (Vice Chair), Arambula, Coto, Hancock, Huff, Liu, Mullin, Pavley, Richman, and Umberg. 1020 N Street, Room 159. Phone 319-2087.

ELECTIONS AND REDISTRICTING (6)

Umberg (Chair), Wyland (Vice Chair), Klehs, Leno, Levine, and Villines. 1020 N Street, Room 152. Phone 319-2094.

ENVIRONMENTAL SAFETY AND
TOXIC MATERIALS (7)

Ruskin (Chair), Tran (Vice Chair), Chu, De La Torre, Goldberg, Strickland, and vacancy. 1020 N Street, Suite 171. Phone 319-3965.

GOVERNMENTAL ORGANIZATION (15)

J. Horton (Chair), Plescia (Vice Chair), Aghazarian, Bermúdez, Calderon, Chavez, Coto, Garcia, La Suer, Levine, Liu, Mountjoy, Negrete McLeod, Torrico, and Yee. 1020 N Street, Room 156. Phone 319-2531.

HEALTH (14)

Chan (Chair), Aghazarian (Vice Chair), Berg, Cohn, Dymally, Frommer, Jones, Montañez, Nakanishi, Negrete McLeod, Richman, Ridley-Thomas. Strickland, and vacancy. Room 6005. Phone 319-2097.

HIGHER EDUCATION (7)

Liu (Chair), Leslie (Vice Chair), Bass, S. Horton, Matthews, Nava, and Ruskin. 1020 N Street, Room 173. Phone 319-3960.

STANDING COMMITTEES OF THE
ASSEMBLY—Continued

HOUSING AND COMMUNITY
DEVELOPMENT (7)

Mullin (Chair), Garcia (Vice Chair), Baca, Hancock, La Suer, Salinas, and Torrico. 1020 N Street, Room 167A. Phone 319-2085.

HUMAN SERVICES (7)

Evans (Chair), Haynes (Vice Chair), Arambula, Bass, Coto, Nation, and Spitzer. Room 6025. Phone 319-2089.

INSURANCE (10)

Vargas (Chair), Benoit (Vice Chair), Bogh, Calderon, Frommer, Karnette, Lieber, Mountjoy, Nava, and Umberg. Room 2013. Phone 319-2086.

JOBS, ECONOMIC DEVELOPMENT,
AND THE ECONOMY (6)

Arambula (Chair), Houston (Vice Chair), Baca, Canciamilla, Garcia, and Oropeza. 1020 N Street, Room 369. Phone 319-2090.

JUDICIARY (9)

Jones (Chair), Harman (Vice Chair), Evans, Haynes, Laird, Leslie, Levine, Lieber, and Montañez. 1020 N Street, Room 104. Phone 319-2334.

LABOR AND EMPLOYMENT (8)

Koretz (Chair), Nakanishi (Vice Chair), Chan, Chu, Houston, Klehs, Laird, and Leno. 1020 N Street, Room 155. Phone 319-2091.

LOCAL GOVERNMENT (7)

Salinas (Chair), Emmerson (Vice Chair), De La Torre, Houston, Lieber, Nation, and Wolk. 1020 N Street, Room 157. Phone 319-3958.

NATURAL RESOURCES (10)

Hancock (Chair), La Malfa (Vice Chair), Harman, Keene, Koretz, Laird, Nava, Saldaña, Wolk, and vacancy. 1020 N Street, Room 164. Phone 319-2092.

**STANDING COMMITTEES OF THE
ASSEMBLY—Continued**

PUBLIC EMPLOYEES, RETIREMENT
AND SOCIAL SECURITY (6)

Torrico (Chair), Blakeslee (Vice Chair), Jones, Mullin, Negrete McLeod, and Niello. 1020 N Street, Room 153. Phone 319-3957.

PUBLIC SAFETY (7)

Leno (Chair), La Suer (Vice Chair), Cohn, Dymally, Goldberg, Spitzer and vacancy. 1020 N Street, Room 111. Phone 319-3744.

REVENUE AND TAXATION (7)

Klehs (Chair), Walters (Vice Chair), Canciamilla, Chu, DeVore, Jones, and Lieber. 1020 N Street, Room 162. Phone 319-2098.

RULES (8)

Montañez (Chair), Cogdill (Vice Chair), Baca, Benoit, Coto, Dymally, Karnette, and Villines. (Alternates: 2 vacancies). Chief Administrative Officer: Jonathon Waldie. Secretary: Anna McCabe. Room 3016. Phone 319-2800.

TRANSPORTATION (13)

Oropeza (Chair), Huff (Vice Chair), Bogh, Chan, S. Horton, Karnette, Liu, Mountjoy, Niello, Pavley, Ridley-Thomas, Salinas, and Torrico. 1020 N Street, Room 112. Phone 319-2093.

UTILITIES AND COMMERCE (11)

Levine (Chair), Bogh (Vice Chair), Baca, Blakeslee, Cohn, De La Torre, J. Horton, Keene, Montañez, Ridley-Thomas, and Wyland. Room 5136. Phone 319-2083.

VETERANS AFFAIRS (9)

Vacancy (Chair), DeVore (Vice Chair), Canciamilla, Chavez, Evans, Oropeza, Plescia, Runner, and Saldaña. 1020 N Street, Room 389. Phone 319-3550.

STANDING COMMITTEES OF THE
ASSEMBLY—Continued

WATER, PARKS AND WILDLIFE (14)

Wolk (Chair), Villines (Vice Chair), Baca, Berg, Bermúdez, Daucher, Dymally, Emmerson, Matthews, Maze, Parra, Pavley, Runner, and Saldaña. 1020 N Street, Room 160. Phone 319-2096.

SUBCOMMITTEES OF THE ASSEMBLY STANDING COMMITTEES

2005–06 REGULAR SESSION

BUDGET—

No. 1—**Health and Human Services**—De La Torre (Chair), Blakeslee, Hancock, Keene, and Mullin.

No. 2—**Education Finance**—Dymally (Chair), Chan, Coto, Daucher, Goldberg, and Huff.

No. 3—**Resources**—Pavley (Chair), Cogdill, Evans, Montañez, and Plescia.

No. 4—**State Administration**—Bermúdez (Chair), Arambula, DeVore, Parra, and Villines.

No. 5—**Information Technology/Transportation**—Nava (Chair), Benoit, and Wolk.

RULES—

Sexual Harassment Prevention and Response (6)—*(Assembly Rule 14.5)*—6 vacancies.

SELECT COMMITTEES OF THE ASSEMBLY

(SUBCOMMITTEES OF THE GENERAL RESEARCH COMMITTEE)

2005–06 REGULAR SESSION

Select Committee on Adult Education—Liu (Chair).

Select Committee on Aerospace—Vacancy (Chair).

Select Committee on Air and Water Quality—Pavley (Chair).

Select Committee on the Alameda Corridor East—Negrete McLeod (Chair).

Select Committee on Bioethics, Medicine and Technology—Saldaña (Chair).

Select Committee on Biotechnology—Mullin (Chair).

Select Committee on California Horseracing Industry—J. Horton (Chair).

Select Committee on California and Latin American Affairs—Vargas (Chair).

Select Committee on Children's Physical and Mental Well Being in Diverse California Communities—Yee (Chair).

Select Committee on Community Colleges—Dymally (Chair).

Select Committee on Critical Issues—Dymally (Chair).

Select Committee on the Development of a 10th University of California, Merced Campus—Matthews (Chair).

Select Committee on Domestic Violence—Cohn (Chair).

Select Committee on Environmental Justice—Montañez (Chair).

Select Committee on Growth and Infrastructure—Canciamilla (Chair).

2005–06 REGULAR SESSION

Select Committee on Gun Violence Prevention— Koretz (Chair).

Select Committee on Hate Crimes—Chu (Chair).

Select Committee on the Los Angeles Health Care Crisis—Ridley-Thomas (Chair), Bass, Chan, De La Torre, Dymally, Frommer, Goldberg, Koretz, Montañez, Richman, and Runner.

Select Committee on Mobilehomes—Lieber (Chair).

Select Committee on Nanotechnology and Emerging Technologies—Ruskin (Chair).

Select Committee on Olmstead Implementation— Daucher (Chair).

Select Committee on Perchlorate Contamination— Baca (Chair).

Select Committee on Ports—Karnette (Chair).

Select Committee on Prison Construction and Operations— Bermúdez (Chair).

Select Committee on Runaway Production— Frommer (Chair).

Select Committee on Rural Economic Development— Salinas (Chair).

Select Committee on Sustainability—Berg (Chair).

Select Committee on Title IX—Oropeza (Chair).

Select Committee on Urban Education in California— Coto (Chair).

Select Committee on Water, Infrastructure and the Economy—Parra (Chair).

Select Committee on Wine—Evans (Chair).

SPECIAL COMMITTEES
OF THE ASSEMBLY

2005–06 REGULAR SESSION

Assembly Legislative Ethics (6)—(*Assembly Rule 22.5)*—Negrete McLeod (Co-Chair), Cogdill (Co-Chair), and 4 vacancies. 1020 N Street, Room 351. Consultant: Scott Hallabrin. Phone 319-3752.

Special Committee on Rail Safety—Frommer (Chair), Bass, Bermudez, Calderon, Coto, Mountjoy, Oropeza, and Runner.

JOINT COMMITTEES

(See Joint Rules 36.5 and 36.7)

2005–06 REGULAR SESSION

Joint Committee on Boards, Commissions and Consumer Protection (6)—*(Business and Professions Code, Section 473. Expires January 1, 2012.)*
—Assembly: Negrete McLeod, Koretz, and Spitzer.
—Senate: Figueroa (Chair), Aanestad, and Vincent.
1020 N Street, Room 521.
Phone 324-2506.

Joint Committee on Rules (22)—*(Joint Rule 40. Continuous existence.)*
—Assembly: Montañez (Chair), Baca, Benoit, Cogdill, Coto, Dymally, Frommer, Karnette, McCarthy, Núñez, and Villines.
—Senate: Battin (Vice Chair), Ashburn, Bowen, Cedillo, Dunn, Escutia, Murray, Ortiz, Perata, Poochigian, and Romero.
Chief Administrative Officer: Jonathon Waldie.
Room 3016.
Phone 319-2804.

Joint Legislative Audit (14)—*(Government Code Sections 10501, 10502, Joint Rule 37.3. Continuous existence.)*
—Assembly: Parra (Chair), Aghazarian, Cogdill,* Goldberg, Klehs, Leslie, and Nava.
[*Keene will serve in place of Cogdill for hearings related to "Secretary of State: Help America Vote Act of 2002". *See Assembly Journal, January 6, 2005, pp. 141–142.]*
—Senate: Poochigian (Vice Chair), Cedillo, McClintock, Morrow, Ortiz, Romero, and Speier.
1020 N Street, Room 107.
Phone 319-3300. Fax: 319-2352.

JOINT COMMITTEES—Continued

2005–06 REGULAR SESSION

Joint Legislative Budget (16)—*(Government Code Sections 9140, 9141, Joint Rule 37. Continuous existence.)*
—Assembly: Laird (Vice Chair), Chu, De La Torre, Goldberg, Keene, McCarthy, Nava, and Runner.
—Senate: Chesbro (Chair), Battin, Ducheny, Dunn, Hollingsworth, McClintock, Migden, and Scott.

SCHEDULE OF 2005–06 ASSEMBLY COMMITTEE MEETINGS

—

MONDAY

Time	Room	Committee
4:00 p.m.**	444	Banking and Finance
1:30 p.m.*	447	Natural Resources
1:30 p.m.*	126	Revenue and Taxation
!*	3162	Rules
1:30 p.m.*	4202	Transportation
3:00 p.m.*	437	Utilities and Commerce

TUESDAY

Time	Room	Committee
2:00 p.m.**	127	Aging and Long-Term Care
9:00 a.m.**	437	Arts, Entertainment, Sports, Tourism, and Internet Media
9:00 a.m.***	447	Business and Professions
1:30 p.m.**	444	Elections and Redistricting
1:30 p.m.***	444	Environmental Safety and Toxic Materials
1:30 p.m.*	4202	Health
1:30 p.m.**	437	Higher Education
1:30 p.m.***	437	Human Services
9:00 a.m.**	447	Jobs, Economic Development, and the Economy
9:00 a.m.*	4202	Judiciary
9:00 a.m.*	126	Public Safety
4:00 p.m.***	126	Veterans Affairs
9:00 a.m.***	437	Water, Parks and Wildlife

SCHEDULE OF 2005–06 ASSEMBLY
COMMITTEE MEETINGS—Continued

WEDNESDAY

Time	Room	Committee
1:30 p.m.***	4202	Agriculture
9:00 a.m.*	4202	Appropriations
!	4202	Budget
1:30 p.m.*	126	Education
1:30 p.m.**	4202	Governmental Organization
9:00 a.m.***	126	Housing and Community Development
9:00 a.m.*	437	Insurance
1:30 p.m.**	447	Labor and Employment
1:30 p.m.***	447	Local Government
9:00 a.m.**	444	Public Employees, Retirement and Social Security

---

  * Meets every week.
 ** Meets 1st and 3rd week of month as called at time indicated.
*** Meets 2nd and 4th week of the month as called at time indicated.
 ! Upon call of the Chair.

SCHEDULE OF 2005–06
SUBCOMMITTEES

BUDGET

MONDAY

Time	Room	Committee
4:00 p.m.*	127	Subcommittee No. 1— Health and Human Services

TUESDAY

Time	Room	Committee
10:00 a.m.*	444	Subcommittee No. 2— Education Finance
1:30 p.m.*	447	Subcommittee No. 4— State Administration

WEDNESDAY

Time	Room	Committee
1:30 p.m.*	444	Subcommittee No. 1— Health and Human Services
4:00 p.m.*	126	Subcommittee No. 2— Education Finance
8:30 a.m.*	447	Subcommittee No. 3— Resources
1:30 p.m.*	437	Subcommittee No. 4— State Administration
4:00 p.m.*	127	Subcommittee No. 5— Information Technology/ Transportation

OFFICES OF THE ASSEMBLY
2005–06

SPEAKER'S OFFICE—
Hon. Fabian Núñez
State Capitol, Room 219

Dan Eaton, *Chief of Staff*
Steven Maviglio, *Deputy Chief of Staff*
Rick Simpson, *Deputy Chief of Staff*
Arnie Sowell, *Policy Director*
Craig Cornett, *Budget Director*
Bob Giroux, *Chief Advisor to the Speaker*
Fredericka McGee, *Legal Counsel*
Vincent Duffy, *Press Secretary*

REPUBLICAN FLOOR LEADER'S OFFICE—
Hon. Kevin McCarthy
State Capitol, Room 3104

Julie Sauls, *Chief of Staff*
Barbara Brown, *Deputy Chief of Staff*
Richard Mersereau, *Director of Policy*
Morgan Crinklaw, *Press Secretary*
Diana Knoles, *Scheduler*

RULES COMMITTEE—
State Capitol, Room 3016

Jon Waldie, *Chief Administrative Officer*
Lynda Roper, *Deputy Administrative Officer*
Flo Sanchez, *Deputy Administrative Officer*
Diane Griffiths, *Chief Legal Counsel*
Lia Lopez, *Consultant*
Anna McCabe, *Committee Secretary*

CHIEF CLERK'S OFFICE—
Assembly Chamber

E. Dotson Wilson, *Chief Clerk*
Lawrence A. Murman, *Assistant Chief Clerk*
Pam Cavileer, *Chief Assistant Clerk*
Sue Parker, *Minute Clerk*
Amy Leach, *History Clerk*
Brian S. Ebbert, *Daily File Clerk*
Cynthia Perkut-Kelly, *Engrossing and Enrolling Supervisor*
Teri Brown, *Floor Analysis Supervisor*

OFFICES OF THE ASSEMBLY—Continued

SERGEANT AT ARMS' OFFICE—
State Capitol Annex

Ronald E. Pane, *Chief Sergeant at Arms*
Robert V. Delaney, *Deputy Chief Sergeant at Arms*

ADMINISTRATIVE SERVICES—
1020 N Street, Room 300

Gus Demas, *Chief Fiscal Officer*
Rich Wagaman, *Facilities Manager*

PERMANENT
STANDING RULES
OF THE ASSEMBLY

2005–06 Regular Session

House Resolution No. 1 (Montañez)
(Adopted December 6, 2004,
Assembly Journal, p. 56)

RESOLUTION ADOPTING PERMANENT STANDING RULES OF THE ASSEMBLY 2005–06

(December 6, 2004)

By Assembly Member Montañez

House Resolution No. 1—Relative to the Standing Rules of the Assembly for the 2005–06 Regular Session.

Resolved by the Assembly of the State of California, That the following Rules be, and the same are hereby, adopted as the Standing Rules of the Assembly for the 2005–06 Regular Session; and be it further

Resolved, That these rules shall govern the operations of the Assembly.

Adopted December 6, 2004

STANDING RULES OF THE ASSEMBLY
2005–06 REGULAR SESSION
I. LEGISLATIVE ORGANIZATION
Assembly General Officers

1.   (a) The general officers of the Assembly are the following:

(1) Speaker

(2) Speaker pro Tempore

Assistant Speaker pro Tempore

Majority Floor Leader

Minority Floor Leader

(3) Chief Clerk

Sergeant at Arms

Chaplain

(b) Except for the officers listed in paragraph (2) of subdivision (a), each officer listed in subdivision (a) shall be elected by a majority vote of the duly elected and qualified Members.

(c) The Chief Clerk, subject to the approval of the Committee on Rules, shall determine the names and titles that shall appear on the front page of all publications.

Hours of Meeting

2.   The Speaker, or, in his or her absence, the Speaker pro Tempore, shall determine the time for convening the session, unless otherwise ordered by a majority vote of the Members present and voting.

Speaker to Call Assembly to Order

3.   The Speaker, or, in his or her absence, the Speaker pro Tempore, shall, at the hour appointed for meeting, call the Assembly to order.

Roll Call and Quorum

4.   Before proceeding with the business of the Assembly, both of the following shall be completed:

(1) The roll of the Members shall be called, and the names of those present shall be entered in the Journal. Forty-one Members constitute a quorum.

(2) The presiding officer shall announce the names of all Members who will be absent from that day's session and the reason for their absence.

Organization of Assembly

5.   For the purposes of the organization of any regular session of the Assembly pursuant to Section 9023 of the Government Code, the person who was the Speaker when the previous regular session adjourned *sine die*, if he or she is reelected to the Assembly, shall be deemed to be the senior member elect.

II.   RULES
Adoption of Standing Rules

6.   The adoption of the Standing Rules requires an affirmative recorded vote of a majority of the duly elected and qualified Members. When once adopted, the Standing Rules shall remain in effect unless suspended or amended as provided in these rules.

Suspension of Rules

7.   Unless specified otherwise in these rules, any Standing Rule of the Assembly not requiring more than a majority vote, except Rule 8, may be suspended temporarily by a vote of a majority of the Members of the Assembly. A rule requiring a two-thirds vote may be temporarily suspended by a two-thirds vote of the Members of the Assembly. A temporary suspension applies only to the matter under immediate consideration, and in no case may it extend beyond an adjournment.

Amending Standing Rules

8.   A standing rule of the Assembly may not be amended except by a resolution adopted by an affirmative recorded vote of a majority of the duly elected and qualified Members.

Mason's Manual

10.   In all cases not provided for by the California Constitution, by the Assembly Rules, by the Joint Rules

of the Senate and Assembly, or by statute, the authority is the latest edition of Mason's Manual.

III. ORGANIZATION OF COMMITTEES
Standing Committees

11. Twenty-nine standing committees of the Assembly are hereby created, upon the several subjects, and titled respectively, as follows:

Aging and Long-Term Care
Agriculture
Appropriations
Arts, Entertainment, Sports, Tourism, and Internet Media
Banking and Finance
Budget
Business and Professions
Education
Elections and Redistricting
Environmental Safety and Toxic Materials
Governmental Organization
Health
Higher Education
Housing and Community Development
Human Services
Insurance
Jobs, Economic Development, and the Economy
Judiciary
Labor and Employment
Local Government
Natural Resources
Public Employees, Retirement and Social Security
Public Safety
Revenue and Taxation
Rules
Transportation
Utilities and Commerce
Veterans Affairs
Water, Parks and Wildlife

Open Meetings

11.3. (a) Except as otherwise provided in this rule, all meetings of the Assembly or a committee thereof shall be open and public, and all persons shall be permitted to attend the meetings. As used in this rule, "meeting" means a gathering of a quorum of the Members of the Assembly or a committee in one place for the purpose of discussing legislative or other official matters within the jurisdiction of the Assembly or committee. As used in this rule, "committee" includes a standing committee, joint committee, conference committee, subcommittee, select committee, special committee, research committee, or any similar body.

(b) Any meeting that is required to be open and public pursuant to this rule, including any closed session held pursuant to subdivision (c), may be held only after full and timely notice to the public as provided by the Joint Rules of the Assembly and Senate.

(c) The Assembly or a committee thereof may hold a closed session solely for any of the following purposes:

(1) To consider the appointment, employment, evaluation of performance, or dismissal of a public officer or employee, to consider or hear complaints or charges brought against a Member of the Legislature or other public officer or employee, or to establish the classification or compensation of an employee of the Assembly.

(2) To consider matters affecting the safety and security of Members of the Legislature or its employees, or the safety and security of any buildings and grounds used by the Legislature.

(3) To confer with, or receive advice from, its legal counsel regarding pending or reasonably anticipated litigation, or whether to initiate litigation, when discussion in open session would not protect the interests of the Assembly or committee regarding the litigation.

(d) A caucus of the Members of the Assembly that is composed of members of the same political party may meet in closed session.

(e) A closed session may be held pursuant to paragraph (3) of subdivision (c) under any of the following circumstances:

(1) An adjudicatory proceeding before a court, administrative body exercising its adjudicatory authority, hearing officer, or arbitrator, to which the Assembly or a committee, Member, or employee thereof is a party, has been initiated formally.

(2) Based on existing facts and circumstances, a point has been reached where, in the opinion of the Assembly or a committee thereof, on the advice of its legal counsel, litigation against the Assembly or a committee, Member, or employee thereof is reasonably anticipated.

(3) Based on existing facts and circumstances, the Assembly or a committee thereof has decided to initiate, or is deciding whether to initiate, litigation.

(4) To confer with, or receive advice from, its legal counsel and negotiator prior to the purchase, sale, exchange, or lease of real property by or for the Assembly or a committee thereof regarding the price and terms of payment for the purchase, sale, exchange, or lease.

(f) Prior to holding a closed session pursuant to paragraph (3) of subdivision (c), the presiding officer of the Assembly or the chair of the committee, as appropriate, shall state publicly which paragraph of subdivision (e) is applicable. If the closed session is held pursuant to paragraph (1) of subdivision (e), the presiding officer or chair shall state the title of or otherwise specifically identify the litigation to be discussed, unless the presiding officer or chair states that to do so would jeopardize the ability to effectuate service of process upon one or more unserved parties, or that to do so would jeopardize the ability of the Assembly or the committee to conclude existing settlement negotiations to its advantage. If the closed session is held pursuant to paragraph (4) of subdivision (e), the notice of the closed session shall identify the real property that the negotiations may concern and the person with whom the negotiations may take place.

(g) The legal counsel for the Assembly or the committee shall prepare and submit to the Assembly or the committee a memorandum stating the specific reasons and legal authority for the closed session. If the closed session is held pursuant to paragraph (1) of subdivision (e), the memorandum shall include the title of or other identification of the litigation. If the closed session is held pursuant to paragraph (2), (3), or (4) of subdivision (e), the memorandum shall set forth the existing facts and circumstances on which the closed session is based. The legal counsel shall submit the memorandum to the Assembly or the committee prior to the closed session, if feasible, or, in any case, not later than one week after the closed session. The memorandum is exempt from disclosure under the Legislative Open Records Act contained in Article 3.5 (commencing with Section 9070) of Chapter 1.5 of Part 1 of Division 2 of Title 2 of the Government Code.

(h) For purposes of paragraph (3) of subdivision (c), "litigation" includes any adjudicatory proceeding, including eminent domain, before a court, administrative body exercising its adjudicatory authority, hearing officer, or arbitrator.

(i) For purposes of this rule, all expressions of the lawyer-client privilege other than those provided in this rule are hereby abrogated. This rule is the exclusive expression of the lawyer-client privilege for the purposes of conducting closed-session meetings pursuant to this rule.

(j) Disclosure of a memorandum required under this rule shall not be deemed a waiver of the lawyer-client privilege provided for under Article 3 (commencing with Section 950) of Chapter 4 of Division 8 of the Evidence Code.

Conference Committee Meetings

11.4.   A Member may not participate in a meeting of a conference committee considering any bill that is not open to the public.

Assembly Investigating Committees

11.5. (a) The standing committees of the Assembly created pursuant to Rule 11, with the exception of the Committee on Rules, are hereby constituted Assembly investigating committees and are authorized and directed to ascertain, study, and analyze all facts relating to any subjects or matters which the Committee on Rules shall assign to them upon request of the Assembly or upon its own initiative.

(b) Each of the Assembly investigating committees consists of the members of the standing committee on the same subject as most recently constituted. The chairperson and vice chairperson is the chairperson and vice chairperson of the standing committee. Vacancies occurring in the membership of the committee shall be filled by the appointing authority.

(c) Each committee and any subcommittee, and its members, have and may exercise all the rights, duties, and powers conferred upon investigating committees and their members by law and by the Joint Rules of the Senate and Assembly and the Standing Rules of the Assembly as they are adopted and amended from time to time, which rules are incorporated herein and made applicable to the committee or subcommittee and their members.

(d) In order to prevent duplication and overlapping of studies between the various investigating committees herein created, a committee may not commence the study of any subject or matter not specifically authorized herein or assigned to it unless and until prior written approval thereof has been obtained from the Committee on Rules.

(e) The Committee on Rules shall provide for the expenses of the above committees and their members and for any charges, expenses, or claims they may incur under this rule, to be paid from the Assembly Operating Fund and disbursed, after certification by the Chairperson of the Committee on Rules or his or her authorized representative, upon warrants drawn by the Controller upon the State Treasury.

Membership of Standing Committees

12. The Speaker shall determine the size, and appoint the membership and the chairperson and vice chairperson, of all standing committees and subcommittees. In appointing Members to serve on committees, the Speaker shall consider the preferences of the Members.

Committee on Rules

13. There is a Committee on Rules, which acts as the executive committee of the Assembly. No regular member of the Committee on Rules may simultaneously serve as a chairperson of any standing committee. All meetings of the Committee on Rules that are required to be open and public shall be held in a room of appropriate size, and audio or video transmission of those meetings shall be provided.

Organization of Party Caucuses

13.1. Within two days after the general election held in November of each even-numbered year, the caucus of the political party having the greatest number of Members in the Assembly, and the caucus of the political party having the second greatest number of Members, each shall meet for the purpose of selecting their officers for the next regular session. The rules and procedures of each caucus shall be determined by that caucus, but may not be inconsistent with these rules.

Powers of the Committee on Rules

14. (a) The Committee on Rules has the following powers:

(1) To refer each bill and house resolution to a committee, as provided by these rules.

(2) To appoint all employees of the Assembly not otherwise provided for by statute. It has authority to terminate, to discipline, to establish, and to modify the terms and conditions of employment of, or to suspend, with or without pay, any employee of the Assembly.

(3) To make studies and recommendations designed to promote, improve, and expedite the business and

procedure of the Assembly and of the committees thereof, and to propose any amendments to the Rules deemed necessary to accomplish these purposes.

(4) To adopt additional policies or requirements regarding the use of cameras and other recording equipment at committee hearings or Assembly floor sessions.

(5) To contract with other agencies, public or private, as it deems necessary for the rendition and affording of those services, facilities, studies, and reports to the committee that will best assist it to carry out the purposes for which it is created.

(6) To cooperate with and secure the cooperation of county, city, city and county, and other local law enforcement agencies in investigating any matter within the scope of these rules and to direct the sheriff of any county to serve subpoenas, orders, and other process issued by the committee.

(7) To report its findings and recommendations to the Legislature and to the people from time to time and at any time.

(8) To do any and all other things necessary or convenient to enable it fully and adequately to exercise its powers, perform its duties, and accomplish the objects and purposes of these rules.

(9) To make available to the Assembly, or to any Assembly or joint committee, or to any Member of the Assembly assistance in connection with the duties of the committee or other legislative matters as the personnel under direction of the committee or its other facilities permit.

(10) To make available to and furnish to the Assembly, and to Assembly investigating committees created at this session and to each of the members thereof, clerical, secretarial, and stenographic help as may be reasonably necessary for the Assembly to carry out its work, and for the committees and each of the members thereof, to make and carry on the studies and investigations required by or of them by the resolutions creating the committees, and for these purposes to employ additional stenographic and secretarial assistants as may be necessary, assign, reassign, and dis-

charge these assistants and prescribe amounts, times, and methods of payment of their compensation. The committee shall allocate annually an amount for the operation of each investigating committee, which shall constitute the annual budget of the committee.

(b) During the times as the Assembly is not in session, the committee is authorized and directed to incur and pay expenses of the Assembly not otherwise provided for that the committee determines are reasonably necessary, including the repair, alteration, improvement, and equipping of the Assembly Chamber and the offices provided for the Assembly in the State Capitol and the Capitol Annex.

(c) The committee shall allocate sufficient moneys from the Assembly Operating Fund to support the Assembly's share of joint operations.

(d) The chairperson of the Committee on Rules shall appoint a Chief Administrative Officer of the Assembly, subject to the ratification of the Committee on Rules, who has duties relating to the administrative, fiscal, and business affairs of the Assembly that the committee shall prescribe. The Chairperson of the Committee on Rules or a majority of the membership of the Committee on Rules may terminate the services of the Chief Administrative Officer at any time. Notwithstanding the foregoing, the Speaker may appoint a temporary chief administrative officer for up to 90 days following the beginning of the session.

(e) The Committee on Rules shall provide for the publication of a compilation of the photographs of accredited press representatives.

(f) The Committee on Rules may delegate powers to the Speaker by a majority vote of the membership of the committee.

Subcommittee on Sexual Harassment Prevention and Response

14.5. (a) The Subcommittee on Sexual Harassment Prevention and Response is created as a subcommittee of the Committee on Rules. The subcommittee is composed of a total of six members, with the following four members appointed by the Chairperson of the

Committee on Rules: two members of the Committee on Rules from the political party having the greatest number of Members in the Assembly and two members of the Committee on Rules from the political party having the second greatest number of Members. The two members from the political party having the second greatest number of Members shall be appointed from a list of nominees that the vice chairperson of the committee provides to the chairperson. The co-chairs of the Assembly Legislative Ethics Committee also shall be members of the subcommittee. The Chairperson of the Committee on Rules shall designate one of the members of the subcommittee to serve as chair of the subcommittee.

(b) The subcommittee shall formulate and recommend to the Committee on Rules procedures for the handling of any complaint of sexual harassment lodged against a Member of the Assembly or an Assembly employee. Those recommendations shall be submitted to the Committee on Rules no later than 30 days following the appointment of the membership of this subcommittee.

(c) Following the submission of the recommendations pursuant to subdivision (b), the chair of the subcommittee may cause the subcommittee to convene to review and recommend further changes in procedures as subsequent events may require.

Committee on Rules

15. The Committee on Rules shall continue in existence during any recess of the Legislature and after final adjournment and until the convening of the next regular session, and shall have the same powers and duties as while the Assembly is in session. In dealing with any matter within its jurisdiction, the committee and its members have and may exercise all of the rights, duties, and powers conferred upon investigating committees and their members by the Joint Rules of the Senate and Assembly as they are adopted and amended from time to time, which rules are incorporated herein and made applicable to the Committee on Rules and its members.

Operating Fund Report

15.5. The Committee on Rules shall annually prepare a report to the public of expenditures as required by Section 9131 of the Government Code.

Independent Audit of Operating Funds

15.6. The Committee on Rules shall annually contract for an independent audit of the revenues and expenditures, for each fiscal year, from the Assembly Operating Fund. The organization performing the audit shall be selected by a majority of the membership of the Committee on Rules. The contract for the audit shall be awarded through a competitive bidding procedure. The audit shall be prepared in a manner and form to be determined by the organization performing the audit, and shall be consistent with generally accepted accounting principles.

The audit shall be completed and made available to the public within 180 calendar days following the completion of the fiscal year for which the audit is performed.

Performance Audit

15.7. In addition to the annual financial audit required by Rule 15.6, the Committee on Rules shall contract for an audit of the administrative operations of the Assembly each session. The administrative departments to be audited shall be determined by the Committee on Rules. An organization performing an audit pursuant to this rule shall be selected by a majority of the membership of the Committee on Rules. A contract for an audit shall be awarded through a competitive bidding procedure. Audits shall be prepared in a manner and form to be determined by the organization performing the audit, and shall be consistent with generally accepted accounting principles.

All findings and recommendations reported by an auditing firm shall be made available to Members and to the public.

Rules Committee Resolutions

16. The Committee on Rules, acting unanimously by appropriate resolution, on behalf of and in the name of the Assembly, may extend congratulations, commendations, sympathy, or regret to any person, group, or organization, and may authorize the presentation of suitably prepared copies of these resolutions to the persons concerned and to their relatives.

Assembly Operating Fund

17. The Committee on Rules is the committee identified in Section 9127 of the Government Code. The balance of all money in the Assembly Operating Fund, including money now or hereafter appropriated, except the sums that are made available specifically for the expense of designated committees or for other purposes, is hereby made available to the Committee on Rules for any charges or claims it may incur in carrying out the duties imposed upon it by these rules or by Assembly or concurrent resolution. The money made available by this rule includes the unencumbered balances of all sums heretofore made available to any Assembly or joint committee by the Assembly, upon the expiration of that committee, and shall be expended as provided in these rules.

Expenditures

18. A Member or committee may not incur any expense except as authorized pursuant to these rules or the Joint Rules of the Senate and Assembly, or as authorized by the Assembly or the Committee on Rules.

The Committee on Rules shall provide, by rules and regulations, for the manner of authorizing expenditures by Members, committees, officers, and employees of the Assembly that are not otherwise authorized by law, these rules, or the Joint Rules of the Senate and Assembly. These rules and regulations shall incorporate a provision whereby construction, alteration, improvement, repair, or maintenance of real or personal property, and the purchase of supplies and equipment, shall be governed by competitive bidding. Further, the rules and regulations shall provide for the payment of expenditures, as authorized by these rules and regulations, from the Assembly Operating Fund upon certification of claims therefor to the Controller by the Committee on Rules or its authorized representative.

A Member may not be reimbursed for travel outside the State of California without prior approval of the Speaker or the Committee on Rules.

Rules and Regulations Governing Committees

20. All claims for expenses incurred by investigating committees of the Assembly shall be approved by the Committee on Rules, or its authorized representative, before the claims are presented to the Controller.

All proposed expenditures, other than expenditures of the funds of an investigating committee, shall be approved by the Committee on Rules or its authorized representative before the expenses are incurred, unless the expenditure is specifically exempted from this requirement by the resolution authorizing it.

No warrant may be drawn in payment of any claim for expenses until the approval of the Committee on Rules, or its authorized representative, has been obtained in accordance with this rule.

The Committee on Rules shall adopt rules and regulations governing the awarding of any contract by an investigating committee, and rules and regulations limiting the amount, time, and place of expenses and allowances to be paid to employees of Assembly investigating committees or other Assembly committees.

These rules may provide for allowances to committee employees in lieu of actual expenses.

Mileage is an allowance to a committee employee in lieu of actual expenses of travel. When travel is by private conveyance, mileage may be allowed only to the operator of, and not to passengers in, a private vehicle. Claims for mileage by private conveyance must be accompanied by the license number of the vehicle and the names of state officers and employees riding as passengers.

Copies of all rules and regulations adopted pursuant to this rule shall be distributed to the chairperson of every investigating committee and of any other Assembly committee that has employees.

Fees for Witnesses

21.   Each witness summoned to appear before the Assembly or any of its committees shall be reimbursed at a rate set by the Committee on Rules.

Assembly General Research Committee

22.   (a) The Assembly General Research Committee is hereby continued as a permanent fact-finding committee pursuant to Section 11 of Article IV of the California Constitution. The committee is allocated all subjects within the scope of legislative regulation and control, but may not undertake any investigation that another committee has been specifically requested or directed to undertake. The Assembly General Research Committee may act through subcommittees appointed by the Speaker in consultation with the Committee on Rules, and each of these subcommittees may act only on the particular study or investigation assigned by the Speaker in consultation with the Committee on Rules to that subcommittee. Each subcommittee shall be known and designated as a select committee. The Speaker is the Chairperson of the Assembly General Research Committee and may be a voting member of any subcommittee. Each member of the Assembly General Research Committee is authorized and directed to receive and investigate requests for legislative action made by individuals or groups, and to report thereon to the full committee. The Committee on Rules is authorized to allocate to any subcommittee from the Assembly Operating Fund those sums that the Committee on Rules deems necessary to complete the investigation or study conferred upon that subcommittee. The Committee on Rules shall further allocate, from time to time, to the Assembly General Research Committee from the Assembly Operating Fund those sums that are necessary to permit the Assembly General Research Committee and the members thereof to carry out the duties

imposed on them. The committee has continuous existence until the time that its existence is terminated by a resolution adopted by the Assembly, and the committee is authorized to act both during and between sessions of the Legislature, including any recess.

(b) The committee and its members shall have and exercise all the rights, duties, and powers conferred upon investigating committees and their members by the Joint Rules of the Senate and Assembly and the Standing Rules of the Assembly as they are adopted and amended from time to time at this session, which provisions are incorporated herein and made applicable to the committee and its members.

(c) The committee has the following additional powers and duties:

(1) To contract with other agencies, public or private, for the rendition and affording of services, facilities, studies, and reports to the committee as the committee deems necessary to assist it to carry out the purposes for which it is created.

(2) To cooperate with and secure the cooperation of county, city, city and county, and other local law enforcement agencies in investigating any matter within the scope of this rule and to direct the sheriff of any county to serve subpoenas, orders, and other process issued by the committee.

(3) To report its findings and recommendations to the Legislature and the people from time to time.

(4) To do any and all other things necessary or convenient to enable it fully and adequately to exercise its powers, perform its duties, and accomplish the objects and purposes of this rule.

Assembly Legislative Ethics Committee

22.5. (a) The Assembly Legislative Ethics Committee is hereby created. The committee shall consist of six Members of the Assembly, appointed by the Speaker. Notwithstanding any other rule of the Assembly, three members of the committee shall be from the political party having the greatest number of Members in the Assembly and three members shall be from the political party having the second greatest number of

Members. Any temporary or permanent vacancy on the committee shall be filled within 10 days by a member from the same political party. All appointments, including appointments to fill permanent or temporary vacancies, of members from the political party having the second greatest number of Members in the Assembly shall be made from a list of nominees that the Minority Floor Leader provides to the Speaker. The Speaker shall designate one member of the committee from the political party having the greatest number of Members in the Assembly and one member of the committee from the political party having the second greatest number of Members to serve as co-chairs of the committee. The Speaker shall designate one of the co-chairs to serve as the presiding officer at any meeting or hearing conducted by the committee.

If a verified complaint is filed against a member of the committee, the Speaker shall temporarily replace the member with a Member from the same political party, who shall serve until the complaint is dismissed or the Assembly takes final action on the complaint, whichever occurs first.

(b) The provisions of this rule, and of Rule 11.5 related to investigating committees, apply to the committee and govern its proceedings.

Prior to the issuance of any subpoena by the committee with respect to any matter before the committee, it shall, by a resolution adopted by the committee pursuant to a vote in accordance with subdivision (n), define the nature and scope of its investigation in the matter before it.

(c) Funds for the support of the committee shall be provided from the Assembly Operating Fund in the same manner that those funds are made available to other committees of the Assembly.

(d) (1) The committee has the power, pursuant to this rule and Article 3 (commencing with Section 8940) of Chapter 1 of Part 1 of Division 2 of Title 2 of the Government Code, to investigate and make findings and recommendations concerning violations by Members of the Assembly of any provision of Article 2 (commencing with Section 8920) of Chapter 1 of Part 1 of Division 2 of Title 2 of the Government Code or of any other provision of law or legislative rule that governs the conduct of Members of the Assembly, hereafter collectively referred to as "standards of conduct."

(2) The committee may, on its own action pursuant to a vote in accordance with subdivision (n), initiate an investigation of a Member of the Assembly.

(e) Any person may file with the committee a verified complaint in writing, which shall state the name of the Member of the Assembly alleged to have violated any standard of conduct, and which shall set forth the particulars thereof with sufficient clarity and detail to enable the committee to make a determination. The person filing the complaint thereafter shall be designated the complainant.

If a verified complaint is filed with the committee, the committee promptly shall send a copy of the complaint to the Member of the Assembly alleged to have committed the violation complained of, who thereafter shall be designated the respondent.

A complaint may not be filed with the committee after the expiration of 12 months from the date the alleged violation is discovered or three years from the date of the alleged violation, whichever occurs first.

(f) (1) If the committee determines that the verified complaint does not allege facts, directly or upon information and belief, sufficient to constitute a violation of any standard of conduct, it shall dismiss the complaint and so notify the complainant and respondent.

(2) (i) If the committee determines that the verified complaint does allege facts, directly or upon information and belief, sufficient to constitute a violation of any standard of conduct, the committee promptly shall investigate the alleged violation and if, after this preliminary investigation, the committee finds that reasonable cause exists for believing the allegations of the complaint, it shall fix a time for a hearing in the matter, which shall be not more than 30 days after that finding. The committee may, however, seek an extension of this

period, not to exceed an additional 30 days, which may be granted by a majority vote of the Committee on Rules.

(ii) If, after preliminary investigation, the committee does not find that reasonable cause exists for believing the allegations of the complaint, the committee shall dismiss the complaint. In either event, the committee shall notify the complainant and the respondent of its determination.

(3) The committee shall make its determination under paragraph (1) or (2) of this subdivision, pursuant to a vote in accordance with subdivision (n), not later than 90 days after first receiving a complaint that satisfies subdivision (e). The committee may, however, seek an extension, not to exceed 30 days, which may be granted by a majority vote of the membership of the Committee on Rules. If the committee has requested a law enforcement agency to investigate the complaint or if the committee knows the complaint is being investigated by a law enforcement agency, the time limits set forth in this subdivision shall be tolled until the investigation is completed.

(4) The committee's determination under paragraph (1) or (2) of this subdivision shall be stated in writing, with reasons given therefor, and shall be provided to the Assembly, and, in any case concerning an alleged violation of Article 2 (commencing with Section 8920) of Chapter 1 of Part 1 of Division 2 of Title 2 of the Government Code, shall be provided to the appropriate law enforcement agency. This written determination is a public record and is open to public inspection.

(5) Any deliberations of the committee from the time of receipt of a complaint until it decides to dismiss the complaint or to set a hearing shall not be open to the public unless the respondent requests a public meeting.

(g) After the complaint has been filed, the respondent shall be entitled to examine and make copies of all evidence in the possession of the committee relating to the complaint.

(h) If a hearing is held pursuant to subdivision (f), the committee, before the hearing has commenced, shall issue subpoenas and subpoenas duces tecum at the request of any party in accordance with Chapter 4 (commencing with Section 9400) of Part 1 of Division 2 of Title 2 of the Government Code. All of the provisions of that chapter, except Section 9410 of the Government Code, shall apply to the committee and the witnesses before it.

(i) At any hearing held by the committee:

(1) Oral evidence shall be taken on oath or affirmation.

(2) Each party shall have these rights: to be represented by legal counsel; to call and examine witnesses; to introduce exhibits; and to cross-examine opposing witnesses.

(3) The hearing shall be open to the public.

(j) Any official or other person whose name is mentioned at any investigation or hearing of the committee, and who believes that testimony has been given that adversely affects him or her, shall have the right to testify or, at the discretion of the committee, to testify under oath relating solely to the material relevant to the testimony regarding which he or she complains.

(k) The committee shall have 15 days following the hearing within which to deliberate and reach its final determination on the matter as follows:

(1) If the committee finds that the respondent has not violated any standard of conduct, it shall order the action dismissed, shall notify the respondent and complainant thereof, and, in cases concerning an alleged violation of Article 2 (commencing with Section 8920) of Chapter 1 of Part 1 of Division 2 of Title 2 of the Government Code, shall transmit a copy of the complaint and the fact of dismissal to the appropriate law enforcement agency. The complaint and the fact of dismissal transmitted pursuant to this paragraph are public records and open to public inspection.

(2) If the committee finds that the respondent has violated any standard of conduct, it shall state its findings of fact and submit a report thereon to the Assembly. This report shall be accompanied by a House Resolution, authored by the committee, which shall be introduced at the Chief Clerk's desk and then referred by the Committee on Rules to the Ethics Committee.

The House Resolution shall include a statement of the committee's findings and the committee's recommendation for disciplinary action. Within seven days, the committee shall adopt the final form of the House Resolution and report it to the Assembly for placement on the Daily File. The committee also shall send a copy of those findings and report to the complainant and respondent, and, in cases concerning an alleged violation of Article 2 (commencing with Section 8920) of Chapter 1 of Part 1 of Division 2 of Title 2 of the Government Code, shall report thereon to the appropriate law enforcement agency. The report submitted pursuant to this paragraph is a public record and open to public inspection.

After the receipt of a copy of the committee's final report and House Resolution, the Assembly expeditiously shall take appropriate action with respect to the respondent.

(*l*) The filing of a complaint with the committee pursuant to this rule suspends the running of the statute of limitations applicable to any violation of any standard of conduct alleged in the substance of that complaint while the complaint is pending.

(m) The committee shall maintain a record of its investigations, inquiries, and proceedings. All records, complaints, documents, and reports filed with or submitted to or made by the committee, and all records and transcripts of any investigations, inquiries, or hearings of the committee under this rule shall be deemed confidential and shall not be open to inspection, without the express permission of the committee, by any person other than a member of the committee, or an employee of the committee or other state employee designated to assist the committee, except as otherwise specifically provided in this rule. The committee may, by adoption of a resolution, authorize the release to the Attorney General or a district attorney of the appropriate county of any information, records, complaints, documents, reports, and transcripts in its possession that are material to any matter pending before the Attorney General or that district attorney. All matters presented at a public hearing of the committee and all reports of the committee stating a final finding of fact pursuant to subdivision (k) shall be public records and open to public inspection. Any employee of the committee who divulges any matter that is deemed to be confidential by this subdivision shall be subject to discipline by the Committee on Rules.

(n) The committee may take any action authorized by this rule only upon the vote of not less than two members from the registered political party having the greatest number of Members in the Assembly and two members from the registered political party having the second greatest number of Members. Any vacancy on the committee does not reduce the votes required to take action.

(o) The committee may render advisory opinions to Members of the Assembly with respect to the standards of conduct and their application and construction. The committee may secure an opinion from the Legislative Counsel for this purpose or issue its own opinion. Any committee advisory opinion shall be prepared by committee members or staff and shall be adopted by the committee pursuant to subdivision (n).

(p) The committee shall conduct, at least semiannually, an orientation course on the relevant statutes and regulations governing official conduct. The curriculum and presentation of the course shall be established by the Committee on Rules.

Pursuant to Section 8956 of the Government Code, the committee shall conduct, at least annually, an orientation course on the relevant ethical issues and laws relating to lobbying. The committee shall impose fees on lobbyists for attending this course at an amount that will permit the participation of lobbyists to the fullest extent possible.

At least once each biennial session, each Member of the Assembly and each designated employee of the Assembly shall attend one of these courses.

Printing of Committee Reports

23. All requests for the printing of reports of Assembly committees shall be referred to the Committee on Rules. The Committee on Rules shall determine

the number of copies needed and whether the report shall be printed in the Journal. In no event may more than 1,000 copies of any committee report be authorized by the Committee on Rules on the first printing, exclusive of the Journal copies if the report is to be printed therein, unless the Committee on Rules finds and determines that there is a special need for that report in greater numbers.

Upon determination by the Committee on Rules that additional copies of an Assembly committee report are required at any time following the first printing of the authorized number of copies, the Committee on Rules may authorize one or more additional printings in the numbers found by it to be necessary and may make funds available therefor.

An Assembly committee report may not contain more than 100 pages, including the front and back cover thereof and any appendix, unless a greater number of pages has been approved and authorized by the Committee on Rules.

Assembly Employees

24. Every employee who works for a committee of the Assembly or a subcommittee of a committee, for a Member of the Assembly, for the Chief Clerk's office, or for the Sergeant at Arms, is an employee of the Assembly. All employees of the Assembly serve at the pleasure of the Assembly and the terms and conditions of their employment may be modified, or their employment may be terminated at will, at any time and without notice, by the Committee on Rules.

Every applicant for employment by the Assembly shall prepare a formal application for employment on forms prescribed by the Committee on Rules. The application shall include a statement of his or her present employment, his or her employment during the preceding two years, and other pertinent information that the Committee on Rules may require. The application shall be certified under penalty of perjury, and any willful false statement or omission of a material fact shall be punishable as perjury. If the application discloses any fact that indicates that the applicant has a personal interest that would conflict with the faithful performance of his or her duties, the applicant shall not be employed. All applications shall be retained in the records of the committee.

Every employee shall complete the Assembly ethics course in the first six months of his or her employment. Thereafter, every employee shall take the course in the first six months of every legislative session.

Every employee shall, within the first six months of every legislative session, take a course on sexual harassment prevention. The content of the course shall be determined by the Committee on Rules and shall include the Assembly's policy on sexual harassment prevention and response.

An employee may not engage in any outside business activity or outside employment that is inconsistent, incompatible, or in conflict with his or her functions or responsibilities as an employee of the Assembly. Any employee who engages in any outside business activity or employment that is in any way related to his or her functions or responsibilities as an employee shall promptly notify the Committee on Rules of that business activity or employment.

Assembly Proceedings

25. Accredited press representatives may not be excluded from any public legislative meeting or hearing and may not be prohibited from taking photographs of, televising, or recording the committee or house hearings, subject to the following conditions:

(1) This rule shall extend to all public legislative meetings.

(2) Lights shall be used only when cameras are filming, and, when possible, proceedings in hearing rooms and the Chamber shall be filmed without lights.

(3) Every effort should be made to set up filming equipment before hearings or sessions begin.

(4) The committee chairperson or the Speaker shall be notified, as far in advance of the proceedings as possible, that recordings and television cameras will be present and filming.

(5) To the extent practical, flash cameras shall not be used.

(6) Photographs shall be taken in an orderly and expeditious manner so as to cause the least possible inconvenience to the committee or to the Members in the Chamber.

IV. ASSEMBLY FUNCTIONS

A. Duties of Assembly Officers

Duties of the Speaker

26. (a) The Speaker possesses the powers and shall perform the duties prescribed as follows:

(1) To preserve order and decorum; he or she may speak to points of order in preference to the other Members, rising from his or her chair for that purpose.

(2) To decide all questions of order subject to appeal to the Assembly by any Member. On every appeal, the Speaker shall have the right to assign the reason for his or her decision.

(3) To name any Member to perform the duties of the Speaker, except that any substitution may not extend beyond adjournment.

(4) To have general direction over the Assembly chamber and rooms set aside for the use of the Assembly, including the rooms for use by Members as private offices.

(5) To allocate funds, staffing, and other resources for the effective operation of the Assembly.

(6) To appoint the membership of all standing and special committees, including the Committee on Rules, and their respective chairpersons and vice-chairpersons. The Speaker has approval power over the appointment of subcommittees of standing and special committees, except as otherwise provided in Rule 14.5. The Committee on Rules consists of the Chairperson, Vice Chairperson and six other Members who shall be appointed by the Speaker in accordance with the process for appointing the membership of standing committees pursuant to this rule. Two alternate members of the Committee on Rules shall be appointed in accordance with the process for appointing members to

the Committee on Rules. Members and alternates so appointed shall remain in office until their successors are selected as provided for in these rules. The Speaker may designate any member in lieu of or in addition to the alternate member to fill a temporary vacancy. An alternate member may serve when a committee member is absent.

(7) To establish a schedule of meetings of standing committees or subcommittees and to approve special meetings at a time different from the scheduled time.

(8) To have general control and direction over the Journals, papers, and bills of the Assembly and to establish a procedure in accordance with Assembly Rule 118 for admitting employees of the Legislature to the Assembly Chambers, including the lobby in the rear of the chambers and any hallway or area of the floor that is adjacent to the desks occupied by the assistants to the Chief Clerk.

(9) To act as Chairperson of the Committee of the Whole.

(10) To order the Lobby and Gallery cleared whenever he or she deems it necessary.

(11) To authenticate by his or her signature, when necessary or required by law, all bills, memorials, resolutions, orders, proceedings, writs, warrants, and subpoenas issued by order of the Assembly.

(b) The Speaker is an ex officio member of all Assembly and joint committees with all of the rights and privileges of that membership, except the right to vote. In counting a quorum of any of those committees, the Speaker shall not be counted as a member.

(c) The Speaker shall, at each regular session, appoint a Member of the Assembly to serve on the Judicial Council pursuant to Section 6 of Article VI of the California Constitution.

Funerals and Other Ceremonies and Events

27.   The Speaker may designate any one or more of the Members of the Assembly as the representatives of the Assembly to attend funerals and other ceremonies and events in appropriate circumstances. The Members

so designated shall receive their expenses as provided in Joint Rule 35.

Selection of Officers

28.   (a) The Speaker shall appoint all nonelected officers of the Assembly except the Minority Floor Leader.

(b) The Minority Floor Leader shall be selected by the caucus of the political party having the second greatest number of Members in the Assembly.

Duties of the Speaker pro Tempore

29.   The Speaker pro Tempore shall perform those duties assigned by the Speaker, including the responsibility of presiding over sessions of the Assembly and advising the Members on parliamentary procedures of the house.

Majority Floor Leader

30.   It is the duty of the Majority Floor Leader to make those appropriate motions, points of order, or other arrangements that may be necessary to expedite the proceedings of the Assembly, and he or she is responsible for the presentation of all matters that relate to the order of business, and to the promotion of harmony among the membership.

Caucus Chairpersons

31.   The chairperson of the caucus of the political party having the greatest number of Members in the Assembly, and the chairperson of the caucus of the political party having the second greatest number of Members in the Assembly, shall perform those duties that are prescribed by their respective party caucuses.

Chief Clerk

32.   The Chief Clerk of the Assembly has the following duties, powers, and responsibilities:

(a) To keep the bills, papers, and records of the proceedings and actions of the Assembly and to have charge of the publication and distribution of those publications related thereto.

(b) To supervise Assembly employees who are engaged in duties related to subdivision (a).

(c) To act as Parliamentarian of the Assembly and to advise the officers of the Assembly and the Committee on Rules on parliamentary procedure and the Rules of the Assembly when called upon to do so.

(d) To prepare all bills, resolutions, histories, journals, and related publications for printing.

(e) To refuse to permit any bills, papers, or records to be removed from his or her office or out of his or her custody, except upon duly signed receipts from persons authorized.

(f) To mail, before the commencement of each regular session of the Legislature, to each Member a blank form on which the Member may indicate his or her committee preferences. Accompanying the blank form shall be mailed a stamped envelope addressed to the Chief Clerk of the Assembly for returning the form. After their receipt, all those communications shall be held by the Chief Clerk of the Assembly and the information contained in the forms shall be forwarded to the Speaker.

(g) To perform other duties that are prescribed by law or the Committee on Rules.

(h) To make technical changes in measures and amendments pending before the Assembly. The Chief Clerk shall notify the Speaker and the author of the measure of any such change.

(i) To compare all bills, ordered or considered engrossed by the Assembly, with the engrossed copies thereof; before they pass out of the possession of the Assembly, to see that each engrossed bill is a true copy of the original, with those amendments that may have been made thereto; and to see that all engrossed bills are reported back in the order in which they were ordered engrossed.

(j) To assist the Committee on Rules, upon its request, in recommending the reference of bills to the appropriate standing committee.

The Assistant Chief Clerk shall have the powers and perform the duties of the Chief Clerk during his or her absence.

Sergeant at Arms

33. The Sergeant at Arms has the following duties, powers, and responsibilities:

(a) To attend the Assembly during its session, preserve order, announce all official messengers, and serve all process issued by authority of the Assembly and directed by the Speaker; the Sergeant at Arms shall receive actual expenses for himself or herself, or for an assistant, incurred in executing any process.

(b) To see that no person is admitted to the Assembly Chamber except in accordance with these rules.

(c) To have general supervision over the Assistant Sergeants at Arms and be responsible for their official acts and their performance of and regular attendance upon their duties.

(d) To execute all commands of the Speaker.

(e) To perform all other duties pertaining to his or her office as prescribed by law or Assembly rule.

The Chief Assistant Sergeant at Arms shall have the powers and perform the duties of the Sergeant at Arms during his or her absence.

Filling Interim Vacancies— Assembly Elected Officers

34. In the event a vacancy in any office, except Speaker, elected by the membership of the Assembly occurs during joint recesses, the Committee on Rules shall fill the office until the session reconvenes. If a vacancy occurs in the office of the Speaker during a joint recess, the Committee on Rules shall notify the membership within 15 days from the time the vacancy occurs and shall call a caucus of the membership of the Assembly for the purpose of filling the vacancy. This caucus shall be held at the State Capitol within 30 days from the time the vacancy occurs. Notice of the caucus shall be in writing and shall be mailed not less than 10 days prior to the meeting of the caucus. If the Committee on Rules fails to act within 15 days from the time

the vacancy in the office of Speaker occurs, the Chief
Clerk of the Assembly shall act in its place, following
the procedure set forth in this rule. Any person selected
to fill any vacancy pursuant to this rule holds the office
until the session reconvenes.

An affirmative recorded vote of a majority of the
duly elected and qualified Members is required for the
selection by the Assembly caucus of a person to fill a
vacancy pursuant to this rule. The procedure for selecting the Speaker at the caucus is the same as the
procedure required for the election of the Speaker at a
session.

B. Printing
Authority for Printing

35.   The State Printer may not charge any printing
or other work to the Assembly other than as provided by
law or Assembly rule, except upon a written order
signed by the Chief Clerk of the Assembly or the Chief
Administrative Officer of the Assembly. All invoices
for printing furnished to the Assembly shall be itemized
and rendered by the State Printer within 30 days after
completion of the printing. When necessary, the Chief
Clerk of the Assembly or the Chief Administrative
Officer of the Assembly may order certain printed
matter completed in advance of its regular order by the
issuance of a rush order.

Ordering of Printing

36.   The Chief Clerk is authorized to, and is
responsible for, ordering, the printing of bills, resolutions, journals, daily files, histories, and related documents.

The Chief Clerk of the Assembly, or the Chief
Administrative Officer of the Assembly, shall order
other printing as directed or authorized by the Committee on Rules, and the written order for that printing shall
be countersigned by the Speaker or a person designated
by the Speaker. The Chief Clerk of the Assembly or the
Chief Administrative Officer of the Assembly shall also

order other printing as directed or authorized by resolution or motion of the Assembly.

Printing Assembly History and Legislative Handbook

37.   During the session, the Chief Clerk shall cause to be printed and placed upon each Member's desk, prior to convening on Monday of each week, a complete history showing all actions taken upon each measure up to and including the legislative day preceding its issuance. For each legislative day intervening between the issuance of each Weekly History, there shall be printed a Daily Supplemental History showing only actions taken upon any measure since the issuance of the preceding Weekly History.

The Chief Clerk of the Assembly shall, as soon as practicable, in each even-numbered year, commence to compile a legislative manual or handbook, pursuant to Section 9740 of the Government Code.

V.   LEGISLATIVE PROCEDURE
Order of Business

40.   (a) The order of business of the Assembly shall be as follows:

1. Roll Call
2. Prayer by the Chaplain
3. Reading of the Previous Day's Journal
4. Presentation of Petitions
5. Introduction and Reference of Bills
6. Reports of Committees
7. Messages From the Governor
8. Messages From the Senate
9. Motions and Resolutions
10. Business on the Daily File
11. Announcements
12. Adjournment

(b) With the exception of Special Orders of Business, the Speaker may determine that a different order of business will result in a more expeditious processing of the business of the Assembly by ordering resolutions honoring an individual or an organization, introductions, and adjournments in memory of individuals to be taken up in a different order than that listed in subdivision (a).

Pledging of Allegiance to the Flag

41.   At each session, following the prayer by the Chaplain, the Members of the Assembly and its officers and employees present in the Assembly Chamber shall pledge their allegiance to the Flag of the United States of America. The Speaker shall invite guests present in the Assembly Chamber to join in the pledge of allegiance to the Flag of the United States of America.

Reading and Correcting Journals

42.   (a) The reading of the Journal of the previous day may be dispensed with, on motion, by a majority vote of the Members present and voting.

(b) All journals of the Assembly shall be corrected by the Minute Clerk and delivered to the Chief Clerk.

(c) A motion to correct any day's Journal or to print a letter in the Journal shall always be in order and shall require a majority vote of the Members present and voting.

Presentation of Petitions

43.   Whenever petitions, memorials, or other papers are presented by a Member, a brief statement of the contents thereof may be made verbally by the introducer. Petitions are not debatable and shall be filed, or referred to a committee as the Speaker shall determine. Receipt of that presentation and its disposition shall be noted in the Journal.

Upon receipt of a petition for the impeachment of any person subject to impeachment by the Legislature, the Speaker shall, without comment or debate, forthwith refer the petition to committee.

Messages From the Governor

44.   Messages from the Governor shall be delivered to the Chief Clerk or an assistant, and shall be read

and ordered printed in the Journal unless otherwise ordered by an affirmative recorded vote of 54 or more Members.

Messages From the Senate

45. Messages from the Senate shall be delivered to the Chief Clerk or an assistant, and shall be read and ordered printed in the Journal. The Committee on Rules shall refer each bill to a committee, unless upon a motion the Assembly, by an affirmative recorded vote of 41 or more Members, refers it to some other committee. The action to refer a bill is not debatable. The reference shall be entered in the Journal. Assembly bills that have been passed without amendment by the Senate shall be ordered to enrollment.

An Assembly bill amended by the Senate shall be placed upon the unfinished business file but shall not be eligible to be acted upon until it is on the unfinished business file for one legislative day, except that when the Assembly bill is placed upon the unfinished business file during the last two legislative days preceding (1) the January 31 bill passage deadline specified by Section 10 of Article IV of the California Constitution, (2) the scheduled commencement of the interim study recess, or (3) the scheduled commencement of the final recess as specified by the Joint Rules of the Senate and Assembly, it may be acted upon immediately.

Presentation of Guests or Memorials in the Assembly

45.5. These rules do not prohibit the Speaker or Speaker pro Tempore from permitting the introduction of a special guest or guests. A request that a session of the Assembly adjourn in memory of a person shall be made in writing. The request shall be read by the presiding officer immediately prior to adjournment.

A. Bills and Resolutions
Bills Defined

46. (a) The word "bill," as used in these rules, includes a constitutional amendment, a concurrent reso-

lution, and a joint resolution, except as otherwise specifically provided.

(b) A concurrent resolution and a joint resolution, other than a resolution ratifying proposed amendments to the United States Constitution and a resolution calling for a constitutional convention, shall be treated in all respects as a bill except as follows:

(1) It shall be given only one formal reading.

(2) It shall not be deemed a bill within the meaning of subdivision (a) of Section 8 of Article IV of the California Constitution.

Introduction and Reference of Bills

47.   (a) Each bill shall be signed by each Member who is an author or coauthor of the bill before it is introduced. If any bill is introduced that does not contain the signature of its author or coauthor, the bill, on motion of the Member whose name appears thereon without that signature, shall be stricken from the file by an affirmative recorded vote of 41 or more Members. In each legislative session, on the first day when bills are introduced under "Introduction and Reference of Bills," the roll shall be called from A to Z and, as each Member's name is called, the Member may introduce one bill, constitutional amendment, or concurrent or joint resolution. After this roll call, the preprint bills shall be introduced in numerical order.

(b) After the introduction of preprinted bills, and subject to the provisions of the Joint Rules of the Senate and Assembly, any Member desiring to introduce a bill, constitutional amendment, or concurrent or joint resolution may at any time during a session send the same to the Chief Clerk's desk.

(c) When received at the Chief Clerk's desk each bill shall, under the proper order of business, be numbered, read the first time, printed, and referred to a standing committee, and a copy thereof shall be placed upon the desk of each Member before final passage.

All bills, constitutional amendments, and concurrent or joint resolutions introduced before the standing committees of the Assembly are appointed shall be referred to committee, the references to take effect when the committees are appointed.

(d) The Committee on Budget may introduce a bill germane to any subject within the jurisdiction of the committee in the same manner as any member. Any other standing committee may introduce a total of five bills in each year of a biennial session that are germane to any subject within the proper consideration of the committee.

(e) No committee, except the Committee on Budget, may introduce or author a House Resolution, Concurrent Resolution, or Joint Resolution.

(f) A committee bill may not be introduced unless it contains the signatures of a majority of all of the members, including the chairperson, of the committee. If all of the members of a committee sign the bill, at the option of the committee chairperson the committee members' names need not appear as authors in the heading of the printed bill.

(g) Subdivision (d) or (e) of this rule may be suspended with respect to a particular bill or resolution by approval of the Committee on Rules.

Bills Authored by a Former Member

47.1.   Whenever the author of a bill in the Assembly is no longer a Member of the Legislature, upon a request of a committee or current Member of the house in which the bill was introduced, the Assembly Committee on Rules may authorize that committee or Member to be the author of that bill. Absent that authorization, an action may not be taken by a committee or the Assembly with respect to a bill authored by a former Member.

Limitation on the Introduction of Bills

49.   (a) A Member may introduce not more than 40 bills in the regular session. As used in this rule, "bills" includes constitutional amendments.

(b) Notwithstanding subdivision (a) of this rule, a Member may introduce not more than five resolutions in the regular session. As used in this rule, "resolutions" include House, Concurrent and Joint Resolutions, but do not include resolutions introduced by a Member for the specific purpose of organizing a session that is convened pursuant to Article IV, Section 3 (a) of the State Constitution or resolutions introduced by the Speaker as part of a session honoring a retiring Assembly Member.

(c) This rule may be suspended with respect to a particular bill or resolution by approval of the Committee on Rules.

Reference of Bills to Committee

51.   Except as otherwise provided in this rule, the Committee on Rules shall refer each bill to a committee by a majority vote of the membership of the committee, unless upon a motion the Assembly, by an affirmative recorded vote of 41 or more Members, refer it to some other committee. A motion to refer a bill is not debatable, except as to the propriety of the motion, and it may not open the main question to debate.

The Committee on Rules may require that, if a bill is reported out of the committee to which it has been referred, it shall be re-referred to another committee that shares jurisdiction of the subject matter of the bill.

Spot Bills

51.5.   A bill that upon introduction makes no substantive change in or addition to existing law, and would not otherwise affect the ongoing operations of state or local government, except a bill stating legislative intent to make necessary statutory changes to implement the Budget Bill, may not be referred to a committee by the Committee on Rules. If the author subsequently proposes to the Committee on Rules to make substantive changes in the bill as introduced, the Committee on Rules may refer the bill to a committee, together with the proposed changes for consideration as author's amendments. A vote on passage of the bill may not be taken, however, until the bill with its amendments, if adopted, has been in print for at least 15 days.

Delivery of Bills to State Printer

52.   After introduction and first reading, all bills shall be delivered to the State Printer.

Introduction of House Resolutions

53.   All house resolutions shall be numbered and shall be referred to the appropriate committee by the Committee on Rules.

Each house resolution shall be signed by each Member who is an author or coauthor of the house resolution before it is introduced.

Resolutions by Member

54.   A concurrent resolution or a house resolution may be introduced relating to a present or former state or federal elected official or a member of his or her immediate family. Other resolutions for the purpose of commendation or congratulation of any person, group, or organization, or for the purpose of expressing sympathy, regret, or sorrow on the death of any person, shall be prepared as a Rules Committee Resolution and presented to the committee for appropriate action.

The Committee on Rules may approve exceptions to this rule for house resolutions. The Chief Clerk may not accept for introduction any house resolution that is contrary to this rule unless it is accompanied by the approval of the Committee on Rules.

B.   Standing Committee Functions
Standing Committee Rules

55.   Subject to the Joint Rules of the Senate and Assembly, the Rules of the Assembly shall govern the conduct of all committee and subcommittee meetings.

Meetings of Standing Committees and Subcommittees

56.   All standing committees and subcommittees shall meet at the hour and place provided by the schedule established by the Speaker, unless permission for a different hearing time is granted by the Speaker. A committee or subcommittee may not meet during any

session of the Assembly, nor may any Member of the Assembly attend a conference committee meeting on any bill during any session of the Assembly without first obtaining permission from the Assembly.

When an unscheduled meeting of a standing committee or subcommittee has been so ordered, the meeting shall convene in an area that is readily accessible to the public and the Assembly shall take care that every effort is made to inform the public that a meeting has been called. An unscheduled meeting of a committee or subcommittee may not be held in the Assembly Chamber.

No bill may be set for hearing, nor may any notice thereof be published by any Assembly committee or subcommittee, until the bill has been referred to the committee or subcommittee. Nothing in this paragraph shall prevent a committee or subcommittee from acting with regard to a bill referred to it where the only action taken is to cause the bill to be reported to the Assembly with the recommendation that amendments be adopted and the bill be reprinted as amended and re-referred to the committee or subcommittee.

The several standing committees and subcommittees and their chairpersons may adopt a procedure under which bills are scheduled for hearing on the basis of like subject matter groupings.

Setting and Hearing Bills in Committee

56.1.   All bills referred to a standing committee pursuant to Assembly Rule 51 shall be set and heard, if requested by the author, as specified by the Joint Rules. If the analysis of an author's amendment that is subsequently adopted pursuant to Assembly Rule 68 discloses that the amendment makes a substantial substantive change to the original bill as referred by the Rules Committee, the bill as amended shall either be set and heard by the committee having jurisdiction of the bill as amended or re-referred to the Committee on Rules pursuant to the Assembly Rules.

Committee Analyses

56.5.   Except as otherwise provided in this rule, each standing committee and subcommittee shall prepare an analysis of every bill it has set for hearing, which shall be available to the public in the office of the committee or subcommittee one working day prior to the date on which the hearing is to be held. In the case of a special meeting, or a meeting of the Committee on Appropriations or the Committee on Budget, or their subcommittees, the analysis shall be available to the public at the beginning of the hearing. No question concerning a committee's compliance with this rule with regard to any bill shall be in order following a vote on passage of the bill in that committee. As used in this rule, a "working day" is any day on which a house file is published.

A copy of each committee analysis shall be transmitted by the committee secretary to the Assembly Floor Analysis Unit at the same time it is made available to the public.

Committee Consultants: Floor Analyses

56.6.   Except as otherwise provided in this rule, the consultants of a standing committee or subcommittee are responsible for monitoring bills assigned to their respective committee or subcommittee throughout the entire legislative process. Except for resolutions and bills on the Consent Calendar, a consultant of the appropriate standing committee shall prepare, in a timely fashion, an analysis of every bill on third reading or the unfinished business file, and of any amendment to a bill that is on the Assembly floor, as directed by the Assembly Floor Analysis Unit.

The committee consultant who prepares the analysis shall transmit a copy of the completed analysis to the Assembly Floor Analysis Unit. The Assembly Floor Analysis Unit is responsible for final editing for grammar and format of all floor analyses.

Consent Calendar

56.7. If the chairperson of a committee or subcommittee, in advance of a hearing, proposes to recommend any bills for consideration on the Consent Calendar without hearing testimony on those bills in committee, a list of those bills shall be made available to the public at the same time as the committee analysis required under Rule 56.5.

Committee Quorum

57. Except as otherwise provided in this rule, a majority of the membership of any standing committee constitutes a quorum for the transaction of its business, including the decision to recommend the adoption of any amendments to any bill. A majority of the membership of the committee, or a subcommittee thereof, is required to report a bill out of the committee or subcommittee, respectively. Any vacancy on a standing committee shall not reduce the votes required to take action on a bill in that committee.

Whenever a member is disqualified pursuant to Joint Rule 44 or the Political Reform Act of 1974 (Title 9 (commencing with Section 81000) of the Government Code) from voting or taking any other action related to the passage, defeat, or amendment of a bill in committee, that disqualification shall be treated the same as a vacancy. The member shall advise the chairperson of a disqualification, and the chairperson shall announce which members are so disqualified at the commencement of the hearing on the bill.

Reconsideration

57.1. After a committee has voted on a bill, reconsideration may be granted only one time. Pursuant to subdivision (a) of Joint Rule 62, reconsideration may be granted within 15 legislative days or prior to the interim study joint recess, whichever occurs first. A vote on reconsideration may not be taken without the same notice required to set a bill for hearing unless that vote is taken at the same meeting at which the vote to be reconsidered was taken and the author is present. An action taken by a committee may not be reconsidered except by a majority vote of the membership of the committee.

Bills Reported Back to Assembly

58. All committees shall act upon bills referred to them as soon as practicable, and when acted upon each bill shall be reported back to the Assembly forthwith; the chairperson of each committee is charged with the observance of this rule. The chairperson of each committee shall, insofar as practicable, report back bills in the same order as they were acted upon by the committee.

Appropriations Suspense File

58.2. The Committee on Appropriations may maintain a suspense file, to which bills may be referred by vote of a majority of the members of the committee present and voting, pending further consideration by the committee. A bill may be taken off the suspense file and heard, upon two days' notice published in the file, by a vote of a majority of the members of the committee present and voting. A bill removed from the suspense file for the purpose of amendment only, pursuant to Rule 68, shall be re-referred to the committee and shall be placed on the suspense file pending further consideration by the committee.

Voting in Committee

58.5. When a standing committee or subcommittee takes action on a bill, including reconsideration, the vote may be by roll call vote only. All roll call votes taken in a standing committee or subcommittee shall be recorded by the committee secretary on forms provided by the Chief Clerk of the Assembly. The record of a roll call vote shall show, for each proposal voted upon: all votes for and against, all members absent, and all members not voting. The chairperson of each standing committee or subcommittee shall promptly transmit a copy of the record of the roll call votes to the Chief

Clerk of the Assembly, who shall cause the votes to be published in an appendix to the Journal on a monthly basis.

The committee secretary of each standing committee or subcommittee shall promptly transmit a copy of the record of the roll call votes to the Assembly Floor Analysis Unit.

A member may submit a written explanation of his or her vote, absence, or failure to vote on any bill or resolution, and that explanation shall be printed in the appendix to the Journal in the appropriate place, provided that no explanation may exceed 50 words in length.

At the request of the author or any member of the committee, the committee shall hold the roll open on any Assembly bill until the adjournment of the committee meeting. At no time may a bill be passed out by a committee without a quorum being present.

This rule does not apply to any of the following:

(a) Adoption of author's amendments to a bill.

(b) Withdrawal of a bill from a committee calendar at the request of an author.

(c) Return of bills to the house where the bills have not been voted on by the committee.

(d) Votes of subcommittees of the Committee on Budget when considering the Budget Bill.

(e) Votes of the Committee on Rules when referring bills to committees.

Subject Matter of Bill Recommended for Interim Study

59. Whenever it is the decision of a standing committee that a bill referred to that committee shall not be given a do-pass recommendation, but that the subject matter of the bill should be referred for study, that standing committee shall retain the bill in its possession and report its recommendation to the Assembly that the subject matter of the bill be referred to the Committee on Rules for that committee's assignment of the subject matter to an appropriate committee.

Nothing in this rule shall be construed to prohibit a committee from subsequently reporting the bill to the

Assembly with a do-pass or do-pass as amended recommendation or from reporting it out of committee without further action on the final day of the session.

Committee Chairperson as Author

60.   A chairperson of a standing committee may not preside at a committee hearing to consider a bill of which he or she is the sole author or the lead author, except that the Chairperson of the Committee on Budget may preside at the hearing of the Budget Bill by the Committee on Budget.

Reports of Committees

61.   Specially prepared reports of standing and special committees shall be delivered to the Chief Clerk or an assistant, and shall be read and ordered printed in the Journal unless otherwise ordered by the Speaker or a majority vote of the Members present and voting.

When a report of a joint legislative committee is delivered to the Assembly Desk, the Speaker shall refer it to a standing committee for review and appropriate action.

Constitutional Amendments

62.5.   All constitutional amendments shall be referred to the policy standing committee having jurisdiction of that subject matter and, upon being reported out of that committee, shall be re-referred to the committee having constitutional amendments within its jurisdiction.

C.   Passage of Bills
Daily File

63.   There shall be printed an Assembly Daily File for each legislative day. The following listing shall constitute the order of business on the Daily File:

1. Special Orders of the Day
2. Second Reading, Assembly Bills
3. Second Reading, Senate Bills
4. Unfinished Business

5. Third Reading, Assembly Bills
6. Third Reading, Senate Bills

All bills on the Daily File shall be called for consideration, provided that Rule 58 has been complied with in the order of their listing. All scheduled committee hearings, together with the list of bills to be heard, shall be published in the Daily File.

Copies of Bills for Action on Floor

64.   A bill may not be considered or acted upon on the floor of the Assembly unless and until a copy of the bill as introduced, and a copy of each amended form of the bill, has been distributed to the desk of each Member in hard copy or in portable document format (PDF) via computer.

Second Reading of Bills

66.   All bills shall be read by title the second time in the order of their appearance upon the second reading file. Upon second reading, Assembly bills reported without amendments shall be ordered engrossed, and Senate bills reported without amendments shall be ordered to third reading. All bills reported out of committee shall be placed on the second reading file for the next legislative day, and may not be read a second time until the next legislative day under that order of business. As used in this rule, "bill" does not include a joint or concurrent resolution, but does include a constitutional amendment.

Bills Requiring General Fund Appropriation

66.6.   Until the Budget Bill has been enacted, the Assembly may not send to the Governor for consideration any bill appropriating funds for expenditure during the fiscal year for which the Budget Bill is to be enacted, except emergency bills recommended by the Governor or appropriations for the salaries and expenses of the Legislature.

Passage of Budget Bill

66.7.   The Budget Bill may not be voted upon for final passage on the floor of the Assembly unless it complies with subdivision (f) of Section 12 of Article IV and Sections 1.3 and 20 of Article XVI of the California Constitution.

Committee Amendments

67.   Committee amendments reported with bills shall be considered upon their second reading, and the amendments may be adopted by majority vote of the Members present and voting. Assembly and Senate bills amended on second reading by committee amendment shall be ordered reprinted and returned to the second reading file. Assembly bills so amended shall be engrossed after printing.

Committee amendments reported with bills shall be prepared, or approved as to form, by the Legislative Counsel. Five copies of the committee amendments to Assembly bills and five copies of the committee amendments to Senate bills shall be delivered to the Chief Clerk's desk.

The Chief Clerk shall cause to be transmitted to the Assembly Floor Analysis Unit a copy of each committee report and committee amendment, unless the committee report or committee amendment is relative to a joint, concurrent, or house resolution.

Adoption of amendments to any bill in the Assembly prior to third reading, other than by a roll call, shall not preclude subsequent consideration in committee, or on the third reading by the Assembly, of the bill, those amendments, or any part thereof.

Author's Amendments

68.   Upon request of the author of a bill, the chairperson of the committee to which the bill has been referred may, by his or her individual action taken independently of any committee meeting, cause the bill to be reported to the Assembly with the recommendation that amendments submitted by the author be

adopted and the bill be reprinted as amended and re-referred to the committee.

Notwithstanding any other rule, a bill to be amended pursuant to this rule may not be placed on the second reading file for the adoption of those amendments.

Vote on Passage of Bill as Amended

68.5.   Except as otherwise provided in this rule, a vote on passage of any bill in a standing committee or subcommittee shall be taken only when the bill is in print, including any previously adopted amendments to the bill. A vote on passage of an amended bill, when the amended form of the bill is not in print, may be taken only if the sole effect of the amendment is to add coauthors to the bill or if the committee determines that the effect of the amendment upon the bill can be readily understood by all of the members and audience present at the hearing. In that circumstance, any member may require that the amendments be in writing at the time of their adoption.

Bill Analysis Prior to Third Reading

68.6.   A bill, concurrent resolution, or joint resolution may not be considered on third reading unless and until an analysis of the measure has been distributed by the Assembly Floor Analysis Unit and placed upon the desks of the Members, unless otherwise ordered by the Speaker.

Analysis of Conference Committee Amendments

68.7.   A report of a conference committee on any bill, other than the Budget Bill, that recommends the substantive amendment of a bill may not be considered unless and until an analysis of the proposed amendment has been distributed by the Assembly Floor Analysis Unit and placed upon the desks of the Members, unless otherwise ordered by the Speaker.

Printing of Conference Committee Reports

68.8. A conference report may not be heard by the Assembly until it has been in print for two days prior to being taken up by the house.

Conference Committee: Substantial Policy Change

68.9. (a) A conference committee on any bill, other than the Budget Bill or a bill that is making statutory changes to implement the Budget Bill, may not approve any substantial policy change in any bill if that substantial policy change has been defeated in a policy committee of the Assembly within the current legislative session. For purposes of this rule, the most recent action of a policy committee with regard to a substantial policy change is deemed the only action taken when the policy committee has taken inconsistent actions with respect to a substantial policy change.

(b) For purposes of subdivision (d) of Joint Rule 29.5, the term "heard" means that a printed bill with substantially similar language was before the appropriate committee and taken up at a regular or special hearing of the committee during the current legislative session; or that an amendment, which was drafted and given a request number or approved as to form by the Legislative Counsel, was before the committee and taken up at a regular or special hearing of the committee.

Amendments From the Floor

69. (a) Any Member may move to amend a bill during its second or third reading, and that motion to amend may be adopted by a majority vote of the Members present and voting.

Amendments to a bill offered from the floor, except committee amendments reported with bills, amendments offered with a motion to amend and re-refer a bill to committee, amendments deleting any number of words, or amendments previously printed in the Journal, are not in order unless and until a copy of the proposed amendments has been placed upon the desks of the Members. A copy of a bill that has been amended only to add coauthors to the bill is not required to be placed upon the desks of the Members if both the Speaker and Minority Leader grant an exemption.

Amendments offered from the floor during a bill's second or third reading shall be prepared, or approved as to form, by the Legislative Counsel.

Before debate five copies of the proposed amendment to Assembly bills, and five copies of the proposed amendments to Senate bills, shall be delivered to the Chief Clerk's desk. One copy of the proposed amendment shall be transmitted by the Chief Clerk to the Assembly Floor Analysis Unit. Bills so amended upon second or third reading shall be reprinted and re-engrossed. The Chief Clerk shall order printed as many copies of all amended bills as he or she may determine to be necessary.

(b) (1) Amendments from the floor during a bill's second or third reading that would make a substantive change in the bill shall be submitted to the Chief Clerk's desk by 5:00 p.m. or the time of adjournment, whichever is later, the business day before the start of session on the legislative day at which they are to be considered.

(2) Upon receipt of the proposed amendments by the Chief Clerk, an analysis shall be prepared by the committee of origin in conjunction with the Assembly Floor Analysis Unit, and a copy of that analysis shall be distributed to each Member's desk prior to the beginning of debate on adoption of the proposed amendments, unless otherwise ordered by the Speaker.

(3) As used in this subdivision, "bill" does not include a joint or concurrent resolution, but does include a constitutional amendment.

(c) Paragraph (1) of subdivision (b) does not apply to (1) amendments to a bill taken up without reference to file, (2) amendments to a bill to add or delete an urgency clause, (3) amendments to a bill that are identical to other amendments submitted to the Chief Clerk's desk in accordance with the requirements of this rule, (4) amendments to the Budget Bill or to a bill that is making statutory changes necessary to implement the

Budget Bill, or (5) amendments to a bill to make the bill contingent upon the enactment of another bill, or to incorporate one or more statutory amendments proposed in another bill to avoid superseding those amendments.

(d) Any bill amended on the second or third reading file shall be ordered reprinted and returned to the third reading file, and may not be acted on by the Assembly until the bill, as amended, has been on the Daily File for one calendar day. This subdivision does not apply to a bill that is amended to add or delete an urgency clause or to a bill that is amended to make statutory changes to implement the Budget Bill.

(e) A motion to amend a bill on the second or third reading file, other than committee amendments reported pursuant to Rule 57, is not in order on (1) the last two legislative days preceding the January 31 bill passage deadline specified by Section 10 of Article IV of the California Constitution or (2) the last seven days preceding the scheduled commencement of the interim study recess or the scheduled commencement of the final recess as specified by the Joint Rules of the Senate and Assembly. Paragraph (1) or (2) may be suspended temporarily by two-thirds vote of the Members present and voting. This subdivision does not apply to amendments to a bill to add or delete an urgency clause, or to incorporate one or more statutory amendments proposed in another bill to avoid superseding those amendments.

Consideration of Political Reform Act Bills

69.1. Pursuant to Section 81012 of the Government Code, any bill that would amend the Political Reform Act of 1974 (Title 9 (commencing with Section 81000) of the Government Code) may not be passed until, 12 days prior to being considered for passage, the bill in its final form has been delivered by the Chief Clerk to the Fair Political Practices Commission for distribution to the news media and to every person who has requested the commission to send a copy of any such bill to him or her.

Electronic Distribution of Bills, Conference Reports, Amendments, and Analyses

69.5.   Any requirement that bills, conference reports, amendments, or an analysis be placed on the desks of the Members is satisfied by electronic distribution of the same information in portable document format (PDF) via computer to the desk of the Members through the Assembly Floor System, unless otherwise ordered by the Speaker.

Consideration of Bills Re-referred to Committee

70.   Whenever a bill that has been amended and re-referred to committee is reported out by that committee, it shall be placed on the second reading file and may not be transferred therefrom to the third reading file until the following day.

Uncontested Bills

71.   A bill may not be placed on the Assembly Consent Calendar unless it has met the requirements of Joint Rule 22.1 with respect to each Assembly standing committee to which the bill has been referred.

Consideration of Concurrent and Joint Resolutions

73.   A concurrent or joint resolution may be amended by a majority vote of the Members present and voting. The ayes and noes may not be called upon the adoption of concurrent resolutions, except those authorizing expenditures of money, unless regularly demanded, or required by statute or the California Constitution.

Adoption of Resolutions

74.   Any resolution upon which a roll call vote is demanded requires an affirmative recorded vote of 41 or more Members for adoption.

The adoption of any resolution authorizing the expenditure of money requires an affirmative recorded vote of 41 or more Members.

Printing of Resolutions

75.   When any previously printed house resolution is before the Assembly for adoption, it may be printed in the Journal only if amendments to it have been adopted, in which case it shall be printed as amended. In the absence of those amendments, house resolutions before the Assembly for adoption shall be referred to by day and page of the Journal as printed upon introduction. For the purposes of this rule, the adding of a coauthor shall not be deemed an amendment.

Concurrence in Senate Amendments

77.   Concurrence in any Senate Amendment to an Assembly bill requires the same affirmative recorded vote as the vote required by the California Constitution for the passage of the bill. A vote on concurrence may not be taken until the bill has been on the unfinished business file for one calendar day, except that when the bill is placed upon the unfinished business file during the last two legislative days preceding (1) the January 31 bill passage deadline specified by Section 10 of Article IV of the California Constitution, (2) the scheduled commencement of the interim study recess, or (3) the scheduled commencement of the final recess as specified by the Joint Rules of the Senate and Assembly, it may be acted upon immediately. The vote on concurrence shall be deemed the vote upon final passage of the bill.

Senate amendments to Assembly bills may not be concurred in unless and until an analysis of the measure has been distributed by the Assembly Floor Analysis Unit and a copy placed upon the desks of the Members, unless otherwise ordered by the Speaker. As used in this rule, "bill" does not include a joint or concurrent resolution, but does include a constitutional amendment.

Digest of Bills Amended in Senate

77.1.   Whenever the Senate amends and passes an Assembly bill, the Legislative Counsel shall, within one day after the bill is passed by the Senate, prepare and transmit to the Chief Clerk and the Speaker a brief digest summarizing the effect of the Senate amendment. Upon receipt from the Legislative Counsel, the Chief Clerk shall cause the digest to be printed in the Daily File immediately following any reference in the file to the bill covered by the digest.

Substantially Amended Bills

77.2.   If the analysis of an amendment adopted on the floor discloses that the amendment makes a substantial substantive change to a bill as passed by the last committee of reference, the bill, as amended, may be referred by the Speaker to the appropriate committee.

A bill that was previously reported from a policy or fiscal committee of reference in compliance with Joint Rule 61 is not subject to the deadlines in Joint Rule 61 if the bill is subsequently referred to a policy or fiscal committee pursuant to this rule.

If the digest to an Assembly Bill that has been returned to the Assembly by the Senate for concurrence in Senate amendments discloses that the Senate has made a substantial substantive change in the bill as first passed by the Assembly, the bill may be referred by the Speaker to the appropriate committee.

Inactive File

78.   Whenever a bill has been passed twice on the third reading file on two successive legislative days, it shall be placed forthwith upon a special file to be known as the inactive file. A bill also may be placed on the inactive file at the request of the author. When a bill has been placed on the inactive file, it may be returned to the third reading file by request of the author. Notice of the request to return the bill to the third reading file shall be published one day in advance in the Assembly File. The bill, when returned to the third reading file, shall then be placed at the foot of the third reading file.

When a bill, placed on the inactive file from the second reading file or the unfinished business file, is removed from the inactive file, it shall be returned to the foot of the second reading file or the unfinished business file, respectively, in the next published Daily File.

Engrossing and Enrolling Bills

79. The Engrossing and Enrolling Clerk shall engross and enroll all bills that come to his or her hands for that purpose, in compliance with the provisions of Section 9503 of the Government Code, and in the order of time in which the same shall be acted upon by the Assembly.

After final passage by both houses, any Assembly bill not amended by the Senate shall be ordered by the Speaker forthwith to be enrolled, as provided in Sections 9508 and 9509 of the Government Code. The Chief Clerk shall report both the day and hour each enrolled bill is presented to the Governor, which report shall be entered in the Journal.

VI. PARLIAMENTARY PROCEDURE

A. Motions and Questions

Precedence of Motions During Debate

80. When a question is under debate or before the Assembly, no motions shall be received but the following, which shall take precedence in the order named:

First—To adjourn;
Second—To recess to a time certain;
Third—To lay on the table;
Fourth—For the previous question;
Fifth—To set as a special order;
Sixth—To postpone indefinitely;
Seventh—To refer to or to re-refer;
Eighth—To amend.

Questions of Order Decided Without Debate

81. All incidental questions of order, arising after a motion is made for any of the questions named in

Rule 80 and pending that motion, shall be decided by the Speaker without debate, whether on appeal or otherwise.

Appeal From Decision of the Speaker

82. Any Member may appeal from a decision of the Speaker without waiting for recognition by the Speaker, even though another Member has the floor. An appeal is not in order when another is pending, or when other business has been transacted by the Assembly prior to the appeal being taken. Upon the appeal being seconded, the Speaker may give his or her reasons for the decision, and the Member making the appeal may give his or her reasons for the appeal, and the Speaker forthwith shall put one of the following questions to the Assembly:

(1) "Shall the decision of the Speaker be sustained?"

(2) "Shall the decision of the Speaker be overruled?"

An appeal may not be amended and yields only to a motion to recess or adjourn, or to lay on the table, or a question of personal privilege. If an appeal is laid on the table, that action shall have no effect on the pending question.

An appeal may not be debated when relating to indecorum, the transgression of rules, or the priority of business. A majority vote of the Members present and voting decides any appeal. In the event of a tie vote, the appeal is lost.

Speaker Explains Order of Business

83. The Speaker may, on his or her own motion or the motion of any Member, explain the order of business when the motion pending before the Assembly is not debatable. That explanation may not consume more than two minutes.

To Adjourn

84. A motion to adjourn is not debatable and may not be amended, and is always in order, except: (a) when another Member has the floor; (b) when the

Assembly is voting; or (c) during a call of the Assembly. The name of any Member moving an adjournment, and the hour at which the motion was made and adjournment taken, shall be entered in the Journal. A motion to adjourn shall be adopted by a majority vote of the Members present and voting.

When a motion to adjourn is made and seconded, it shall be in order for the Speaker, before putting the question, to permit any Member to state to the Assembly any fact relating to the condition of the business of the Assembly which would seem to render it improper or inadvisable to adjourn. That statement may not occupy more than two minutes and is not debatable.

An affirmative recorded vote of a majority of the duly elected and qualified Members is required to adjourn any session of the Assembly *sine die.*

To Recess to a Time Certain

85. A motion to recess to a time certain is treated the same as a motion to adjourn, except that the motion is debatable when no business is before the Assembly, and can be amended as to the time and duration of the recess. It yields only to a motion to adjourn.

To Lay on the Table

86. A motion to lay on the table is not debatable and may not be amended.

A motion to table a bill, constitutional amendment, or concurrent or joint resolution is adopted by an affirmative recorded vote of 41 or more Members.

Any motion to lay on the table, if carried by 41 or more votes, carries with it the main question and everything that adheres to it, except that a motion to lay an amendment on the table, if adopted, does not carry with it a bill, constitutional amendment, or concurrent, joint, or house resolution.

A motion to lay an amendment on the table is adopted by a majority vote of the Members present and voting.

A motion to lay on the table may not be applied with respect to reconsideration.

The Previous Question

87.   The previous question shall be put only when demanded by five Members, and its effect, when sustained by a majority vote of the Members present and voting, shall be to put an end to all debate and bring the Assembly to a vote only on the question then pending, except that the proponent of the matter pending shall be allowed not more than five minutes to close the debate.

Motion to Set Special Order

88.   A motion to set any matter before the Assembly as a special order of business is adopted by an affirmative recorded vote of 54 or more members. The motion is debatable only as to the propriety of setting the main question as a special order of business, and may be amended only as to the time.

Motion to Postpone to a Time Certain

89.   A motion to postpone to a time certain is deemed and treated as a motion to set as a special order.

Motion to Postpone Indefinitely

90.   The making of a motion to postpone indefinitely any bill, motion, or amendment opens the main question to debate. If the motion to postpone indefinitely prevails by an affirmative recorded vote of 41 or more Members, the main question may not be acted upon again during the session.

Motion to Amend

91.   A motion to amend may itself be amended, but an "amendment to an amendment" may not be amended. A motion to substitute is deemed to be a motion to amend and is considered the same as an amendment.

Only one substitute is in order when an amendment is pending. A motion to amend or to substitute is debatable, except where the main question to be amended is not debatable. Any motion to amend may be adopted by a majority vote of the Members present and voting.

A motion to amend that is decided in the negative is not again in order on the same day, or at the same stage of proceeding. The fact that a motion to amend by striking out certain words is decided in the negative does not preclude a motion to amend by adding words, or a motion to amend by striking out and inserting words, except that in no case may a further amendment be substantially the same as the one rejected.

Subject to the above provisions of this rule and Rule 69, a motion to amend is in order during the second or third reading of any bill.

Amendment To Be Germane

92.   An amendment to any bill, other than a bill stating legislative intent to make necessary statutory changes to implement the Budget Bill, whether reported by a committee or offered by a Member, is not in order when the amendment relates to a different subject than, is intended to accomplish a different purpose than, or requires a title essentially different than, the original bill.

A motion or proposition on a subject different from that under consideration may not be admitted as an amendment.

An amendment is not in order that changes the original number of any bill.

A Member may not be added or deleted as an author or coauthor of a bill or resolution without his or her consent.

Consideration of Motions

93.   A motion, whether oral or written, may not be adopted until it is seconded and distinctly stated to the Assembly by the Speaker.

Motions in Writing

94.   Upon request of the Speaker, all motions shall be reduced to writing and shall be read to the Assembly by the Speaker before being acted upon.

Withdrawal of Motions

95.   After a motion is stated by the Speaker, or a bill, resolution, or petition is read by the Chief Clerk, it is·in the possession of the Assembly.

Motion to Withdraw or Re-refer Bills

96.   (a) A motion to withdraw a bill or resolution from committee, or to re-refer a bill or resolution from one committee to another committee, may be made during the regular order of business. A motion to re-refer may be debated only as to the propriety of the reference, and shall require an affirmative recorded vote of 41 or more Members.

(b) A bill or resolution may not be withdrawn from committee and placed upon the file, unless a motion to withdraw has been heard by, and has been approved by a majority vote of, the Committee on Rules. This subdivision does not apply to a bill in a fiscal committee that has been amended so as not to require its reference to a fiscal committee, as indicated by the Legislative Counsel's Digest.

(c) A motion to continue a motion to withdraw a bill or resolution from committee requires a majority of those members present and voting. A motion to withdraw a motion to withdraw is not in order.

Re-reference of Measures on File

97.   A motion to re-refer a bill or resolution that is on the Assembly Daily File to committee may be made during the regular order of business. The motion is debatable only as to the propriety of that reference and shall require an affirmative recorded vote of 41 or more Members.

Bills Stricken From File

98.   A motion to strike from the file any bill or resolution requires an affirmative recorded vote of 41 or more Members. That bill or resolution may not be acted upon again during the session.

Motion to Rescind Action or Expunge Record

99. Previous to the approval of the Journal by the Assembly, any action may be rescinded and its record ordered expunged by the affirmative recorded vote sufficient to take that action originally, except that an action may not be rescinded and the record expunged by a vote less than an affirmative recorded vote of 41 or more Members. A motion to rescind the action and expunge the record may not be made twice on the same proposition.

A motion to rescind is not in order on any matter upon which a vote to reconsider has previously been taken in the Assembly.

Whenever any action of the Assembly is rescinded and its record ordered expunged, the record of the action expunged may not appear in any form whatsoever, except that the record of the proceedings on the motion to rescind and expunge shall appear in the Journal as and when printed.

Reconsideration of Vote

100. (a) A motion to reconsider a vote on the next legislative day shall be made on the same day the vote to be reconsidered was taken. A motion to reconsider may not adopted unless it receives an affirmative recorded vote of 41 or more Members. A motion to reconsider may be voted on without a second.

A motion to reconsider a vote shall be made by a Member voting on the question, and takes precedence over all motions, except a motion to adjourn. Upon that motion being made, the matter to be reconsidered forthwith shall be placed upon the unfinished business file, and further action may not be taken prior to the next legislative day. When a motion to reconsider has once been made, the motion is the property of the Assembly. When reconsideration is granted, the matter to be reconsidered shall be before the Assembly in the same status it had prior to the vote being reconsidered.

(b) (1) Interim Study Recess:

No motion to reconsider the vote whereby amendments are concurred in on Assembly bills, the vote whereby a Senate bill is passed and returned to the Senate, or the vote whereby a conference committee report is adopted is in order on the last two legislative days preceding the interim study recess.

A motion to reconsider the vote whereby amendments are refused concurrence on Assembly bills, the vote whereby Senate bills are refused passage, or the vote whereby a conference committee report is refused adoption is in order on the last legislative day preceding the interim study recess. The motion may be taken up before the end of that legislative day.

As used in this paragraph, "bill" does not include a joint or concurrent resolution.

(2) January 31—Even-numbered Year:

A motion to reconsider the vote whereby an Assembly bill is passed to the Senate is not in order on the last two legislative days preceding January 31 of the even-numbered year.

A motion to reconsider the vote whereby an Assembly bill is refused passage on its third reading is in order on the last legislative day preceding January 31 of the even-numbered year. The motion must be taken up before the end of that legislative day.

As used in this paragraph, "bill" does not include a Senate bill, a constitutional amendment, or a joint or concurrent resolution.

(3) Spring or Summer Recess:

A motion to reconsider the vote whereby a bill is passed is not in order on the last two legislative days preceding the Spring or Summer Recess as established by the Joint Rules of the Senate and Assembly.

(4) Deadline for Passage by House:

A motion to reconsider the vote whereby an Assembly bill is passed to the Senate is not in order on the last two legislative days preceding the last day for the Assembly to pass a bill introduced in the Assembly, as set forth in the Joint Rules of the Senate and the Assembly.

As used in this paragraph, "bill" does not include a Senate bill, a constitutional amendment, or a joint or concurrent resolution.

(5) Final Recess:

A motion to reconsider the vote whereby a bill is passed is not in order on the last two legislative days preceding the final recess.

A motion to reconsider the vote whereby a bill is defeated is in order on the day of the final recess. The motion must be taken up before the end of that legislative day.

(c) Any Member voting on any matter may move to take up on the same day the motion, previously made by another Member, to reconsider the vote on that matter. A motion to take up on the same day a motion to reconsider the vote on a bill requires an affirmative recorded vote of at least 41 Members. A motion to take up on the same day a motion to reconsider the vote on any motion, amendment, Assembly resolution, or proposition other than a bill requires an affirmative vote of a majority vote of the Members present and voting. The motion to take up the reconsideration on the same day takes precedence over the motion to reconsider and, upon demand of any Member, the motion to take up the reconsideration on the same day shall be put to an immediate vote. If the motion to take up the reconsideration on the same day is adopted, the motion to reconsider is the next order of business before the Assembly.

(d) A second motion to reconsider the same question is not in order, nor is a motion to reconsider reconsideration in order.

(e) A motion to continue a motion to reconsider requires a majority vote of those Members present and voting.

Call of Assembly

101. After the roll has been called, and prior to the announcement of the vote, any Member may move a call of the Assembly. The Members present may order a call of the Assembly by a majority vote of the Members present and voting, and the Speaker shall immediately order the Sergeant at Arms to lock all doors and direct the Chief Clerk to prepare a list of absentees as disclosed by the last roll call. The list of

absentees shall be furnished to the Sergeant at Arms, whereupon no Members shall be permitted to leave the Assembly Chamber except by written permission of the Speaker, and a person may not be permitted to enter except Members, Senators, or officers, or employees of the Legislature in the official performance of their duties.

Each Member who is found to be absent, and for whom a leave of absence has not been granted, shall be forthwith taken into custody wherever found by the Sergeant at Arms, his or her assistants, or any person designated by the Sergeant at Arms, including members of the California Highway Patrol, and sheriffs or their deputies, and brought to the Assembly Chamber.

A recess or adjournment may not be taken during a call of the Assembly. Additional business may be conducted and calls placed regardless of the number of calls in effect. A call of the Assembly may be dispensed with at any time upon a majority vote of the Members present, that action to become effective upon the completion of the roll call and the announcement of the vote upon the matter for which the call was ordered, unless, prior to the announcement of the vote, the call is continued by a majority vote of the Members present.

Division of Question

102.   Any Member may call for a division of the question, and the Speaker shall order the question divided if it comprehends propositions in substance so distinct that, one being taken away, a substantive proposition would remain for the decision of the Assembly. This rule does not apply to an individual bill or resolution.

B.   Voting
Members Voting

104.   Every Member in the Assembly Chamber when a roll call is required shall record his or her vote openly and without debate, unless the Assembly excuses that member by a majority vote of the Members present and voting.

A Member may not operate the voting switch of any other Member, except that a Member presiding at the time of a roll call, who is not the Speaker or the Speaker pro Tempore, may direct another Member on the floor to operate the voting switch of the presiding Member, and any Member so presiding, including the Speaker and the Speaker pro Tempore, may also operate the voting switches at the rostrum of the Speaker and the Speaker pro Tempore, at their direction.

The name of any Member who refuses to vote as required by this rule, after being requested by the Speaker to do so, shall be entered in the Journal, together with a statement that he or she was present and did so refuse to vote. Any Member who refuses so to vote may, if he or she so desires, immediately after the announcement of the vote, submit a written explanation of the failure to vote and that explanation shall be printed in the Journal, provided that no explanation may exceed 50 words in length.

In addition to the entry of his or her name in the Journal, any Member who refuses so to vote when required, and who has not been excused from doing so, may, immediately after the announcement of the vote, at the discretion of the Speaker or upon demand of any Member, be summoned to appear before the bar of the Assembly for public censure by the Speaker or by any Member designated by the Speaker. Censure of a Member as provided by this rule does not constitute a bar to proceedings for his or her expulsion from the Assembly pursuant to Section 5 of Article IV of the California Constitution.

A Member may submit a written explanation of his or her vote on any bill or house resolution, and that explanation shall be printed in the Journal immediately following the vote, provided that no explanation may exceed 50 words in length.

A Member, prior to adjournment on the same legislative day, in the absence of any objection, may instruct the Chief Clerk to add his or her vote to any previously announced vote that had been taken during his or her absence, so long as the outcome of the vote is not thereby changed. The Chief Clerk shall record any vote additions or vote changes in the order signed by the Members at the Clerk's desk.

Ayes and Noes

105.   The ayes and noes shall be recorded by the electrical voting system on the final passage of all bills, when an affirmative recorded vote of 41 Members or any vote above that number is required, when demanded by three Members, or when ordered by the Speaker. The names of the Members so voting shall be entered in the Journal.

Voting and Vote Changes

106.   When once begun, voting may not be interrupted, except that, before the vote is announced, any Member may have the total pending vote flashed on the visible vote recorder. Prior to the announcement of the vote, the presiding officer shall instruct the Chief Clerk to record verbal votes from Members not at their desks. Any Member may move a call of the Assembly after the completion of the roll. A Member, prior to adjournment on the same legislative day, and in the absence of any objection, may instruct the Chief Clerk to change his or her recorded vote after the vote is announced, so long as the outcome of the vote is not thereby changed. The Chief Clerk may record any vote change only after the Member making the change has announced it to the Assembly.

Tie Vote

107.   In case of an equal division, or tie vote, the question shall be lost.

VII.   MEMBERS' DECORUM AND PRIVILEGES

Order in Speaking to Questions

108.   When a Member desires to address the Assembly, the Member shall rise from his or her seat and respectfully address himself or herself to "Mr. Speaker" or "Madame Speaker." Upon being recognized, the Member may speak, confining himself or

herself to the question under consideration. When two or more Members rise at the same time, the Speaker shall designate the Member who is entitled to the floor.

A Member may not speak more than once during the consideration of any one question on the same day and at the same stage of proceeding, except that the author of a bill or resolution or the mover of a question has the right to open and close the debate thereon. A Member may not be allowed to speak more than five minutes to open and five minutes to close the debate on any question, including amendments, and no Member other than the author or the mover of the question may be allowed to speak more than five minutes thereon. A Member may not yield to any other Member the time for which he or she is entitled to speak on any matter.

Rules of Decorum

108.1.   (a) In accordance with Rule 10, Members of the Assembly shall conduct themselves in accordance with the rules of decorum specified in Sections 120 to 126, inclusive, of Mason's Manual of Legislative Procedure.

(b) Notwithstanding subdivision (a), the Committee on Rules may adopt additional rules of decorum by majority vote of the membership of the committee.

Motions

109.   When a Member desires to make a motion, the Member shall obtain recognition as provided in Rule 108. Upon being recognized, the Member shall open by stating his or her motion, except in the case of a nomination, and in any other case may not speak to the merits of the motion at that time, but shall confine his or her remarks to those necessary to explain the motion. If the motion is in order and is seconded, it shall be stated to the Assembly by the Speaker. If the motion is debated, the Member who made it shall then be entitled to recognition to open the debate on the motion.

When a Member obtains the floor during debate upon any question that is pending before the Assembly and addresses the Assembly regarding the merits of the pending question, the Member may not be permitted to conclude his or her debate by making any motion or by demanding the previous question.

Leave of Absence

110.   A Member may not absent himself or herself from attendance at any session of the Assembly without leave of the Assembly. A Member may not obtain that leave of absence or be excused for nonattendance except by a vote of 54 or more Members or by unanimous consent. A Member who obtains a leave of absence for personal business, or is excused for nonattendance for personal business, thereby waives his or her per diem allowance for attendance upon any session of the Legislature for which he or she secures that leave of absence or excuse. A Member may not obtain a leave of absence for legislative business or be excused for nonattendance for legislative business unless the Member has filed with the Speaker a statement of the legislative business for which he or she seeks that leave of absence or excuse. That statement shall be printed in the Journal.

If a Member is not recorded on the attendance roll within 30 minutes after the scheduled start of the session, the Member shall stand up before the Assembly and explain the reason he or she is late before he or she is recorded on the roll call for any vote. If a Member does not explain his or her reason for being late, any other Member may raise a point of order under this rule, whereupon the tardy Member's vote may not be recorded until an explanation is made.

Personal Privilege

111.   Any Member may rise to explain a matter of personal privilege. A matter of personal privilege is a matter involving the Member's integrity, dignity, or honor. Upon rising to explain such a matter, the Member forthwith shall be recognized by the Speaker, but may not discuss a question in that explanation. Matters of personal privilege yield only to a motion to recess or adjourn.

Objection to Reading of Any Paper

112. Any Member, upon recognition by the Speaker, may object to the reading of any paper before the Assembly. When that objection is made, the question of reading shall be determined without debate by a majority vote of the Members present and voting, upon a brief statement by the Speaker of the substance of the objection.

Members at Chief Clerk's Desk

113. A Member or other person may not be allowed at the Chief Clerk's desk while the ayes and noes are being recorded or the votes counted.

Members Called to Order for Transgressing Rules

114. If any Member transgresses the Rules of the Assembly, the Speaker shall, or any Member may, call the offending Member to order. The Member so called to order immediately shall take his or her seat, until the Speaker, without debate, has determined whether the Member is in order. That decision by the Speaker shall be subject to an appeal to the Assembly.

If any Member is called to order for offensive words spoken in debate, the person calling him or her to order shall state to the Assembly the words to which exception is taken. No Member may be held to answer, or be subject to censure by the Assembly, for language used in debate if other business has been transacted by the Assembly prior to exception being taken to the words spoken.

VIII. MISCELLANEOUS
Committee of the Whole

115. The Assembly may resolve itself into a Committee of the Whole at any time by a majority vote of the Members present and voting. While sitting as that committee, persons other than Members may address the committee. The Speaker of the Assembly, or any Member named by the Speaker, shall preside as Chairperson of the Committee of the Whole.

A motion that the Committee of the Whole "do now rise and report back to the Assembly," shall always be in order and shall be decided without debate. All actions of the Committee of the Whole shall be reported to the Assembly by the chairperson, but may not be entered in the Journal except upon motion and a majority vote of the Members present and voting.

Use of Assembly Chamber

116.   The Assembly Chamber may not be used for any public or private business, other than legislative matters, except upon approval of the Speaker or the Chair of the Committee on Rules.

Use of Assembly Facilities: Smoking

117.   The smoking of tobacco products is prohibited within any building, or portion of a building, occupied or used by Assembly Members or employees if the building or portion of the building is under the jurisdiction or control of the Assembly. This smoking prohibition shall apply to any outdoor area within five feet of an entrance or exit to any building or portion of a building subject to this rule. This smoking prohibition shall apply to the Assembly Chamber, Assembly hearing rooms, and Assembly offices, and to hallways, stairways, and bathrooms within any building or portion of a building subject to this rule.

Floor of the Assembly: Telephones

117.5.   A cellular telephone may not be used on the floor of the Assembly during any session of the Assembly.

Meeting of the Assembly: Firearms

117.7.   A person, except a peace officer acting within the scope of his or her employment, may not carry or possess a firearm on the floor of the Assembly during any session of the Assembly or in a committee hearing room during any meeting of a committee or subcommittee.

Persons Admitted to Floor of the Assembly

118. A person other than Members of the Legislature, officers, employees of the Legislature, accredited members of the press, and guests may not be admitted to the floor of the Assembly during any session of the Assembly. A guest of any Member may be admitted only upon presentation of a guest card of the Member countersigned by the Speaker. A guest card is valid only on the legislative day for which it is issued. A lobbyist, as defined by Section 82039 of the Government Code, may not, under any circumstances, be admitted to the Assembly Chamber while the Assembly is in session.

Persons admitted to the Assembly Chamber, other than Members, may not be permitted to stand in the lobby in the rear of the Assembly Chamber while the Assembly is in session, but shall be required to occupy the seats provided for them.

Guests may be seated only in the chairs in the back of the rail in the rear of the Assembly Chamber, and may not be permitted to sit at the desks of the Members. No person other than an accredited newspaper representative may be permitted to sit at the press desks. A special section in the balcony may be reserved for those holding guest cards. Neither any person mentioned in this rule nor any other person, except a Member of the Legislature, may engage in influencing the passage or defeat of legislation in the Assembly Chamber.

A person other than a Member of the Legislature, the Sergeant at Arms or his or her assistants, the Chief Clerk or his or her assistants, or the Legislative Counsel or his or her representatives, may not be permitted in the area of the floor of the chamber which is occupied by the desks of the Members.

Business Attire

118.1. Notwithstanding any other provision of these Rules, a Member of the Legislature, officer or employee of the Legislature, accredited member of the press, or any other person may be admitted to the floor of the Assembly during any session only if dressed in appropriate business attire.

Qualifications and Elections of Members

119.   An affirmative vote of 41 or more Members shall be required to determine the qualifications and election of any Member pursuant to Section 5 of Article IV of the California Constitution. A motion to disqualify a Member is not in order at the convening of a legislative session until a Speaker has been elected in accordance with Section 9023 of the Government Code.

Compensation and Expenses of Member Convicted of Felony

120.   If a Member of the Assembly is convicted of a felony by a superior court, his or her right to further compensation or expenses is thereupon suspended, and his or her membership on any committee is thereupon suspended. If the conviction becomes final, the right of the Member to further compensation or expenses shall terminate and any compensation or expenses withheld shall be forfeited to the state. If the conviction is reversed by an appellate court or a motion for a new trial is granted, and the Member is thereafter found not guilty or the charges against him or her are dismissed, the amounts of the withheld compensation or expenses shall be paid to the Member and the suspension of his or her committee membership shall terminate.

Whenever a Member is convicted of a felony in the superior court, the Committee on Rules shall give written notice thereof to the Controller, directing him or her to discontinue any further payments to the Member unless and until the Committee on Rules notifies the Controller that the Member has been found not guilty or that the charges against him or her are dismissed. The Controller may not draw any warrant payable to that Member except as provided in this rule.

The Seal of the Assembly

121.   The Seal of the Assembly may be used only by or on behalf of a Member of the Assembly, or when specifically authorized by the Committee on Rules.

INDEX TO PERMANENT
STANDING RULES OF ASSEMBLY

A

J

L

N

O

P

RULES COMMITTEE

CONSTITUTION
OF THE
STATE OF CALIFORNIA

ARTICLE IV
LEGISLATURE

CONSTITUTION
of the
STATE OF CALIFORNIA

ARTICLE IV

LEGISLATIVE

[*Heading as amended November 8, 1966.*]

[*Legislative Power*]

SEC. 1.   The legislative power of this State is vested in the California Legislature which consists of the Senate and Assembly, but the people reserve to themselves the powers of initiative and referendum. [*New section adopted November 8, 1966.*]

[*Legislators—Limitation on Incumbency—*
Restriction of Retirement Benefits—
Limitation of Staff and Support Services—
Number of Terms]

SEC. 1.5.   The people find and declare that the Founding Fathers established a system of representative government based upon free, fair, and competitive elections. The increased concentration of political power in the hands of incumbent representatives has made our electoral system less free, less competitive, and less representative.

The ability of legislators to serve unlimited number of terms, to establish their own retirement system, and to pay for staff and support services at state expense contribute heavily to the extremely high number of incumbents who are reelected. These unfair incumbent advantages discourage qualified candidates from seeking public office and create a class of career politicians, instead of the citizen representatives envisioned by the Founding Fathers. These career politicians become representatives of the bureaucracy, rather than of the people whom they are elected to represent.

To restore a free and democratic system of fair elections, and to encourage qualified candidates to seek public office, the people find and declare that the powers of incumbency must be limited. Retirement benefits must be restricted, state-financed incumbent staff and support services limited, and limitations placed upon the number of terms which may be served. [*New section adopted November 6, 1990. Initiative measure.*]

[*Senate and Assembly—Membership— Elections—Number of Terms— Qualifications—Vacancies*]

Sec. 2. (a) The Senate has a membership of 40 Senators elected for 4-year terms, 20 to begin every 2 years. No Senator may serve more than 2 terms.

The Assembly has a membership of 80 members elected for 2-year terms. No member of the Assembly may serve more than 3 terms.

Their terms shall commence on the first Monday in December next following their election.

(b) Election of members of the Assembly shall be on the first Tuesday after the first Monday in November of even-numbered years unless otherwise prescribed by the Legislature. Senators shall be elected at the same time and places as members of the Assembly.

(c) A person is ineligible to be a member of the Legislature unless the person is an elector and has been a resident of the legislative district for one year, and a citizen of the United States and a resident of California for 3 years, immediately preceding the election.

(d) When a vacancy occurs in the Legislature the Governor immediately shall call an election to fill the vacancy. [*As amended November 6, 1990. Initiative measure.*]

[*Legislative Sessions—Regular and Special Sessions*]

Sec. 3. (a) The Legislature shall convene in regular session at noon on the first Monday in December of each even-numbered year and each house shall immediately organize. Each session of the Legislature shall adjourn sine die by operation of the Constitution at midnight on November 30 of the following even-numbered year.

(b) On extraordinary occasions the Governor by proclamation may cause the Legislature to assemble in special session. When so assembled it has power to legislate only on subjects specified in the proclamation but may provide for expenses and other matters incidental to the session. [*As amended June 8, 1976.*]

[*Legislators—Conflict of Interest—Prohibited Compensation—Earned Income*]

Sec. 4. (a) To eliminate any appearance of a conflict with the proper discharge of his or her duties and responsibilities, no Member of the Legislature may knowingly receive any salary, wages, commissions, or other similar earned income from a lobbyist or lobbying firm, as defined by the Political Reform Act of 1974, or from a person who, during the previous 12 months, has been under a contract with the Legislature. The Legislature shall enact laws that define earned income. However, earned income does not include any community property interest in the income of a spouse. Any Member who knowingly receives any salary, wages, commissions, or other similar earned income from a lobbyist employer, as defined by the Political Reform Act of 1974, may not, for a period of one year following its receipt, vote upon or make, participate in making, or in any way attempt to use his or her official position to influence an action or decision before the Legislature, other than an action or decision involving a bill described in subdivision (c) of Section 12 of this article, which he or she knows, or has reason to know, would have a direct and significant financial impact on the lobbyist employer and would not impact the public generally or a significant segment of the public in a similar manner. As used in this subdivision, "public generally" includes an industry, trade, or profession.

[*Legislators—Travel and Living Expenses*]

(b) Travel and living expenses for Members of the Legislature in connection with their official duties shall be prescribed by statute passed by rollcall vote entered in the journal, two-thirds of the membership of each house concurring. A Member may not receive travel and living expenses during the times that the Legislature is in recess for more than three calendar days, unless the Member is traveling to or from, or is in attendance at, any meeting of a committee of which he or she is a member, or a meeting, conference, or other legislative function or responsibility as authorized by the rules of the house of which he or she is a member, which is held at a location at least 20 miles from his or her place of residence.

[*Legislators—Retirement*]

(c) The Legislature may not provide retirement benefits based on any portion of a monthly salary in excess of five hundred dollars ($500) paid to any Member of the Legislature unless the Member receives the greater amount while serving as a Member in the Legislature. The Legislature may, prior to their retirement, limit the retirement benefits payable to Members of the Legislature who serve during or after the term commencing in 1967.

When computing the retirement allowance of a Member who serves in the Legislature during the term commencing in 1967 or later, allowance may be made for increases in cost of living if so provided by statute, but only with respect to increases in the cost of living occurring after retirement of the Member. However, the Legislature may provide that no Member shall be deprived of a cost of living adjustment based on a monthly salary of five hundred dollars ($500) which has accrued prior to the commencement of the 1967 Regular Session of the Legislature. [*As amended June 5, 1990.*]

[*Legislators—Retirement*]

Sec. 4.5. Notwithstanding any other provision of this Constitution or existing law, a person elected to or serving in the Legislature on or after November 1, 1990, shall participate in the Federal Social Security (Retirement, Disability, Health Insurance) Program and the State shall pay only the employer's share of the contribution necessary to such participation. No other pension or retirement benefit shall accrue as a result of service in the Legislature, such service not being intended as a career occupation. This Section shall not be construed to abrogate or diminish any vested pension or retirement benefit which may have accrued under an existing law to a person holding or having held office in the Legislature, but upon adoption of this Act no further entitlement to nor vesting in any existing program shall accrue to any such person, other than Social Security to the extent herein provided. [*New section adopted November 6, 1990. Initiative measure.*]

[*Legislators—Qualifications—Expulsion*]

Sec. 5. (a) Each house shall judge the qualifications and elections of its Members and, by rollcall vote entered in the journal, two thirds of the membership concurring, may expel a Member.

[*Legislators—Honoraria*]

(b) No Member of the Legislature may accept any honorarium. The Legislature shall enact laws that implement this subdivision.

[*Legislators—Gifts—Conflict of Interest*]

(c) The Legislature shall enact laws that ban or strictly limit the acceptance of a gift by a Member of the Legislature from any source if the acceptance of the gift might create a conflict of interest.

[*Legislators—Prohibited Compensation or Activity*]

(d) No Member of the Legislature may knowingly accept any compensation for appearing, agreeing to appear, or taking any other action on behalf of another person before any state government board or agency. If a Member knowingly accepts any compensation for appearing, agreeing to appear, or taking any other action on behalf of another person before any local government board or agency, the Member may not, for a period of one year following the acceptance of the compensation, vote upon or make, participate in making, or in any way attempt to use his or her official position to influence an action or decision before the Legislature, other than an action or decision involving a bill described in subdivision (c) of Section 12 of this article, which he or she knows, or has reason to know, would have a direct and significant financial impact on that person and would not impact the public generally or a significant segment of the public in a similar manner. As used in this subdivision, "public generally" includes an industry, trade, or profession. However, a Member may engage in activities involving a board or agency which are strictly on his or her own behalf, appear in the capacity of an attorney before any court or the Workers' Compensation Appeals Board, or act as an advocate without compensation or make an inquiry for information on behalf of a person before a board or agency. This subdivision does not prohibit any action of a partnership or firm of which the Member is a member if the Member does not share directly or indirectly in the fee, less any expenses attributable to that fee, resulting from that action.

[*Legislators—Lobbying*]

(e) The Legislature shall enact laws that prohibit a Member of the Legislature whose term of office commences on or after December 3, 1990, from lobbying, for compensation, as governed by the Political Reform Act of 1974, before the Legislature for 12 months after leaving office.

[*Legislators—Conflict of Interest*]

(f) The Legislature shall enact new laws, and strengthen the enforcement of existing laws, prohibiting Members of the Legislature from engaging in activities or having interests which conflict with the proper discharge of their duties and responsibilities. However, the people reserve to themselves the power to implement this requirement pursuant to Article II. [*As amended June 5, 1990. Subdivision (b) operative December 3, 1990.*]

[*Senatorial and Assembly Districts*]

SEC. 6.   For the purpose of choosing members of the Legislature, the State shall be divided into 40 Senatorial and 80 Assembly districts to be called Senatorial and Assembly Districts. Each Senatorial district shall choose one Senator and each Assembly district shall choose one member of the Assembly. [*New section adopted June 3, 1980.*]

[*House Rules—Officers—Quorum*]

SEC. 7.   (a) Each   house   shall   choose   its officers and adopt rules for its proceedings. A majority of the membership constitutes a quorum, but a smaller number may recess from day to day and compel the attendance of absent members.

[*Journals*]

(b) Each house shall keep and publish a journal of its proceedings. The rollcall vote of the members on a question shall be taken and entered in the journal at the request of 3 members present.

[*Public Proceedings—Closed Sessions*]

(c) (1) The proceedings of each house and the committees thereof shall be open and public. However, closed sessions may be held solely for any of the following purposes:

(A) To consider the appointment, employment, evaluation of performance, or dismissal of a public officer or employee, to consider or hear complaints or charges brought against a Member of the Legislature or other public officer or employee, or to establish the classification or compensation of an employee of the Legislature.

(B) To consider matters affecting the safety and security of Members of the Legislature or its employees or the safety and security of any buildings and grounds used by the Legislature.

(C) To confer with, or receive advice from, its legal counsel regarding pending or reasonably anticipated, or whether to initiate, litigation when discussion in open session would not protect the interests of the house or committee regarding the litigation.

(2) A caucus of the Members of the Senate, the Members of the Assembly, or the Members of both houses, which is composed of the members of the same political party, may meet in closed session.

(3) The Legislature shall implement this subdivision by concurrent resolution adopted by rollcall vote entered in the journal, two-thirds of the membership of each house concurring, or by statute, and shall prescribe that, when a closed session is held pursuant to paragraph (1), reasonable notice of the closed session and the purpose of the closed session shall be provided to the public. If there is a conflict between a concurrent resolution and statute, the last adopted or enacted shall prevail.

[*Recess*]

(d) Neither house without the consent of the other may recess for more than 10 days or to any other place. [*As amended June 5, 1990. Subdivision (c) operative December 3, 1990.*]

[*Legislature—Total Aggregate Expenditures*]

Sec. 7.5. In the fiscal year immediately following the adoption of this Act, the total aggregate expenditures of the Legislature for the compensation of members and employees of, and the operating expenses and equipment for, the Legislature may not exceed an amount equal to nine hundred fifty thousand dollars ($950,000) per member for that fiscal year or 80 percent of the amount of money expended for those purposes in the preceding fiscal year, whichever is less. For each fiscal year thereafter, the total aggregate expenditures may not exceed an amount equal to that expended for those purposes in the preceding fiscal year, adjusted and compounded by an amount equal to the percentage increase in the appropriations limit for the State established pursuant to Article XIII B. [*New section adopted November 6, 1990. Initiative measure.*]

[*Bills and Statutes—30-day Waiting Period*]

SEC. 8. (a) At regular sessions no bill other than the budget bill may be heard or acted on by committee or either house until the 31st day after the bill is introduced unless the house dispenses with this requirement by rollcall vote entered in the journal, three fourths of the membership concurring.

[*Bills and Statutes—3 Readings*]

(b) The Legislature may make no law except by statute and may enact no statute except by bill. No bill may be passed unless it is read by title on 3 days in each house except that the house may dispense with this requirement by rollcall vote entered in the journal, two thirds of the membership concurring. No bill may be passed until the bill with amendments has been printed and distributed to the members. No bill may be passed unless, by rollcall vote entered in the journal, a majority of the membership of each house concurs.

[*Bills and Statutes—Effective Date*]

(c) (1) Except as provided in paragraphs (2) and (3) of this subdivision, a statute enacted at a regular session shall go into effect on January 1 next following a 90-day period from the date of enactment of the statute and a statute enacted at a special session shall go into

effect on the 91st day after adjournment of the special
session at which the bill was passed.

(2) A statute, other than a statute establishing or
changing boundaries of any legislative, congressional,
or other election district, enacted by a bill passed by the
Legislature on or before the date the Legislature adjourns for a joint recess to reconvene in the second
calendar year of the biennium of the legislative session,
and in the possession of the Governor after that date,
shall go into effect on January 1 next following the
enactment date of the statute unless, before January 1, a
copy of a referendum petition affecting the statute is
submitted to the Attorney General pursuant to subdivision (d) of Section 10 of Article II, in which event the
statute shall go into effect on the 91st day after the
enactment date unless the petition has been presented to
the Secretary of State pursuant to subdivision (b) of
Section 9 of Article II.

(3) Statutes calling elections, statutes providing for
tax levies or appropriations for the usual current
expenses of the State, and urgency statutes shall go into
effect immediately upon their enactment.

[*Bills and Statutes—Urgency Statutes*]

(d) Urgency statutes are those necessary for immediate preservation of the public peace, health, or safety.
A statement of facts constituting the necessity shall be
set forth in one section of the bill. In each house the
section and the bill shall be passed separately, each by
rollcall vote entered in the journal, two thirds of the
membership concurring. An urgency statute may not
create or abolish any office or change the salary, term,
or duties of any office, or grant any franchise or special
privilege, or create any vested right or interest.
[*As amended June 5, 1990.*]

[*Ballot Measures—Application*]

SEC. 8.5.   An act amending an initiative statute, an
act providing for the issuance of bonds, or a constitutional amendment proposed by the Legislature and

submitted to the voters for approval may not do either of the following:

(a) Include or exclude any political subdivision of the State from the application or effect of its provisions based upon approval or disapproval of the measure, or based upon the casting of a specified percentage of votes in favor of the measure, by the electors of that political subdivision.

(b) Contain alternative or cumulative provisions wherein one or more of those provisions would become law depending upon the casting of a specified percentage of votes for or against the measure. [*New section adopted June 2, 1998.*]

[*Statutes—Title—Section*]

SEC. 9. A statute shall embrace but one subject, which shall be expressed in its title. If a statute embraces a subject not expressed in its title, only the part not expressed is void. A statute may not be amended by reference to its title. A section of a statute may not be amended unless the section is re-enacted as amended. [*New section adopted November 8, 1966.*]

[*Governor's Veto—Bill Introduction in Biennial Session*]

SEC. 10. (a) Each bill passed by the Legislature shall be presented to the Governor. It becomes a statute if it is signed by the Governor. The Governor may veto it by returning it with any objections to the house of origin, which shall enter the objections in the journal and proceed to reconsider it. If each house then passes the bill by rollcall vote entered in the journal, two thirds of the membership concurring, it becomes a statute.

(b) (1) Any bill, other than a bill which would establish or change boundaries of any legislative, congressional, or other election district, passed by the Legislature on or before the date the Legislature adjourns for a joint recess to reconvene in the second calendar year of the biennium of the legislative session, and in the possession of the Governor after that date, that is not returned within 30 days after that date becomes a statute.

(2) Any bill passed by the Legislature before September 1 of the second calendar year of the biennium of the legislative session and in the possession of the Governor on or after September 1 that is not returned on or before September 30 of that year becomes a statute.

(3) Any other bill presented to the Governor that is not returned within 12 days becomes a statute.

(4) If the Legislature by adjournment of a special session prevents the return of a bill with the veto message, the bill becomes a statute unless the Governor vetoes the bill within 12 days after it is presented by depositing it and the veto message in the office of the Secretary of State.

(5) If the 12th day of the period within which the Governor is required to perform an act pursuant to paragraph (3) or (4) of this subdivision is a Saturday, Sunday, or holiday, the period is extended to the next day that is not a Saturday, Sunday, or holiday.

(c) Any bill introduced during the first year of the biennium of the legislative session that has not been passed by the house of origin by January 31 of the second calendar year of the biennium may no longer be acted on by the house. No bill may be passed by either house on or after September 1 of an even-numbered year except statutes calling elections, statutes providing for tax levies or appropriations for the usual current expenses of the State, and urgency statutes, and bills passed after being vetoed by the Governor.

(d) The Legislature may not present any bill to the Governor after November 15 of the second calendar year of the biennium of the legislative session.

(e) The Governor may reduce or eliminate one or more items of appropriation while approving other portions of a bill. The Governor shall append to the bill a statement of the items reduced or eliminated with the reasons for the action. The Governor shall transmit to the house originating the bill a copy of the statement and reasons. Items reduced or eliminated shall be separately reconsidered and may be passed over the Governor's veto in the same manner as bills. [*As amended June 5, 1990.*]

[*Committees*]

Sec. 11. The Legislature or either house may by resolution provide for the selection of committees necessary for the conduct of its business, including committees to ascertain facts and make recommendations to the Legislature on a subject within the scope of legislative control. [*As amended November 7, 1972.*]

[*Governor's Budget—Budget Bill—Other Appropriations*]

Sec. 12. (a) Within the first 10 days of each calendar year, the Governor shall submit to the Legislature, with an explanatory message, a budget for the ensuing fiscal year containing itemized statements for recommended state expenditures and estimated state revenues. If recommended expenditures exceed estimated revenues, the Governor shall recommend the sources from which the additional revenues should be provided.

(b) The Governor and the Governor-elect may require a state agency, officer or employee to furnish whatever information is deemed necessary to prepare the budget.

(c) The budget shall be accompanied by a budget bill itemizing recommended expenditures. The bill shall be introduced immediately in each house by the persons chairing the committees that consider appropriations. The Legislature shall pass the budget bill by midnight on June 15 of each year. Until the budget bill has been enacted, the Legislature shall not send to the Governor for consideration any bill appropriating funds for expenditure during the fiscal year for which the budget bill is to be enacted, except emergency bills recommended by the Governor or appropriations for the salaries and expenses of the Legislature.

(d) No bill except the budget bill may contain more than one item of appropriation, and that for one certain, expressed purpose. Appropriations from the General Fund of the State, except appropriations for the public schools, are void unless passed in each house by rollcall vote entered in the journal, two thirds of the membership concurring.

(e) The Legislature may control the submission, approval, and enforcement of budgets and the filing of claims for all state agencies. [*As amended June 4, 1974, and November 5, 1974.*]

[*Legislators—Ineligible for Certain Offices*]

SEC. 13. A member of the Legislature may not, during the term for which the member is elected, hold any office or employment under the State other than an elective office. [*As amended November 5, 1974.*]

[*Members—Not Subject to Civil Process*]

SEC. 14. A member of the Legislature is not subject to civil process during a session of the Legislature or for 5 days before and after a session. [*New section adopted November 8, 1966.*]

[*Influencing Action or Vote of a Member— Felony*]

SEC. 15. A person who seeks to influence the vote or action of a member of the Legislature in the member's legislative capacity by bribery, promise of reward, intimidation, or other dishonest means, or a member of the Legislature so influenced, is guilty of a felony. [*As amended November 5, 1974.*]

[*Uniform Operation of General Laws— Special Statute—Invalid*]

SEC. 16. (a) All laws of a general nature have uniform operation.

(b) A local or special statute is invalid in any case if a general statute can be made applicable. [*As amended November 5, 1974.*]

[*Grant of Extra Compensation or
Allowance Prohibited*]

SEC. 17.   The Legislature has no power to grant, or
to authorize a city, county, or other public body to grant,
extra compensation or extra allowance to a public
officer, public employee, or contractor after service has
been rendered or a contract has been entered into and
performed in whole or in part, or to authorize the
payment of a claim against the State or a city, county, or
other public body under an agreement made without
authority of law. [*New section adopted November 8,
1966.*]

[*Impeachment*]

SEC. 18.   (a) The Assembly has the sole power of
impeachment. Impeachments shall be tried by the
Senate. A person may not be convicted unless, by
rollcall vote entered in the journal, two thirds of the
membership of the Senate concurs.

(b) State officers elected on a statewide basis, members of the State Board of Equalization, and judges of
state courts are subject to impeachment for misconduct
in office. Judgment may extend only to removal from
office and disqualification to hold any office under the
State, but the person convicted or acquitted remains
subject to criminal punishment according to law.
[*New section adopted November 8, 1966.*]

[*Lotteries—Horse Races Regulated—
Bingo Games and Raffles for
Charitable Purposes—
Gaming on Tribal Lands*]

SEC. 19.   (a) The Legislature has no power to authorize lotteries and shall prohibit the sale of lottery
tickets in the State.

(b) The Legislature may provide for the regulation
of horse races and horse race meetings and wagering on
the results.

(c) Notwithstanding subdivision (a), the Legislature by statute may authorize cities and counties to provide for bingo games, but only for charitable purposes.

(d) Notwithstanding subdivision (a), there is authorized the establishment of a California State Lottery.

(e) The Legislature has no power to authorize, and shall prohibit casinos of the type currently operating in Nevada and New Jersey.

(f) [1] Notwithstanding subdivisions (a) and (e), and any other provision of state law, the Governor is authorized to negotiate and conclude compacts, subject to ratification by the Legislature, for the operation of slot machines and for the conduct of lottery games and banking and percentage card games by federally recognized Indian tribes on Indian lands in California in accordance with federal law. Accordingly, slot machines, lottery games, and banking and percentage card games are hereby permitted to be conducted and operated on tribal lands subject to those compacts.

(f) [2] Notwithstanding subdivision (a), the Legislature may authorize private, nonprofit, eligible organizations, as defined by the Legislature, to conduct raffles as a funding mechanism to provide support for their own or another private, nonprofit, eligible organization's beneficial and charitable works, provided that (1) at least 90 percent of the gross receipts from the raffle go directly to beneficial or charitable purposes in California, and (2) any person who receives compensation in connection with the operation of a raffle is an employee of the private nonprofit organization that is conducting the raffle. The Legislature, two-thirds of the membership of each house concurring, may amend the percentage of gross receipts required by this subdivision to be dedicated to beneficial or charitable purposes by means of a statute that is signed by the Governor. [*As amended March 7, 2000.*]

---

[1] Ballot Proposition 1A (SCA 11) March 7, 2000.
[2] Ballot Proposition 17 (SCA 4) March 7, 2000.

[*Fish and Game—Districts and Commission*]

SEC. 20. (a) The Legislature may provide for division of the State into fish and game districts and may protect fish and game in districts or parts of districts.

(b) There is a Fish and Game Commission of 5 members appointed by the Governor and approved by the Senate, a majority of the membership concurring, for 6-year terms and until their successors are appointed and qualified. Appointment to fill a vacancy is for the unexpired portion of the term. The Legislature may delegate to the commission such powers relating to the protection and propagation of fish and game as the Legislature sees fit. A member of the commission may be removed by concurrent resolution adopted by each house, a majority of the membership concurring. [*New section adopted November 8, 1966.*]

[*War- or Enemy-Caused Disaster*]

SEC. 21. To meet the needs resulting from war-caused or enemy-caused disaster in California, the Legislature may provide for:

(a) Filling the offices of members of the Legislature should at least one fifth of the membership of either house be killed, missing, or disabled, until they are able to perform their duties or successors are elected.

(b) Filling the office of Governor should the Governor be killed, missing, or disabled, until the Governor or the successor designated in this Constitution is able to perform the duties of the office of Governor or a successor is elected.

(c) Convening the Legislature.

(d) Holding elections to fill offices that are elective under this Constitution and that are either vacant or occupied by persons not elected thereto.

(e) Selecting a temporary seat of state or county government. [*As amended November 5, 1974.*]

[*Accountability—Session Goals and Objectives*]

SEC. 22.   It is the right of the people to hold their legislators accountable. To assist the people in exercising this right, at the convening of each regular session of the Legislature, the President pro Tempore of the Senate, the Speaker of the Assembly, and the minority leader of each house shall report to their house the goals and objectives of that house during that session and, at the close of each regular session, the progress made toward meeting those goals and objectives. [*New section adopted June 5, 1990.*]

[*State Capitol Maintenance—Appropriations*]

SEC. 28.   (a) Notwithstanding any other provision of this Constitution, no bill shall take effect as an urgency statute if it authorizes or contains an appropriation for either (1) the alteration or modification of the color, detail, design, structure or fixtures of the historically restored areas of the first, second, and third floors and the exterior of the west wing of the State Capitol from that existing upon the completion of the project of restoration or rehabilitation of the building conducted pursuant to Section 9124 of the Government Code as such section read upon the effective date of this section, or (2) the purchase of furniture of different design to replace that restored, replicated, or designed to conform to the historic period of the historically restored areas specified above, including the legislators' chairs and desks in the Senate and Assembly Chambers.

(b) No expenditures shall be made in payment for any of the purposes described in subdivision (a) of this section unless funds are appropriated expressly for such purposes.

(c) This section shall not apply to appropriations or expenditures for ordinary repair and maintenance of the State Capitol building, fixtures and furniture. [*New Section adopted June 3, 1980.*]

INDEX TO
CALIFORNIA CONSTITUTION

GENERAL INFORMATION

LEGISLATIVE SESSIONS

SESSIONS OF THE CALIFORNIA LEGISLATURE

The first two sessions were held in San Jose; the Third Session met at Vallejo and later removed to Sacramento; the Fourth Session met at Vallejo and later removed to Benicia; the Fifth Session met at Benicia and later removed to Sacramento. Beginning with the Sixth Session all Legislatures have met in Sacramento, except the Thirteenth which convened at Sacramento but later removed to San Francisco; the 1958 session met at Benicia for one day.

Session	Convened			Adjourned			Legislative days †		
							Assembly	Senate	Length *
1	Dec.	15,	1849	April	22,	1850	103	103	129
2	Jan.	6,	1851	May	1,	1851	98	98	116
3	Jan.	5,	1852	May	4,	1852	96	96	120
4	Jan.	3,	1853	May	19,	1853	108	109	137
5	Jan.	2,	1854	May	15,	1854	110	108	134
6	Jan.	1,	1855	May	7,	1855	103	102	127
7	Jan.	7,	1856	April	21,	1856	87	85	106
8	Jan.	5,	1857	April	30,	1857	99	100	116
9	Jan.	4,	1858	April	26,	1858	93	96	113
10	Jan.	3,	1859	April	19,	1859	89	88	107
11	Jan.	2,	1860	April	30,	1860	100	96	120

	Convened	Adjourned			
12	Jan. 7, 1861	May 20, 1861	108	106	134
13	Jan. 6, 1862	May 15, 1862	101	106	130
14	Jan. 5, 1863	April 27, 1863	93	94	113
15	Dec. 7, 1863	April 4, 1864	88	89	120
16	Dec. 4, 1865	April 2, 1866	87	85	120
17	Dec. 2, 1867	Mar. 30, 1868	85	82	120
18	Dec. 6, 1869	April 4, 1870	88	86	120
19	Dec. 4, 1871	April 1, 1872	86	85	120
20	Dec. 1, 1873	Mar. 30, 1874	88	89	120
21	Dec. 6, 1875	April 3, 1876	90	86	120
22	Dec. 3, 1877	April 1, 1878	84	84	120
23	Jan. 5, 1880	April 16, 1880	87	84	103
24	Jan. 3, 1881	Mar. 4, 1881	49	51	61
24 ex.	April 4, 1881	May 13, 1881	34	35	40
25	Jan. 8, 1883	Mar. 13, 1883	53	52	65
25 ex.	Mar. 24, 1884	May 13, 1884	40	38	51
26	Jan. 5, 1885	Mar. 11, 1885	52	51	66

† Actual days in session.

* The length of session is by calendar days, excluding constitutional recesses during the sessions of 1913 through 1957.

SESSIONS OF THE CALIFORNIA LEGISLATURE—Continued

Session	Convened	Adjourned	Legislative days †		Length *
			Assembly	Senate	
26 ex.	July 20, 1886	Aug. 20, 1886	25	26	54
	(Reconvened)	(Proclamation)‡			
27	Sept. 7, 1886	Sept. 11, 1886	55	53	69
28	Jan. 3, 1887	Mar. 12, 1887	55	54	69
29	Jan. 7, 1889	Mar. 16, 1889	63	64	80
30	Jan. 5, 1891	Mar. 25, 1891	58	57	72
31	Jan. 2, 1893	Mar. 14, 1893	55	54	69
32	Jan. 7, 1895	Mar. 16, 1895	61	61	76
33	Jan. 4, 1897	Mar. 20, 1897	66	67	77
33 ex.	Jan. 2, 1899	Mar. 19, 1899	12	12	13
34	Jan. 29, 1900	Feb. 10, 1900	55	52	69
35	Jan. 7, 1901	Mar. 16, 1901	57	52	69
	Jan. 5, 1903	Mar. 14, 1903			

	Convened		Adjourned				
36	Jan.	2, 1905	Mar.	10, 1905	52	50	68
36 ex.	June	2, 1906	June	12, 1906	11	10	11
37	Jan.	7, 1907	Mar.	12, 1907	55	52	65
37, 1st ex.	Nov.	19, 1907	Nov.	23, 1907	5	5	5
37, 2d ex.	Nov.	23, 1907 (1 p.m.)	Nov.	23, 1907 (2:30 p.m.)	1	1	1
38	Jan.	4, 1909	Mar.	24, 1909	66	60	80
38, 1st ex.	Sept.	6, 1910	Sept.	9, 1910	4	4	4
38, 2d ex.	Oct.	3, 1910	Oct.	5, 1910	3	3	3
39	Jan.	2, 1911	Mar.	27, 1911	69	68	85
39, 1st ex.	Nov.	27, 1911	Dec.	24, 1911	27	24	28
39, 2d ex.	Dec.	24, 1911 (12:05 p.m.)	Dec.	24, 1911 (3:30 p.m.)	1	1	1
40, 1st part	Jan.	6, 1913	Feb.	4, 1913	79	79	94
2d part	Mar.	10, 1913	May	12, 1913			
41, 1st part	Jan.	4, 1915	Jan.	30, 1915	72	69	90
2d part	Mar.	8, 1915	May	9, 1915			

† Actual days in session.

* The length of session is by calendar days, excluding constitutional recesses during the sessions of 1913 through 1957.

‡ Governor Stoneman adjourned the extraordinary session by proclamation from August 20 to September 7, 1886.

SESSIONS OF THE CALIFORNIA LEGISLATURE—Continued

Session	Convened	Adjourned	Legislative days †		Length *
			Assembly	Senate	
41 ex.	Jan. 5, 1916	Jan. 11, 1916	6	7	7
42, 1st part	Jan. 8, 1917	Jan. 26, 1917	66	61	80
2d part	Feb. 26, 1917	April 27, 1917	63	59	77
43, 1st part	Jan. 6, 1919	Jan. 24, 1919			
2d part	Feb. 24, 1919	April 22, 1919			
43 ex.	Nov. 1, 1919 (2 p.m.)	Nov. 1, 1919 (6 p.m.)	1	1	1
44, 1st part	Jan. 3, 1921	Jan. 24, 1921	71	66	87
2d part	Feb. 24, 1921	April 29, 1921			
45, 1st part	Jan. 8, 1923	Feb. 2, 1923	78	74	101
2d part	Mar. 5, 1923	May 18, 1923			
46, 1st part	Jan. 5, 1925	Jan. 24, 1925	63	60	80
2d part	Feb. 24, 1925	April 24, 1925			
46 ex.	Oct. 22, 1926 (10 a.m.)	Oct. 22, 1926 (2 p.m.)	1	1	1

	Convened	Adjourned			
47, 1st part	Jan. 3, 1927	Jan. 21, 1927	63	63	85
2d part	Feb. 23, 1927	April 29, 1927			
47 ex.	Sept. 4, 1928	Sept. 5, 1928	2	2	2
48, 1st part	Jan. 7, 1929	Jan. 18, 1929	72	73	99
2d part	Feb. 18, 1929	May 15, 1929			
49, 1st part	Jan. 5, 1931	Jan. 23, 1931	74	74	100
2d part	Feb. 24, 1931	May 15, 1931			
50, 1st part	Jan. 2, 1933	Jan. 28, 1933	88	88	111
2d part	Feb. 28, 1933	May 12, 1933			
3d part	July 17, 1933	July 26, 1933			
50 ex.	Sept. 12, 1934	Sept. 15, 1934	4	4	4
51, 1st part	Jan. 7, 1935	Jan. 26, 1935	98	95	125
2d part	Mar. 4, 1935	June 16, 1935			
51 ex.	May 25, 1936	May 26, 1936	2	2	2
52, 1st part	Jan. 4, 1937	Jan. 22, 1937	82	81	108
2d part	Mar. 1, 1937	May 28, 1937			
52 ex.	Mar. 7, 1938	Mar. 12, 1938	6	6	6
53, 1st part	Jan. 2, 1939	Jan. 25, 1939	99	97	131
2d part	Mar. 6, 1939	June 20, 1939			

† Actual days in session.

* The length of session is by calendar days, excluding constitutional recesses during the sessions of 1913 through 1957.

SESSIONS OF THE CALIFORNIA LEGISLATURE—Continued

Session	Convened	Adjourned	Legislative days [†]		Length [*]
			Assembly	Senate	
53. 1st ex.	Jan. 29, 1940 May 13, 1940 Sept. 21, 1940 Dec. 2, 1940 (2 p.m.)	Feb. 25, 1940 May 24, 1940 Sept. 22, 1940 Dec. 5, 1940 (9 p.m.)	40	40	312
2d ex.	May 13, 1940	May 24, 1940	10	10	12
3d ex.	Sept. 13, 1940	Sept. 13, 1940	1	1	1
4th ex.	Sept. 21, 1940 Dec. 2, 1940	Sept. 22, 1940 Dec. 5, 1940	6	6	76
5th ex.	Dec. 2, 1940	Dec. 5, 1940	4	4	4
54. 1st part 2d part	Jan. 6, 1941 Mar. 3, 1941	Jan. 25, 1941 June 14, 1941	94	93	124
54 1st ex.	Dec. 19, 1941 Jan. 12, 1942	Dec. 22, 1941 Jan. 22, 1942	15	15	35
2d ex.	Jan. 17, 1942	Jan. 18, 1942	2	2	2

	Convened	Adjourned			
55, 1st part	Jan. 4, 1943	Jan. 31, 1943			
2d part	Mar. 8, 1943	May 5, 1943	71	71	87
55, 1st ex.	Jan. 28, 1943	Jan. 30, 1943	3	3	3
2d ex.	Mar. 20, 1943	Mar. 25, 1943	5	5	6
3d ex.	Jan. 27, 1944	Jan. 31, 1944	5	5	5
4th ex.	June 5, 1944	June 13, 1944	8	8	9
56, 1st part	Jan. 8, 1945	Jan. 27, 1945			
2d part	Mar. 5, 1945	June 16, 1945	97	97	124
56 1st ex.	Jan. 7, 1946	Feb. 19, 1946	33	33	44
2d ex.	July 22, 1946	July 25, 1946	4	4	4
57, 1st part	Jan. 6, 1947	Feb. 5, 1947			
2d part	Mar. 17, 1947	June 20, 1947	94	92	127
57, 1st ex.	Jan. 13, 1947	Feb. 5, 1947			
	Mar. 3, 1947	June 24, 1947	84	63	138
1948	Mar. 1, 1948	Mar. 27, 1948	20	20	27
1949, 1st part	Jan. 3, 1949	Jan. 29, 1949			
2d part	Mar. 7, 1949	July 2, 1949	106	108	145
1st ex.	Dec. 12, 1949	Dec. 21, 1949	8	9	10

† Actual days in session.

* The length of session is by calendar days, excluding constitutional recesses during the sessions of 1913 through 1957.

SESSIONS OF THE CALIFORNIA LEGISLATURE—Continued

Session	Convened	Adjourned	Legislative days †		Length *
			Assembly	Senate	
1950	Mar. 6, 1950	April 4, 1950	20	21	30
1st ex.	Mar. 6, 1950	April 15, 1950	28	26	41
2d ex.	Mar. 6, 1950 (12:15 p.m.)	Mar. 6, 1950 (6 p.m.)	1	1	1
3d ex.	Sept. 20, 1950	Sept. 26, 1950	6	6	7
1951, 1st part	Jan. 8, 1951	Jan. 23, 1951	88	88	120
2d part.	Mar. 12, 1951	June 23, 1951			
1952	Mar. 3, 1952	April 1, 1952	20	21	30
1st ex.	Mar. 3, 1952	April 2, 1952	21	22	31
2d ex.	Aug. 4, 1952	Aug. 13, 1952	9	9	10
1953, 1st part	Jan. 5, 1953	Jan. 17, 1953	91	91	120
2d part.	Feb. 24, 1953	June 10, 1953			
1954	Mar. 1, 1954	Mar. 30, 1954	21	21	30
1st ex.	Mar. 1, 1954	April 1, 1954	22	23	32

Session	Convened			Adjourned					
1955, 1st part	Jan.	3,	1955	Jan.	21,	1955	93	89	120
2d part	Feb.	28,	1955	June	8,	1955			
1956	Mar.	5,	1956	April	3,	1956	21	21	30
1st ex.	Mar.	5,	1956	April	5,	1956	23	23	32
1957, 1st part	Jan.	7,	1957	Jan.	25,	1957	97	91	120
2d part	Mar.	4,	1957	June	12,	1957			
1958, 1st part	Feb.	3,	1958	Feb.	4,	1958	24	24	30
2d part	Mar.	3,	1958	Mar.	30,	1958			
1st ex	Mar.	4,	1958	April	23,	1958	36	35	51
2d ex	Mar.	31,	1958	April	24,	1958	17	17	25
1959	Jan.	5,	1959	June	19,	1959	113	112	166
1960	Feb.	1,	1960	Mar.	26,	1960	22	21	30
1st ex	Feb.	1,	1960	April	7,	1960	31	30	67
2d ex	Mar.	2,	1960	Mar.	10,	1960	6	4	9
1961	Jan.	2,	1961	June	16,	1961	114	116	166
1962	Feb.	5,	1962	April	3,	1962	22	20	30
1st ex	Mar.	7,	1962	April	13,	1962	25	24	38
2d ex	April	9,	1962	April	13,	1962	5	4	5
3d ex	June	26,	1962	June	28,	1962	3	3	3

† Actual days in session.

* The length of session is by calendar days, excluding constitutional recesses during the sessions of 1913 through 1957.

SESSIONS OF THE CALIFORNIA LEGISLATURE—Continued

Session	Convened	Adjourned	Legislative days†		Length *
			Assembly	Senate	
1963	Jan. 7, 1963	June 21, 1963	109	109	166
1st ex.	July 8, 1963	Aug. 1, 1963	16	16	25
1964	Feb. 3, 1964	Mar. 26, 1964	18	17	30
1st ex.	Feb. 3, 1964	May 23, 1964	56	55	111
2d ex.	Mar. 30, 1964	May 23, 1964	34	24	55
1965	Jan. 4, 1965	June 18, 1965	106	107	166
1st ex.	June 25, 1965	July 6, 1965	8	8	12
2d ex.	Sept. 20, 1965	Nov. 4, 1965	28	27	46
1966	Feb. 7, 1966	April 4, 1966	18	19	30
1st ex.	Feb. 10, 1966	July 7, 1966	81	81	148
2d ex.	April 5, 1966	July 8, 1966	52	36	95
1967	Jan. 2, 1967	Sept. 8, 1967	142	143	250
1st ex.	Sept. 5, 1967	Sept. 7, 1967	3	3	3
2d ex.	Nov. 6, 1967	Dec. 8, 1967	21	21	33

	Convened	Adjourned			
1968	Jan. 8, 1968 (Reconvened)	Aug. 3, 1968 (Proclamation)‡	131	137	250
1st ex.	Sept. 9, 1968	Sept. 13, 1968	10	10	12
1969	Sept. 9, 1968	Sept. 20, 1968	140	136	248
1970	Jan. 6, 1969	Sept. 10, 1969	141	150	262
1971	Jan. 5, 1970	Sept. 23, 1970	193	199	365
1st ex.	Jan. 4, 1971	Jan. 3, 1972	29	36	87
1972	Dec. 6, 1971	Mar. 1, 1972	139	148	369
1973–74	Jan. 3, 1972	Jan. 5, 1973	239	254	692
1st ex.	Jan. 8, 1973	Nov. 30, 1974	1	1	1
	Dec. 4, 1973 (12 noon)	Dec. 4, 1973 (1 p.m.)			
2d ex.	Sept. 25, 1974	Oct. 2, 1974	4	4	8

† Actual days in session.

* The length of session is by calendar days, excluding constitutional recesses during the sessions of 1913 through 1957.

‡ Acting Governor Burns adjourned the regular session by proclamation from August 3, 1968 to September 9, 1968.

SESSIONS OF THE CALIFORNIA LEGISLATURE—Continued

Session	Convened	Adjourned	Legislative days †		Length *
			Assembly	Senate	
1975–76	Dec. 2, 1974	Nov. 30, 1976	256	255	674
1st ex.	Feb. 17, 1975	June 27, 1975	76	46	131
2d ex.	May 19, 1975	Sept. 12, 1975	56	44	117
3d ex.	May 20, 1975	May 29, 1975	7	5	10
1977–78	Dec. 6, 1976	Nov. 30, 1978	256	260	725
1st ex.	Jan. 5, 1978	April 24, 1978	58	59	110
1979–80	Dec. 4, 1978	Nov. 30, 1980	251	262	728
1981–82	Dec. 1, 1980	Nov. 30, 1982	248	257	729
1st ex.	Nov. 9, 1981	Feb. 25, 1982	29	23	109
1983–84	Dec. 6, 1982	Nov. 30, 1984	262	266	666
1st ex.	Dec. 6, 1982	July 19, 1983	68	72	226
2nd ex.	Jan. 19, 1984	Feb. 17, 1984	5	3	30
1985–86	Dec. 3, 1984	Nov. 30, 1986	251	254	718
1st ex.	Sept. 8, 1986	Nov. 30, 1986	68	65	84

1987–88	Dec.	1,	1986	Nov.	30,	1988	246	253	731
1st ex.	Nov.	9,	1987	Nov.	10,	1987	2	2	2
1989–90	Dec.	5,	1988	Nov.	30,	1990	264	269	726
1st ex.	Nov.	2,	1989	Sept.	1,	1990	44	66	305
1991–92	Dec.	3,	1990	Nov.	30,	1992	292	284	728
1st ex.	Dec.	3,	1990	Nov.	30,	1992	141	127	728
2nd ex.	Oct.	8,	1992	Nov.	30,	1992	2	2	54
1993–94	Dec.	7,	1992	Nov.	30,	1994	245	255	724
1st ex.	Jan.	4,	1993	Aug.	31,	1994	124	142	605
1995–96	Dec.	5,	1994	Nov.	30,	1996	264	265	637
1st ex.	Jan.	19,	1995	Sept.	1,	1996	79	98	592
2nd ex.	Feb.	17,	1995	Sept.	1,	1996	65	87	563
3rd ex.	Jan.	4,	1996	Mar.	15,	1996	19	15	71
4th ex.	Feb.	13,	1996	Mar.	28,	1996	16	9	45
1997–98	Dec.	2,	1996	Nov.	30,	1998 [2]	268	271	729
1st ex.	Jan.	13,	1997 [1]	Aug.	31,	1998 [2]	86	113	597

† Actual days in session.

* The length of session is by calendar days, excluding constitutional recesses during the sessions of 1913 through 1957.

[1] Assembly convened the 1997–98 1st Ex. Session January 14, 1997.

[2] Assembly adjourned the 1997–98 1st Ex. Session September 1, 1998.

SESSIONS OF THE CALIFORNIA LEGISLATURE—Continued

Session	Convened	Adjourned	Legislative days †		Length *
			Assembly	Senate	
1999–2000	Dec. 7, 1998	Nov. 30, 2000	222	240	725
1st ex.	Jan. 19, 1999	Mar. 26, 1999	26	22	67
2001–02	Dec. 4, 2000	Nov. 30, 2002	262	262	727
1st ex.	Jan. 3, 2001	May 14, 2001	68	66	132
2nd ex.	May 14, 2001	May 9, 2002	82	76	361
3rd ex.	Jan. 10, 2002	May 2, 2002	27	31	113
2003–04	Dec. 2, 2002	Nov. 30, 2002	248	263	730
1st ex.	Dec. 9, 2002	July 29, 2003	45	49	233
2nd ex.	Jan. 23, 2003	Feb. 18, 2003	7	10	27
3rd ex.	Nov. 18, 2003	Jan. 15, 2004	5	7	59
4th ex.	Nov. 18, 2003	Nov. 30, 2004	49	61	379
5th ex.	Nov. 18, 2003	Nov. 30, 2004	35	41	379

2005–06	Dec.	6,	2004	—				—
1st ex.	Jan.	6,	2005		—	—	—	

† Actual days in session.
* The length of session is by calendar days, excluding constitutional recesses during the sessions of 1913 through 1957.

GOVERNORS OF CALIFORNIA, 1849–2004

Name	Politics	Date of election	Date of inauguration	Notes
Burnett, Peter H.	Ind. D.	Nov. 13, 1849	Dec. 20, 1849	Resigned January 8, 1851.
McDougal, John.	Ind. D.		Jan. 9, 1851	Lieutenant Governor succeeded Burnett.
Bigler, John.	D.	Sept. 3, 1851	Jan. 8, 1852	Assemblyman, 1849–1851.
Bigler, John.		Sept. 7, 1853	Jan. 7, 1854	Re-elected, September 7, 1853.
Johnson, J. Neely.	Amer.	Sept. 5, 1855	Jan. 9, 1856	Assemblyman, 1853.
Weller, John B.	D.	Sept. 2, 1857	Jan. 8, 1858	U.S. Senator, 1851–1857.
Latham, Milton S.	Lecomp. D.	Sept. 7, 1859	Jan. 9, 1860	Resigned Jan. 14, 1860, U.S. Senator, 1860–1863.
Downey, John G.	Lecomp. D.		Jan. 14, 1860	Lieutenant Governor succeeded Latham.
Stanford, Leland	R.	Sept. 4, 1861	Jan. 10, 1862	U.S. Senator, 1885–1897.
Low, Frederick F.	Union	Sept. 2, 1863	Dec. 10, 1863	Representative in Congress, 1861–1863.
Haight, Henry H.	D.	Sept. 4, 1867	Dec. 5, 1867	Member of Second Constitutional Convention.
Booth, Newton.	R.	Sept. 6, 1871	Dec. 8, 1871	Resigned Feb. 27, 1875. U.S. Senator, 1875–1881.
Pacheco, Romualdo.	R.		Feb. 27, 1875	Lieutenant Governor succeeded Booth.
Irwin, William.	D.	Sept. 1, 1875	Dec. 9, 1875	Harbor Commission, 1883–1886.
Perkins, George C.	R.	Sept. 3, 1879	Jan. 8, 1880	U.S. Senator, 1893–1903.
Stoneman, George.	D.	Nov. 7, 1882	Jan. 10, 1883	Transportation Commissioner.
Bartlett, Washington.	D.	Nov. 2, 1886	Jan. 8, 1887	Railroad Commissioner.
Waterman, Robert W.	R.		Sept. 13, 1887	Lieutenant Governor succeeded Bartlett.
Markham, Henry H.	R.	Nov. 4, 1890	Jan. 8, 1891	Representative in Congress, 1885–1887.
Budd, James H.	D.	Nov. 6, 1894	Jan. 11, 1895	Representative in Congress, 1883–1885.

Gage, Henry T.	R.	Nov. 8, 1898	Jan. 3, 1899	Minister to Portugal, Dec. 21, 1909.
Pardee, George C.	R.	Nov. 4, 1902	Jan. 6, 1903	Regent of University of California, 1899.
Gillett, James N.	R.	Nov. 6, 1906	Jan. 8, 1907	Representative in Congress, 1903–1906.
Johnson, Hiram W.	R.	Nov. 8, 1910	Jan. 3, 1911	Re-elected Nov. 3, 1914.
Johnson, Hiram W.	Prog.	Nov. 3, 1914	Jan. 5, 1915	Elected U.S. Senator, Nov. 7, 1916. Resigned as Governor, March 15, 1917.
Stephens, Wm. D.	R.	......	Mar. 15, 1917	Member of Congress, 10th Dist., 1910–1916. Appointed Lieutenant Governor, July 19, 1916.
Stephens, Wm. D.	R.	Nov. 5, 1918	Jan. 7, 1919	Elected 1918.
Richardson, Friend Wm.	R.	Nov. 7, 1922	Jan. 9, 1923	State Treasurer, 1915–1922.
Young, C. C.	R.	Nov. 2, 1926	Jan. 4, 1927	Lieutenant Governor, 1919–1927.
Rolph, James, Jr.	R.	Nov. 4, 1930	Jan. 6, 1931	Mayor of San Francisco, 1911–1930. Deceased, June 2, 1934.
Merriam, Frank F.	R.	......	June 2, 1934	Lieutenant Governor succeeded Rolph.
Merriam, Frank F.	R.	Nov. 6, 1934	Jan. 8, 1935	Lieutenant Governor, 1931–1934.
Olson, Culbert L.	D.	Nov. 8, 1938	Jan. 2, 1939	State Senator, 1935–1938.
Warren, Earl	R.	Nov. 3, 1942	Jan. 4, 1943	Attorney General, 1938–1942.
Warren, Earl	R.-D.	Nov. 5, 1946	Jan. 6, 1947	Re-elected Nov. 5, 1946.
Warren, Earl	R.	Nov. 7, 1950	Jan. 8, 1951	Re-elected Nov. 7, 1950. Appointed Chief Justice U.S. Supreme Court, Oct. 5, 1953.
Knight, Goodwin J.	R.	......	Oct. 5, 1953	Resigned as Governor, Oct. 4, 1953. Lieutenant Governor succeeded Warren.
Knight, Goodwin J.	R.	Nov. 2, 1954	Jan. 3, 1955	Elected Governor Nov. 2, 1954.

GOVERNORS OF CALIFORNIA, 1849–2004—Continued

Name	Politics	Date of election	Date of inauguration	Notes
Brown, Edmund G.	D.	Nov. 4, 1958	Jan. 5, 1959	Attorney General, 1951–1958.
Brown, Edmund G.	D.	Nov. 6, 1962	Jan. 7, 1963	Re-elected Nov. 6, 1962.
Reagan, Ronald............	R.	Nov. 8, 1966	Jan. 5, 1967	
Reagan, Ronald............	R.	Nov. 3, 1970	Jan. 4, 1971	Re-elected Nov. 3, 1970.
Brown, Edmund G. Jr.	D.	Nov. 5, 1974	Jan. 6, 1975	Secretary of State, 1971–1974.
Brown, Edmund G. Jr.	D.	Nov. 7, 1978	Jan. 8, 1979	Re-elected Nov. 7, 1978.
Deukmejian, George....	R.	Nov. 2, 1982	Jan. 3, 1983	Attorney General, 1979–1982.
Deukmejian, George....	R.	Nov. 4, 1986	Jan. 5, 1987	Re-elected Nov. 4, 1986.
Wilson, Pete	R.	Nov. 6, 1990	Jan. 7, 1991	U.S. Senator from 1983–91; Resigned as U.S. Senator Jan. 7, 1991.
Wilson, Pete	R.	Nov. 1, 1994	Jan. 7, 1995	Re-elected Nov. 1, 1994.
Davis, Gray.................	D.	Nov. 3, 1998	Jan. 4, 1999	
Davis, Gray.................	D.	Nov. 5, 2002	Jan. 6, 2003	
Schwarzenegger, Arnold..	R.	Oct. 7, 2003	Nov. 17, 2003	Recalled Oct. 7, 2003.

CALENDAR 2003

JANUARY

S	M	T	W	T	F	S
			1	2	3	4
5	6	7	8	9	10	11
12	13	14	15	16	17	18
19	20	21	22	23	24	25
26	27	28	29	30	31	

FEBRUARY

S	M	T	W	T	F	S
						1
2	3	4	5	6	7	8
9	10	11	12	13	14	15
16	17	18	19	20	21	22
23	24	25	26	27	28	

MARCH

S	M	T	W	T	F	S
						1
2	3	4	5	6	7	8
9	10	11	12	13	14	15
16	17	18	19	20	21	22
23	24	25	26	27	28	29
30	31					

APRIL

S	M	T	W	T	F	S
		1	2	3	4	5
6	7	8	9	10	11	12
13	14	15	16	17	18	19
20	21	22	23	24	25	26
27	28	29	30			

MAY

S	M	T	W	T	F	S
				1	2	3
4	5	6	7	8	9	10
11	12	13	14	15	16	17
18	19	20	21	22	23	24
25	26	27	28	29	30	31

JUNE

S	M	T	W	T	F	S
1	2	3	4	5	6	7
8	9	10	11	12	13	14
15	16	17	18	19	20	21
22	23	24	25	26	27	28
29	30					

JULY

S	M	T	W	T	F	S
		1	2	3	4	5
6	7	8	9	10	11	12
13	14	15	16	17	18	19
20	21	22	23	24	25	26
27	28	29	30	31		

AUGUST

S	M	T	W	T	F	S
					1	2
3	4	5	6	7	8	9
10	11	12	13	14	15	16
17	18	19	20	21	22	23
24	25	26	27	28	29	30
31						

SEPTEMBER

S	M	T	W	T	F	S
	1	2	3	4	5	6
7	8	9	10	11	12	13
14	15	16	17	18	19	20
21	22	23	24	25	26	27
28	29	30				

OCTOBER

S	M	T	W	T	F	S
			1	2	3	4
5	6	7	8	9	10	11
12	13	14	15	16	17	18
19	20	21	22	23	24	25
26	27	28	29	30	31	

NOVEMBER

S	M	T	W	T	F	S
						1
2	3	4	5	6	7	8
9	10	11	12	13	14	15
16	17	18	19	20	21	22
23	24	25	26	27	28	29
30						

DECEMBER

S	M	T	W	T	F	S
	1	2	3	4	5	6
7	8	9	10	11	12	13
14	15	16	17	18	19	20
21	22	23	24	25	26	27
28	29	30	31			

CALENDAR 2004

JANUARY

S	M	T	W	T	F	S
				1	2	3
4	5	6	7	8	9	10
11	12	13	14	15	16	17
18	19	20	21	22	23	24
25	26	27	28	29	30	31

FEBRUARY

S	M	T	W	T	F	S
1	2	3	4	5	6	7
8	9	10	11	12	13	14
15	16	17	18	19	20	21
22	23	24	25	26	27	28
29						

MARCH

S	M	T	W	T	F	S
	1	2	3	4	5	6
7	8	9	10	11	12	13
14	15	16	17	18	19	20
21	22	23	24	25	26	27
28	29	30	31			

APRIL

S	M	T	W	T	F	S
				1	2	3
4	5	6	7	8	9	10
11	12	13	14	15	16	17
18	19	20	21	22	23	24
25	26	27	28	29	30	

MAY

S	M	T	W	T	F	S
						1
2	3	4	5	6	7	8
9	10	11	12	13	14	15
16	17	18	19	20	21	22
23	24	25	26	27	28	29
30	31					

JUNE

S	M	T	W	T	F	S
		1	2	3	4	5
6	7	8	9	10	11	12
13	14	15	16	17	18	19
20	21	22	23	24	25	26
27	28	29	30			

JULY

S	M	T	W	T	F	S
				1	2	3
4	5	6	7	8	9	10
11	12	13	14	15	16	17
18	19	20	21	22	23	24
25	26	27	28	29	30	31

AUGUST

S	M	T	W	T	F	S
1	2	3	4	5	6	7
8	9	10	11	12	13	14
15	16	17	18	19	20	21
22	23	24	25	26	27	28
29	30	31				

SEPTEMBER

S	M	T	W	T	F	S
			1	2	3	4
5	6	7	8	9	10	11
12	13	14	15	16	17	18
19	20	21	22	23	24	25
26	27	28	29	30		

OCTOBER

S	M	T	W	T	F	S
					1	2
3	4	5	6	7	8	9
10	11	12	13	14	15	16
17	18	19	20	21	22	23
24	25	26	27	28	29	30
31						

NOVEMBER

S	M	T	W	T	F	S
	1	2	3	4	5	6
7	8	9	10	11	12	13
14	15	16	17	18	19	20
21	22	23	24	25	26	27
28	29	30				

DECEMBER

S	M	T	W	T	F	S
			1	2	3	4
5	6	7	8	9	10	11
12	13	14	15	16	17	18
19	20	21	22	23	24	25
26	27	28	29	30	31	

CALENDAR 2005

JANUARY

S	M	T	W	T	F	S
						1
2	3	4	5	6	7	8
9	10	11	12	13	14	15
16	17	18	19	20	21	22
23	24	25	26	27	28	29
30	31					

FEBRUARY

S	M	T	W	T	F	S
		1	2	3	4	5
6	7	8	9	10	11	12
13	14	15	16	17	18	19
20	21	22	23	24	25	26
27	28					

MARCH

S	M	T	W	T	F	S
		1	2	3	4	5
6	7	8	9	10	11	12
13	14	15	16	17	18	19
20	21	22	23	24	25	26
27	28	29	30	31		

APRIL

S	M	T	W	T	F	S
					1	2
3	4	5	6	7	8	9
10	11	12	13	14	15	16
17	18	19	20	21	22	23
24	25	26	27	28	29	30

MAY

S	M	T	W	T	F	S
1	2	3	4	5	6	7
8	9	10	11	12	13	14
15	16	17	18	19	20	21
22	23	24	25	26	27	28
29	30	31				

JUNE

S	M	T	W	T	F	S
			1	2	3	4
5	6	7	8	9	10	11
12	13	14	15	16	17	18
19	20	21	22	23	24	25
26	27	28	29	30		

JULY

S	M	T	W	T	F	S
					1	2
3	4	5	6	7	8	9
10	11	12	13	14	15	16
17	18	19	20	21	22	23
24	25	26	27	28	29	30
31						

AUGUST

S	M	T	W	T	F	S
	1	2	3	4	5	6
7	8	9	10	11	12	13
14	15	16	17	18	19	20
21	22	23	24	25	26	27
28	29	30	31			

SEPTEMBER

S	M	T	W	T	F	S
				1	2	3
4	5	6	7	8	9	10
11	12	13	14	15	16	17
18	19	20	21	22	23	24
25	26	27	28	29	30	

OCTOBER

S	M	T	W	T	F	S
						1
2	3	4	5	6	7	8
9	10	11	12	13	14	15
16	17	18	19	20	21	22
23	24	25	26	27	28	29
30	31					

NOVEMBER

S	M	T	W	T	F	S
		1	2	3	4	5
6	7	8	9	10	11	12
13	14	15	16	17	18	19
20	21	22	23	24	25	26
27	28	29	30			

DECEMBER

S	M	T	W	T	F	S
				1	2	3
4	5	6	7	8	9	10
11	12	13	14	15	16	17
18	19	20	21	22	23	24
25	26	27	28	29	30	31

CALENDAR 2006

JANUARY						
S	M	T	W	T	F	S
1	2	3	4	5	6	7
8	9	10	11	12	13	14
15	16	17	18	19	20	21
22	23	24	25	26	27	28
29	30	31				

FEBRUARY						
S	M	T	W	T	F	S
			1	2	3	4
5	6	7	8	9	10	11
12	13	14	15	16	17	18
19	20	21	22	23	24	25
26	27	28				

MARCH						
S	M	T	W	T	F	S
			1	2	3	4
5	6	7	8	9	10	11
12	13	14	15	16	17	18
19	20	21	22	23	24	25
26	27	28	29	30	31	

APRIL						
S	M	T	W	T	F	S
						1
2	3	4	5	6	7	8
9	10	11	12	13	14	15
16	17	18	19	20	21	22
23	24	25	26	27	28	29
30						

MAY						
S	M	T	W	T	F	S
	1	2	3	4	5	6
7	8	9	10	11	12	13
14	15	16	17	18	19	20
21	22	23	24	25	26	27
28	29	30	31			

JUNE						
S	M	T	W	T	F	S
				1	2	3
4	5	6	7	8	9	10
11	12	13	14	15	16	17
18	19	20	21	22	23	24
25	26	27	28	29	30	

JULY						
S	M	T	W	T	F	S
						1
2	3	4	5	6	7	8
9	10	11	12	13	14	15
16	17	18	19	20	21	22
23	24	25	26	27	28	29
30	31					

AUGUST						
S	M	T	W	T	F	S
		1	2	3	4	5
6	7	8	9	10	11	12
13	14	15	16	17	18	19
20	21	22	23	24	25	26
27	28	29	30	31		

SEPTEMBER						
S	M	T	W	T	F	S
					1	2
3	4	5	6	7	8	9
10	11	12	13	14	15	16
17	18	19	20	21	22	23
24	25	26	27	28	29	30

OCTOBER						
S	M	T	W	T	F	S
1	2	3	4	5	6	7
8	9	10	11	12	13	14
15	16	17	18	19	20	21
22	23	24	25	26	27	28
29	30	31				

NOVEMBER						
S	M	T	W	T	F	S
			1	2	3	4
5	6	7	8	9	10	11
12	13	14	15	16	17	18
19	20	21	22	23	24	25
26	27	28	29	30		

DECEMBER						
S	M	T	W	T	F	S
					1	2
3	4	5	6	7	8	9
10	11	12	13	14	15	16
17	18	19	20	21	22	23
24	25	26	27	28	29	30
31						

Photoelectronic composition by
CALIFORNIA OFFICE OF STATE PUBLISHING

05   01645—100